Reading for Meaning

FOSTERING COMPREHENSION IN THE MIDDLE GRADES

Edited by

BARBARA M. TAYLOR
MICHAEL F. GRAVES &
PAUL VAN DEN BROEK

International Reading Association
800 Barksdale Road
Newark, DE 19714

Teachers College
Columbia University
New York and London

Published simultaneously by Teachers College Press, 1234 Amsterdam Ave., New York, NY 10027 and The International Reading Association, 800 Barksdale Rd., Newark, Delaware 19714

Library of Congress Cataloging-in-Publication Data

Reading for meaning : fostering comprehension in the middle grades / Barbara M. Taylor, Michael F. Graves, Paul van den Broek, editors.
    p.   cm. — (Language and literacy series)
    Includes bibliographical references and index.
    ISBN 0-8077-3897-2 (cloth). — ISBN 0-8077-3896-4 (pbk.)
    1. Reading comprehension—United States. 2. Reading (Middle school)—United States. I. Taylor, Barbara (Barbara M.) II. Graves, Michael F. III. Broek, Paul van den.
LB1050.45 .R443 2000
428.4'3'071221—dc21   99-045904

ISBN 0-8077-3896-4 (paper)
ISBN 0-8077-3897-2 (cloth)
IRA Inventory Number 9135

Printed on acid-free paper

Manufactured in the United States of America

07   06   05   04   03   02   01   00   8   7   6   5   4   3   2   1

(Continued)

Contents

Introduction

BARBARA M. TAYLOR, MICHAEL F. GRAVES,
AND PAUL VAN DEN BROEK

Reading comprehension is of great concern to many Americans, as evidenced by the mandate in most states today for graduation standards in reading and for assessments aligned to those standards (Jerald & Curran, 1998). Undoubtedly, this call for reading standards and assessments stems, in part, from the less than adequate reading performance of many of our students. Although National Assessment of Educational Progress (NAEP) data make it clear the American students are reading as well or slightly better today than in 1970 (Campbell, Voelkl & Donahue, 1997), many of our children and youth are not reading well enough to keep up with the demands of a technologically advanced society. The 1998 NAEP assessment, for example, shows that only 31% of fourth-graders, 33% of eighth-graders, and 40% of twelfth-graders attained a proficient level in reading (Donahue, Voelkl, Campbell, & Mazzeo, 1999).

Of course, we know all too well that the poverty level of schools affects reading achievement. "School poverty depresses the scores of all students in schools where at least half of the students are eligible for subsidized lunch, and seriously depresses the scores when over 75 percent of students live in low-income households" (Puma et al., 1997 p. 12). Furthermore, the gap between high- and low-poverty schools remains large and has not been diminished through Title I services (Puma et al., 1997). Clearly, there is a lot of work that needs to be done to improve the reading comprehension of many students in the United States.

Fortunately, we know a considerable amount from educational research about improving reading comprehension. For example, teachers who place greater emphasis on comprehension and higher-level thinking skills have been associated with higher student achievement (Puma et al., 1997). Eighth- and twelfth-grade students who are asked by their teacher at least once a week to explain or support their understanding of what they have read and those who are asked to discuss various interpretations of what they have read are more proficient readers than students who do these things less often (Campbell, Donahue, Reese & Phillips, 1996). And students who are taught cognitive strategies such as predicting, questioning, and summarizing have been shown to improve their reading comprehension as measured by both experimenter-constructed and standardized tests (Pressley, 1998; Rosenshine, Meister, & Chapman, 1996).

This book focuses on what we have learned from research about fostering reading comprehension in the middle grades. It is the outgrowth of the second Guy Bond Commemorative Reading Conference, held at the University of Minnesota on October 3–4, 1997. Professor Bond was a distinguished professor of reading who taught at the University of Minnesota from 1937 to 1966 and wrote extensively about reading instruction. Cumulatively, contributors to the volume have spent well over 100 years researching various aspects of reading comprehension, and the chapters assembled here focus on the knowledge and strategies that have been shown to be effective in improving middle-grade students' reading comprehension.

In Chapter 1 Paul van den Broek and Kathleen Kremer discuss the cognitive processes that take place during comprehension and how these processes allow the reader to construct a coherent memory representation of the text to be accessed at a later time. They also describe potential sources of reader failure in this comprehension process as well as guidelines for instruction in and policy issues related to reading comprehension.

In Chapter 2 Michael Pressley traces the history of research in reading comprehension and then moves into a discussion of the value of teaching multiple comprehension strategies in reading. He concludes with the observation that we have made great progress in teaching students to use the processes that good readers use.

In Chapter 3 Janice Dole focuses on the benefits of both explicit and implicit comprehension instruction. She characterizes explicit instruction, an outgrowth of direct instruction in reading skills, as practice in strategies involving the whole process of comprehension and consisting of explanation and demonstration, guided and independent practice, and discussion of when to perform a particular strategy. She characterizes implicit comprehension instruction, stemming from the whole-language tradition, as practice with reading and writing that involves student choice, interest, and purpose. Dole concludes that programs that incorporate the best components of explicit and implicit instruction in reading comprehension—such as Book Club, described in this volume by Taffy Raphael—are the most effective.

The next three chapters are devoted to descriptions of effective comprehension and vocabulary programs designed for use in middle-grade classrooms. In Chapter 4 Taffy Raphael focuses on the role of instruction within Book Club, a literature-based literacy curriculum. After she describes Book Club, she discusses the complexities of teaching and the range of teacher roles within the Book Club framework, from providing explicit instruction on particular strategies to facilitating student-to-student talk in large and small groups.

In Chapter 5 Lynn and Douglas Fuchs describe their research on a promising collaborative learning program, Peer-Assisted Learning Strategies (PALS), which has been found to be effective in improving grade 2–5 students' reading fluency and comprehension. The program involves partner reading, paragraph summarizing, and prediction within a peer-tutoring framework.

In Chapter 6 Michael Graves describes a four-part vocabulary program that includes wide reading, teaching individual words, teaching students strategies for learning words independently, and fostering word consciousness. He provides suggestions for how to provide this instruction in approximately 1 hour spread across a school week and concludes that such instruction will be time well spent in enhancing both students' vocabulary and their comprehension.

In Chapter 7 Donna Alvermann discusses research on the value of discussion in helping middle-grade students comprehend what they read. She also points to the problem of some voices being silenced in peer-led discussions, something about which teachers need to be aware. She concludes by arguing that students' comprehension is maximized when teachers encourage them to view texts as providing messages they can either accept or challenge.

In Chapter 8 Robert Jiménez discusses the research he has done on the effective literacy practices provided for Latina/Latino students by Latina/Latino teachers. In addition to effective instructional practices to enhance students' literacy learning, he discusses some of the ways Latina/Latino teachers develop trust and rapport with Latina/Latino students and techniques used by these teachers to communicate effectively with their students.

In the final chapter, Jere Brophy provides thoughtful reactions to the papers in this volume. He also discusses the need to go beyond merely developing standards for literacy learning, as has been done by many states and by professional organizations. Educators also need to carefully design well-balanced literacy curricula "with options identified for students who have special needs and for teachers who are willing to trade off one set of desired outcomes for another." This needs to be done within a curriculum-planning framework, beginning with the establishment of goals expressed as desired outcomes. Brophy also stresses that educators must insist on credible evidence to support claims of effectiveness made by particular literacy programs.

Taken together, the chapters in this book provide a wealth of information on reading comprehension, effective reading comprehension instruction, and successful reading comprehension programs and practices to enhance middle-grade students' reading comprehension. Our hope is that the information and ideas provided by the authors will help teachers clarify for themselves what they are already doing well and what changes they may need to make to best foster reading comprehension in the middle grades.

REFERENCES

Campbell, J. R., Voelkl, K. E., & Donahue, P. L. (1997). *Report in brief: NAEP 1996 trends in academic progress.* Washington, DC: U.S. Department of Education, Office of Educational Research and Improvement.

Donahue, P. L., Voelkl, K. E., Campbell, J. R. & Mazzeo, J. (1999). *NAEP 1998 reading report card for the nation and states.* Washington, DC: U.S. Department of Education, Office of Educational Research and Improvement.

Jerald, C., & Curran, B. H. (1998, January 8). By the numbers. Quality counts '98: The urban challenge. *Education Week, 17,* pp. 56–59.

Pressley, M. (1998). *Reading instruction that works: The case for balanced teaching.* New York: Guilford.

Puma, M. J., Karweit, N., Price, C., Ricciuti, A., Thompson, W., & Vaden-Kiernan, M. (1997). *Prospects: Student outcomes, final report.* Washington, D.C.: U.S. Department of Education, Office of Educational Research and Improvement.

Rosenshine, B., Meister, C., & Chapman, S. (1996). Teaching students to generate questions: A review of the intervention studies. *Review of Educational Research, 66,* 181–221.

1

The Mind in Action: What It Means to Comprehend During Reading

PAUL VAN DEN BROEK
KATHLEEN E. KREMER

Reading is one of the most uniquely human and complex of all cognitive activities. It also is one that is indispensable for adequate functioning in most current societies. Successful reading requires many basic processes, such as the identification of letters, the mapping of letters onto sounds, and the recognition of words and syntax. The ultimate goal, however, is for readers to *learn* from text: to recognize the depicted facts or events, to connect them to each other and to background knowledge, and to memorize the results so that they can be used later. This goal requires additional, higher-order processes, such as inference making and reasoning. One of the central aims of education is to provide children with the tools to perform these requisite basic and higher-order processes and to assist readers who have difficulty with them.

In the past decade, tremendous advances have been made in understanding how readers with different ability levels comprehend, store, and retrieve text information. Many of these advances have occurred within the cognitive sciences, such as cognitive psychology and neuroscience. The purpose of this chapter is to provide an overview of these advances and to explore their implications for educational practice. The first section outlines the cognitive processes that occur during comprehension, with a focus on higher-order skills. When executed properly, these skills enable readers to construct a coherent memory representation of the text that can be accessed later. The second section explores various ways in which these processes may go awry and comprehension may fail. The final section focuses on implications for education: the prevention and remediation of comprehension problems and the design of reading programs.

READING COMPREHENSION:
BUILDING A REPRESENTATION OF THE TEXT

How do readers comprehend a text? To answer this question, it is important to recognize that *comprehension* may mean a variety of things. For example, it may mean being able to recall the text, to answer questions about character motives, to extract themes, to critique the structure, or a combination of these activities. Although each kind of comprehension leads readers to adopt somewhat different goals and processes, together they share an important feature. They all require that readers construct a mental "picture" of the text: a representation in memory of the textual information and its interpretation. Such mental representations ideally can be easily accessed, manipulated, and applied to any number of situations. Thus they are central to performance on any comprehension task.[1] In order to understand the reading process and why it sometimes fails, it is crucial to find out what these representations look like and how readers construct them.

The Nature of the Mental Representation of a Text

When reading is successful, the result is a coherent and usable mental representation of the text. This representation resembles a network, with nodes that depict the individual text elements (e.g., events, facts, settings) and connections that depict the meaningful relations between the elements (Trabasso, Secco, & van den Broek, 1984; van den Broek, 1990; see also Graesser & Clark, 1985; Schank & Abelson, 1977). To illustrate, a network representation for the simple story in Table 1.1 is given in Figure 1.1. Each node in Figure 1.1 stands for an event corresponding to a different main clause in the text.[2] The connections between the nodes stand for the main relations between the events described by the clauses. For natural texts, the networks can be quite extensive (e.g., Graesser & Clark, 1985; van den Broek, Rohleder, & Narváez, 1996).

What makes a representation coherent and usable for later tasks are the relations between elements that readers must infer. Many possible relations exist, but two types have been found to be particularly important for establishing coherence: referential and causal/logical (van den Broek, 1994). Referential relations enable readers to keep track of elements such as objects, people, and events mentioned in several places within the text (e.g., Gernsbacher, 1990; Kintsch & van Dijk, 1978; O'Brien, 1987). Causal/logical relations enable readers to identify how different events or facts depend on each other (e.g., Fletcher & Bloom, 1988; Goldman & Varnhagen, 1986; Schank & Abelson, 1977; Trabasso & van den Broek, 1985).

Table 1.1. Example narrative text.

1. Once there was a little boy
2. who lived in a hot country.
3. One day his mother told him to take some cake to his grandmother.
4. She warned him to hold it carefully
5. so it wouldn't break into crumbs.
6. The little boy put the cake in a leaf under his arm
7. and carried it to his grandmother's.
8. When he got there
9. the cake had crumbled into tiny pieces.
10. His grandmother told him he was a silly boy
11. and that he should have carried the cake on top of his head
12. so it wouldn't break.
13. Then she gave him a pat of butter to take back to his mother's house.
14. The little boy wanted to be very careful with the butter
15. so he put it on top of his head
16. and carried it home.
17. The sun was shining hard
18. and when he got home
19. the butter had all melted.
20. His mother told him that he was a silly boy
21. and that he should have put the butter in a leaf
22. so that it would have gotten home safe and sound.

For instance, when reading "The lady gave the waiter $10. He returned to give her the change," referential coherence is established by recognizing that "he" refers to the waiter and "her" to the lady. Causal/logical coherence is established by inferring that the waiter is returning change because the lady had given him $10 and that the purchase must have been for a lesser amount.

Many of the referential and causal/logical relations that readers must infer are much more complex than the simple ones in the above example. For instance, they may extend over long distances in the text, may be difficult to interpret, or may require coordinating numerous pieces of information. Examples of each situation are easy to find. Texts frequently introduce a character or object that then disappears from the focus of

Figure 1.1. Partial network of example text in Table 1.1;
numbers refer to clauses, arrows to causal connections.

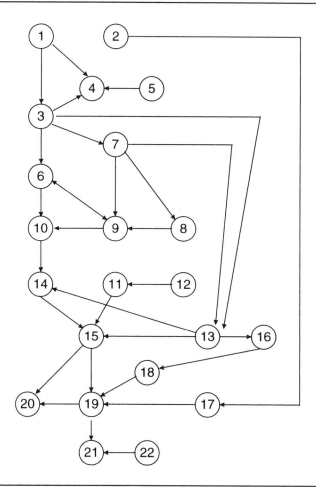

Source: Adapted from Trabasso, Secco, & van den Broek (1984) p. 94.

attention, only to return much later. Readers must realize that both ap-
pearances involve the same person or object, or else establish identity by
paging back. In addition, texts may include relations that are confusing
to readers who lack considerable world experience or background knowledge in a particular subject. For example, few adults know enough about
astronomy to understand the causal relation in the sentence pair "The

presence of the moon exerts a strong gravitational pull on the earth. Thus it has contributed to the emergence of life on earth." The missing information (i.e., that the moon's gravitational pull is instrumental in creating the earth's magnetic field, which in turn shields the earth's surface from lethal cosmic radiation) needs to be explicitly stated for most readers or comprehension suffers. Texts also often include relations that require the coordination of more than two pieces of information. For example, it is the character of Hamlet and the special circumstances in which he finds himself that cause him to act with dramatic effects in the way Shakespeare describes.

These examples illustrate some important aspects of the construction of a coherent representation during reading. First, the number of relational inferences required for its construction is usually quite large, although many inferences may be generated without effort or awareness by skilled readers. Even simple texts, such as "the lady and the waiter" example, consist of multiple relations. Second, readers make extensive use of background knowledge. The need to do so is obvious for complex cases, such as the text about the influence of the moon on the emergence of life on earth. Yet even "the lady and waiter" example relies on substantial prior knowledge, such as that ladies are female and can be referred to by "she," and that waiters work in restaurants where customers consume and pay for drinks and food. Third, as the Hamlet example highlights, the difficulty in constructing a coherent representation may be compounded when multiple factors contribute to a single relation, particularly when each factor is presented in nonadjacent portions of the text.

Considerable empirical evidence supports the view that referential and causal/logical networks are key components of the mental representations that successful readers construct. The evidence is too extensive to be reviewed here in its entirely, but some examples may be helpful (for reviews, see Britton & Graesser, 1996; Gernsbacher, 1994). Upon completing reading, people recall events with many connections to other events more frequently (Fletcher & Bloom, 1988; Graesser & Clark, 1985; J. Miller & Kintsch, 1980; Trabasso & van den Broek, 1985) and more quickly (O'Brien & Myers, 1987) than those with few or no connections. They also judge richly connected events as more essential to the narrative than those with fewer links (Trabasso & Sperry, 1985; van den Broek, 1988). Furthermore, their answers to questions about the text tend to follow the connections captured by the network (Goldman, 1985; Graesser & Clark, 1985; Trabasso, van den Broek, & Liu, 1988). These results are complemented by findings obtained during reading itself. When readers are asked to "think aloud" while proceeding through a text, they most often give responses that reflect attempts to establish referential and causal/logical coherence (Fletcher, 1986; Pressley & Afflerbach, 1995; Trabasso & Suh, 1993).

Evidence for referential and causal/logical networks is found even when readers are not explicitly prompted to recall the text. As above, these patterns hold when measures are taken during or after reading. For instance, when reminded afterwards of a fact or event, readers automatically and spontaneously bring to mind other components directly connected to it on the network more quickly than unconnected ones from the same text (McKoon & Ratcliff, 1980; Trabasso & Suh, 1993; van den Broek & Lorch, 1993). During reading, they also activate information from the preceding text or from their background knowledge more quickly if it is relevant for establishing referential or causal/logical coherence at that point (Gernsbacher, 1990; O'Brien & Albrecht, 1991; Singer & Ritchot, 1996; van den Broek, Rohleder, & Narváez, 1996; van den Broek & Thurlow, 1990).[3] Moreover, the time it takes to read a sentence is directly proportional to the number of inferences needed to be generated for coherence (Bloom, Fletcher, van den Broek, Reitz, & Shapiro, 1990).

In summary, the identification and representation of both referential and causal/logical relations in texts are essential components of reading comprehension.[4] Successful readers consistently engage in higher-order cognitive processes aimed at identifying these relations and at storing them as a coherent network within their memory. These cognitive processes also account for many of the individual and age-related differences found among readers. Recent findings reveal that poorer readers are less likely to engage in these higher-order processes than their more skilled peers (Gernsbacher, 1990; Just & Carpenter, 1992; Kim, van Dusen, Freudenthal, & Williams, 1992; Lee-Sammons & Whitney, 1991; Whitney, Ritchie, & Clark, 1991). Furthermore, as children gain experience with reading and cognitively mature, they gradually develop the ability to infer relations between events and facts in systematic ways (Bourg & Stephenson, 1997; Casteel, 1993; Goldman & Varnhagen, 1986; van den Broek, 1989a; van den Broek, Lorch & Thurlow, 1996; for reviews, see Oakhill, 1994; and van den Broek, 1997).

The Process of Reading Comprehension

So far, this chapter has focused on the product of reading comprehension: a memory representation resembling a network of relations between elements within the text. From an educational perspective, however, the cognitive processes by which readers arrive at this product are much more interesting because that is where failures to comprehend originate. These processes are what teachers hope to affect by instruction. How, then, does comprehension occur? The answer to this question requires detailed consideration of exactly what happens as readers proceed through the text.

At each point during reading, the comprehender attempts to make sense of the information explicitly stated in the current sentence by connecting it to two other sources of information: associated concepts in background knowledge (e.g., Kintsch, 1988) and a subset of concepts from preceding sentences (Fletcher & Bloom, 1988; Kintsch & van Dijk, 1978; van den Broek, 1990).[5] When the reader is satisfied with the attained level of comprehension, he or she proceeds to the next sentence and the process repeats itself.[6] At each cycle, the success of the process depends on a delicate interaction between several factors. The importance of information within the text and of the reader's background knowledge has already been discussed. A further, crucial role in this interaction is played by the reader's attentional capacities. A reader can only identify a meaningful connection between two elements if he or she attends to both of them at the same time (Fletcher & Bloom, 1988; Just & Carpenter, 1992; Kintsch & van Dijk, 1978; Rayner & Pollatsek, 1989; van den Broek, Young, Tzeng, & Linderholm, 1998). Yet human attentional capacities are severely limited (Klatzky, 1980). Consequently, successful comprehension depends in part on readers' ability to allocate their limited attention efficiently and effectively to the most relevant pieces of information within the text and within their memory.[7]

Successful comprehension also depends on readers' standards for coherence. These subjective standards dictate when readers feel that they have achieved adequate understanding of the text and can proceed to the next sentence. They also dictate when readers feel that additional steps should be taken to make sense of the current sentence, such as accessing further information from memory (Goldman & Saul, 1990; R. Lorch, Lorch, & Klusewitz, 1993; van den Broek, Risden, & Husebye-Hartman, 1995). Standards for coherence differ widely as a function of the skill level of the reader. In particular, good readers rely on two kinds of standards: referential and causal/logical coherence. These readers are almost invariably driven by a desire to grasp the referential and causal/logical antecedents to the information in the current sentence (Singer, 1994; van den Broek, 1994). In contrast, less skilled readers set lower standards for comprehension, such as by relaxing or even totally abandoning their need for these kinds of coherence. The standards that readers adopt also differ by such factors as their metacognitive skills, motivation, reading goals, and pragmatic concerns. Indeed, even a given individual may apply different standards of coherence from one reading context to the next, such as school-related versus leisure reading.

The picture of successful text comprehension that emerges is one in which readers' focus of attention continually changes with each new sentence. During each cycle, readers attend to new text elements while letting others fade into the background. Some of the changes in attention are not under the control of readers. Elements of the new sentence and their associated concepts, for example, push out all but a selected few elements from the preceding cycle. Other changes are directed by readers, by applying standards of coherence and reading strategies to select which information from the prior text or background knowledge is needed for comprehending the current sentence. What information readers attend to both enables and limits the meaningful relations that they can identify among the elements in the text. Together, the relations that are identified during each cycle form a coherent mental representation. (For details on the accumulation of relations into a network, see Goldman & Varma, 1995; Langston & Trabasso, 1998; van den Broek, Risden, Fletcher, & Thurlow, 1996).

WHY COMPREHENSION MIGHT FAIL

Good readers are adept at the higher-order processes needed to identify relations within a text. Their processes have become so automatic that frequently they are not even aware of the individual steps they have taken to achieve comprehension. For beginning readers, readers with learning difficulties, and advanced readers confronting novel and complicated materials, however, the application and the outcome of these cognitive processes are much less certain. One or more components may fail, resulting in an incomplete or erroneous mental representation of the text. The next section focuses on the three main sources of such failure: characteristics of the reader, properties of the text, and the reading context (see Figure 1.2).

Characteristics of the Reader

Attention: The Bottleneck in Comprehension. Attention and short-term memory play crucial roles in reading. As children mature, they improve at attending selectively and systematically to relevant information while blocking out distractions in their environment (P. Miller & Seier, 1994; Vurpillot, 1968). The amount of information they can keep in short-term memory and their speed of processing also improve steadily (Dempster, 1981; Dempster & Rohwer, 1983; Kail, 1991). Within an age group, however, individual differences in attentional capacity and short-term mem-

Figure 1.2. Factors that affect success/failure in comprehension.

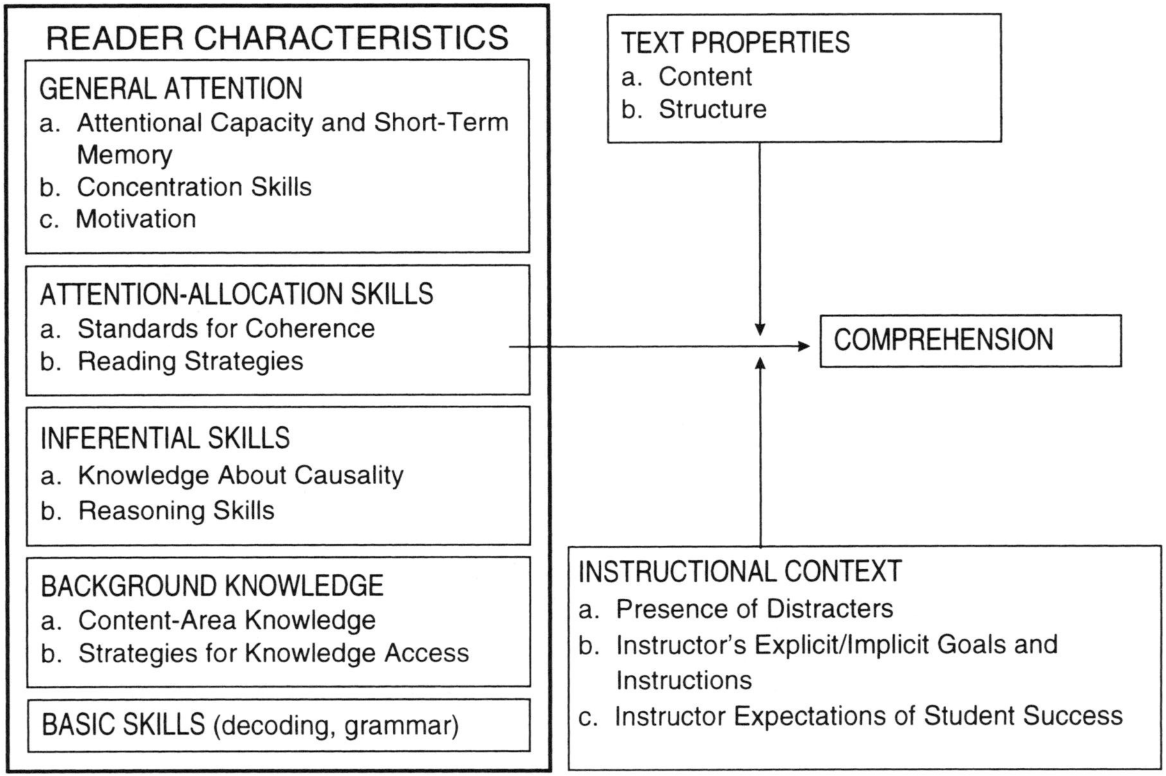

TEXT PROPERTIES
a. Content
b. Structure

COMPREHENSION

INSTRUCTIONAL CONTEXT
a. Presence of Distracters
b. Instructor's Explicit/Implicit Goals and Instructions
c. Instructor Expectations of Student Success

READER CHARACTERISTICS

GENERAL ATTENTION
a. Attentional Capacity and Short-Term Memory
b. Concentration Skills
c. Motivation

ATTENTION-ALLOCATION SKILLS
a. Standards for Coherence
b. Reading Strategies

INFERENTIAL SKILLS
a. Knowledge About Causality
b. Reasoning Skills

BACKGROUND KNOWLEDGE
a. Content-Area Knowledge
b. Strategies for Knowledge Access

BASIC SKILLS (decoding, grammar)

ory ability are remarkably stable across tasks (Daneman & Carpenter, 1980; Dixon, LeFevre, & Twilley, 1988; Just & Carpenter, 1992; Whitney et al., 1991).

Individual differences in processing capacities partially account for difficulties in reading comprehension. For instance, children with attention-deficit disorder do not differ from other children in their memory capacity, but rather in their ability to resist being sidetracked by irrelevant objects and tasks (E. Lorch et al., 1995). When these distracters are absent, their ability to understand stories resembles that of children without this disorder in many ways (Landau, Lorch, & Milich, 1992). Similarly, students with low academic motivation may readily shift their focus of attention to other attractive objects and activities in their environment. By eliminating these attractive options, by developing attention-focusing skills, and by making sure that reading is a rewarding and motivating activity, teachers can ensure that students devote their maximum mental capacities to the most important task during reading: constructing a coherent mental representation of the text.

Reading Strategies and Metacognition: The Allocation of Cognitive Resources During Comprehension. The distribution of attentional resources is also important during the reading process itself. Here, readers must continuously decide what is important in a new sentence, when to integrate the information with background knowledge, when to return to earlier information in the text, when to shift to a new sentence, and when to adjust reading speed. These decisions, whether made consciously or subconsciously, rely on both reading strategies and metacognition.

Reading strategies are mental and behavioral activities that people use to increase their likelihood of comprehending text. Metacognition is the knowledge of when to apply such strategies as a function of text difficulty, situational constraints, and the reader's own cognitive abilities. Both reading strategies and metacognition play important roles in the reading process. For instance, simply teaching children a reading strategy often does not result in their being able to use it in contexts other than that in which they first learned it. For transfer to occur across time and contexts, readers must also acquire a metacognitive awareness of what conditions warrant the use of the strategy as well as the ability to monitor comprehension and the environment to detect when these conditions are met. Comprehension monitoring, in turn, depends on readers' standards for coherence. These subjective standards determine when readers believe that adequate comprehension has been attained and when additional steps are needed to achieve it, such as the application of reading strategies. As noted earlier, skilled readers maintain standards of referential and causal/logical coherence, whereas poor readers do so less consistently. Skilled readers also relax or strengthen their standards to fit the learning environment. For instance, they slow down and engage in more extensive coherence-building activities when reading for a test than when reading for entertainment or general comprehension purposes (Pressley & McCormick, 1995; van den Broek, Lorch, Linderholm, & Gustafson, 1998; Zwaan & Brown, 1996). Thus good readers tend to have available a wide array of standards and knowledge about when to apply them (R. Lorch et al., 1993).[8] With maturation and relevant experiences, children acquire new strategies and then gradually learn to apply them flexibly, accurately, and consistently.

Good and poor readers within an age group differ in their acquisition and use of reading strategies and metacognitive skills. For instance, an important step of the reading process involves selecting which elements from the current sentence to carry over to the next sentence. Skilled readers choose information that is likely to become referentially and causally/logically relevant to subsequent text (Fletcher & Bloom, 1988; Gernsbacher, 1990; Kintsch & van Dijk, 1978). This kind of carryover reduces the need for time-consuming and cognitively demanding retrievals of earlier text. A similar process involves forward inferencing, in which readers draw on background knowledge and text information to anticipate what will be described later. When correct, these inferences help establish the referential and causal/logical connections needed for comprehension. Skilled readers recognize when forward inferences are warranted (Vonk & Noordman, 1990). Poor readers, in contrast, either fail to generate these inferences or jump to conclusions about what will happen next that are well beyond what the text justifies. Such mistakes consume precious attentional resources and require costly and often unsuccessful attempts to "undo" relations that have been established in the meanwhile (van Oostendorp, 1991).

Together, reading strategies and metacognition enable readers to allocate their cognitive resources to what is most important in the text. In doing so, these skills make or break attempts at achieving a coherent mental representation of what is being read. Because reading strategies and metacognitive skills are learned and generalizable to a wide range of contexts, they are at the core of most reading instruction and remediation programs.

Inferential and Reasoning Skills. Although the effective allocation of cognitive resources is a prerequisite for reading, it is not sufficient. To be successful, readers must also have the inferential and reasoning skills to establish meaningful connections between information in the text and relevant background knowledge. Central to these skills is knowing what constitutes a referential or causal/logical relation and being able to recognize or construct one when needed in order to form a coherent mental representation of the text.

Inferential and reasoning skills develop gradually and systematically as children become older and gain experience (e.g., Siegler, 1995; Thompson & Myers, 1985; van den Broek, 1989a). For instance, young children have difficulty remembering goals within stories, focusing instead on overt actions (van den Broek, 1997). This difficulty leads to poor comprehension because goals often provide the rationale for how and why events across episodes are connected. Through the elementary school years, children increasingly remember these internal events and come to judge them as being of central importance, resulting in an improved understanding of the general causal structure of stories. Other inferential and reasoning skills are difficult even for adults. As an example, adults have trouble recognizing that events can have multiple causes, even though these situations are pervasive in texts or everyday life (Shapiro, van den Broek, & Fletcher, 1995). This difficulty can result in the reader's proceeding to the next sentence once a single causal relation has been identified without realizing that the explanation is incomplete.[9] The omission of other causes will be reflected in the memory representation, and comprehension will suffer.

Inferential and reasoning skills are closely related to other reader characteristics that affect text comprehension, such as standards of coherence. On the one hand, the ability to make referential and logical/causal connections determines whether readers attain their subjective standards. On the other hand, the readers' standards dictate when they believe reading comprehension is adequate or when additional relations must be inferred.

Knowledge of Content Area. Another characteristic that influences the chances of comprehending is the amount of background knowledge readers have relevant to the text. Expertise supports the reading process in two ways. First, as people accumulate information about a specific topic, their internal representation of that area becomes richer and more densely interconnected. Additional facts, events, and relations are explicitly encoded. Consequently, readers can use this expanded representation to recognize a wider array of concepts and the causal/logical connections between them in the text. Second, the more extensively interconnected readers' background knowledge is, the more rapidly and easily each piece of information can be accessed from memory (Ericsson & Kintsch, 1995). Efficiency of retrieval frees cognitive resources that can then be devoted to other processes needed for comprehension. Indeed, inferential and reasoning skills tend to improve in conjunction with gaining expertise in a content area (Chi, Feltovich, & Glaser, 1981; Patel, Arocha, & Kaufman, 1994).

The subject matter of the text, therefore, can greatly affect assessments of readers' competencies. Poor readers may seem more skilled when given passages in their area of expertise. Conversely, proficient readers may seem less capable when presented with complex material on a topic in which they have little prior experience. In addition, reading difficulties may occur when the author and comprehender come from very different cultural and social backgrounds.

Access of background knowledge is also affected by specific strategies that readers have available. For example, proficient readers often access background knowledge in a more restrained and effective way than do less proficient readers (Zwaan & Brown, 1996). A related phenomenon occurs when accessing information from prior text rather than from memory. More successful readers "jump back" to where they expect the desired information to be, estimate their location relative to this information, and then search forward (Goldman & Saul, 1990). Poor readers use less efficient strategies, such as reviewing all earlier text from the beginning in a linear fashion. Furthermore, proficient readers flexibly adjust their search strategies to fit the goal of retrieving the information (e.g., O'Brien & Myers, 1987).

Basic Skills. The focus of this chapter is on the higher-order cognitive skills needed for reading comprehension rather than on basic skills such as letter identification, word decoding, and grammatical knowledge. These basic skills, however, are just as essential to the reading process because they provide the initial input from which mental representations of the text are constructed. In addition, well-developed basic skills decrease the demands on readers' cognitive resources. With instruction and experience, readers can automatize these basic components of reading, thereby freeing energy for more advanced components, such as establishing referential and causal/logical connections (Perfetti, 1994; Torgeson & Hecht, 1996; Yuill & Oakhill, 1988).

When children first learn to read, most of their effort must be devoted to deciphering individual words rather than constructing coherent representations of the text. By the time they reach junior high school, this initial task is generally mastered (Sticht & James, 1984). Some individuals, however, continue to struggle with basic reading skills into adulthood. For instance, most people with dyslexia have trouble decoding words into individual sounds. Because this difficulty can lead to incorrect word identification as well as to cognitive resources being unavailable for higher-order cognitive processes, such individuals usually have difficulty understanding and learning from text.

The above findings demonstrate that basic skills are necessary but not sufficient for reading comprehension. Consequently, instructional techniques that focus on these skills are not a substitute for the fostering of higher-order cognitive skills needed to create coherent mental representations of texts. In fact, even the need to teach certain basic skills remains controversial, as evidenced by the ongoing debate among educators over phonological-awareness versus whole-language instruction programs (Goodman, 1989; Stahl & P. D. Miller, 1989). Current research, however, suggests that although some children can develop various basic skills without formal instruction, others depend on such training (Adams, 1990; Adams & Bruck, 1995).

Characteristics of the Reader: Summary. Together, these five sets of traits (general cognitive capacities, reader strategies and metacognition, inferential and reasoning abilities, background knowledge, and basic reading skills) provide readers with the cognitive tools to learn from a text. By guiding each step of the reading process, they determine whether readers construct a coherent memory representation of the content. If any of these components are missing or weak, comprehension is likely to suffer.

Under some circumstances, however, reader characteristics can compensate each other. For instance, strong higher-order cognitive skills can overcome a weakness in basic reading skills or in content knowledge (Schultz, 1982). This situation is readily seen among second-language readers. Lacking vocabulary, they depend even more strongly than do first-language readers on such cognitive abilities as inference making in order to make sense of unknown phrases from the surrounding text (Horiba, van den Broek, & Fletcher, 1993). Thus sometimes people can rely on different strengths to achieve the same goal of comprehending while reading. Compensation can only occur in very selected situations, however, when (1) all skills are present to at least some degree and (2) the compensating skills are very strong.

Properties of the Text

Whether a coherent mental representation is constructed during reading also depends on the properties of the text. The same information can be conveyed in different ways, with certain forms being more user-friendly than others. User-friendly texts reduce the demands on readers' cognitive capacities and inferential skills. In such texts, earlier content is restated when important for understanding a current section, connections that readers must make are clearly delineated, relevant background knowledge is explicitly presented, and distracting information (e.g., details, tangential facts) is kept to a minimum (Graves et al., 1988). These properties are especially important for beginning and poor readers, whose ability to make referential and causal/logical connections between text content and background knowledge is tenuous even under ideal circumstances. Specific methods for making texts more user-friendly are presented later in this chapter.

It is important to note that instructors can use texts for two rather different purposes: to convey information and to help students acquire reading skills. In the former situation, the text should be structured so as to minimize the higher-order cognitive skills needed for comprehension. In the latter situation, the text should be user-friendly in a controlled way in order to provide opportunities to develop appropriate strategies.

Reading Context

In addition to reader characteristics and text properties, the specific context in which reading occurs affects the chances of successful comprehension. The influence of potentially distracting objects or tasks has already been discussed. Furthermore, how readers approach the comprehension process depends on their evaluation of the situational goals. For instance, they may adopt less stringent standards of coherence when reading for entertainment rather than for educational purposes. Such flexibility in response to contextual demands is especially developed among proficient readers.

Even subtle environmental variations, especially within the classroom, can lead readers to adopt very different goals. For example, teachers can explicitly influence goal formation through the specific instructions or rationale that they provide for a reading activity. They can also implicitly affect reading goals, such as by the methods they select to assess comprehension (e.g., literal versus inferential questions, amount of background knowledge required; see Mayer, 1975) or by their expectations of students' achievement (Jussim, 1989; Madon, Jussim, & Eccles, 1997). These reading goals subsequently exert a powerful influence over the amount of effort devoted to the comprehension process and over the final representation of the text. It is therefore crucial that instructors be aware of how their actions affect student effort and set up a classroom environment that evokes the intended educational outcomes.

IMPLICATIONS FOR EDUCATION

The picture of reading comprehension that emerges is rather complex. Readers must simultaneously coordinate multiple tasks requiring various higher-order and basic cognitive skills while ignoring irrelevant information and other distractions. Comprehension suffers if any aspect of the interaction among the reader, text, and immediate context goes awry. Understanding the intricate nature of the reading process and the many possible causes of failure is of great benefit to effective instruction. On one hand, it suggests what techniques educators should include when developing new instructional programs. On the other hand, it elucidates the specific strengths and weaknesses of such programs that are already in use.

Developing Instructional Techniques

An understanding of how readers comprehend text can guide the development and use of instructional techniques in several important ways.

Targeting Instruction. First, knowledge of how readers comprehend indicates which skills educators should target when teaching students to read or when creating intervention programs in this area. As discussed earlier, successful reading comprehension requires making referential and causal/logical connections between text elements and background knowledge. This activity depends on various cognitive processes, including inference making, attention allocation, and reading strategies. Providing training in these processes should therefore be at the core of reading instruction and remediation programs. Which processes to target in instruction will depend in part on the age and experience level of the students. Novice readers may need to devote most of their effort to acquiring such primary skills as phoneme recognition and the decoding of words. Once these fundamentals are mastered, instructors can concentrate more exclusively on teaching the higher-order cognitive skills needed to form a coherent mental representation of the text.

Creating New Methods. Second, an understanding of the cognitive processes involved in reading comprehension can suggest new methods for teaching these requisite skills. One example that has proven very effective while requiring little time and effort involves the use of causal questioning (Trabasso et. al, 1988; van den Broek, Tzeng, Risden, Trabasso, & Basche, 1998). Causal questioning techniques derive from the observation that poor readers have difficulty making the referential and causal/logical inferences needed for comprehension. While reading age-appropriate materials, students are prompted by "Why" and "How" questions placed at locations in the text where inference making is most likely to falter. Such situations include when information must be remembered from a much earlier portion of the text (particularly when the causal relation crosses an episode or paragraph boundary), when considerable background knowledge must be accessed, and when other processes such as word and syntax identification consume a considerable portion of available cognitive resources. The causal questions train readers to focus their attention on the relevant information needed to establish coherence. In doing so, readers gain experience with such higher-order skills as attention allocation, standards of coherence, and reading strategies.

Evidence for the effectiveness of causal questioning techniques comes from a classroom study in which ninth-grade students read narrative texts and were prompted with questions such as those enumerated above (van den Broek, Tzeng, Risden, Trabasso, & Basche, 1998). One-third of the students received the questions during reading, and another third received the same ones afterwards. The final third were not presented with any questions, thus forming a control group. Two hours later, all participants were asked to recall as much as they could from the text. The results can be seen in the right portion of Figure 1.3. Students prompted during reading remembered 30% more of the material than those in the control group. This improved recall primarily reflected an increase in memory for information needed to answer the questions and not simply information found within the questions themselves. The (re)-activation of information during reading that would not have been activated without questioning allowed the identification of additional connections and thus improved memory. Interestingly, students who received the questions after reading did not benefit at all compared with those in the control group. These results suggest that for older students, causal questioning techniques significantly improve understanding and memory of the text, but only when they occur during reading.

The conclusions are rather different when the same techniques are applied to students at a much earlier stage of learning to read. The results for third-grade students are presented in the left portion of Figure 1.3. Here, posing questions during reading actually interfered with comprehension and memory. For these children, such questioning diverted attention from the basic and inferential processes in which they engage spontaneously. Questioning after reading resulted in slightly better recall relative to questioning during reading (while still showing interference compared to the control condition), but, as closer examination showed, only because memory for the information contained in the question itself

Figure 1.3. The effects of causal questioning on memory by third- and ninth-grade students.

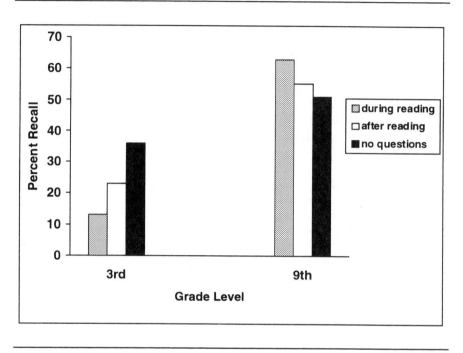

did not suffer as much as the other information in the text. Apparently, the fact that the questions in this condition repeated information somewhat diminished the interference effect. Overall, this study demonstrates that causal questioning techniques (1) can effectively improve comprehension, but only for students who have mastered the basic processes of reading, and (2) are most effective for this group when applied during as opposed to after reading.

Improving Texts. The above instructional implications of understanding the reading process focused on teaching students the cognitive skills required for successful comprehension. A very different application involves using insights in the reading process to revise instructional texts so that readers can more effectively construct a mental representation of the content.[10] Following the earlier model of reading, text revisions are most likely to be useful if they facilitate the identification of referential and causal/logical relations (Beck, McKeown, Sinatra, & Loxterman, 1991;

van den Broek, 1989b) while reducing the cognitive demands on readers (Britton & Gulgoz, 1991; van den Broek, Linderholm, Gaddy, Mischinski, Crittenden, & Samuels, 1998).

To test the effectiveness of text revisions based on the principles of causal/referential coherence and attention allocation, two difficult expository texts were revised using these rules (from van den Broek, Linderholm, Gaddy, Mischinski, Crittenden, & Samuels, 1998):

1. Rearrange information that is presented out of temporal or causal order.
2. Make goal or theme information that is omitted yet can be inferred from the original text explicit.
3. Reduce the risk of breakdown in causal coherence by identifying places where
   a. inadequate explanation is provided by the text
   b. multiple causality is involved
   c. the current sentence and its explanations are separated by large segments of text

   In these cases, explicitly state explanations that can be inferred from the original text and reinstate relevant information from the preceding text.

College students with high reading scores and students with low reading scores were then presented with a modified text and the original version of the other text. After completing reading, participants were asked to recall the texts and to answer comprehension questions. Students with low reading scores remembered more information and were better able to answer questions with the revised text than with the original text. Students with high reading scores showed such improvement only on the comprehension questions. A very different picture emerges when students were presented with simple texts. In this case, revisions did not improve performance for either skilled or poor readers. Thus modifying texts according to rules that reduce attentional and inferential difficulty is a powerful way to improve comprehension and memory, but only when the original text would have challenged the skill level and background knowledge of the reader.

Developing Techniques: Summary. These examples show that knowledge of the cognitive processes involved in comprehension can help educators develop new approaches to reading instruction as well as to the preparation of texts and other written materials in a wide range of academic subjects. In both cases, the core goal should be to guide students' efforts at achieving referentially and causally/logically coherent mental representations of texts. Furthermore, such knowledge ensures that this goal is implemented in ways that are appropriate for the age and reading experience level of the students.

Evaluating Current Instructional Programs

Understanding the reading process can also clarify what it is about successful instructional programs in this area that makes them work. Such classification is important because many such programs are costly and time-consuming. In addition to activities aimed at fostering higher-order cognitive skills needed for reading, they tend to include a large number of other activities. Furthermore, the intensive nature of these programs makes them difficult to implement in a particular situation. By identifying the most effective components, existing programs can be adapted to fit the needs and constraints of the teacher, students, and learning environment.

Fostering Comprehension Skills. At the elementary school level, several instructional programs shown to be efficacious in improving reading comprehension performance focus on fostering attention-allocation and comprehension skills. Examples include the Reading Recovery programs for beginning readers (Clay, 1985, 1991), the Reciprocal Teaching programs for fourth- through sixth-grade children (Palincsar & Brown, 1984), and the Peer-Assisted Learning Strategies (PALS) program for students with learning disabilities (Fuchs & Fuchs, Chapter 5, this volume). Such programs have been called transactional methods for the instruction of comprehension strategies because their core feature is that students are prompted to ask and answer questions throughout the reading (Pressley et al., 1992). Initially, the teacher plays a major role in selecting these questions and assisting with the answers. Gradually, however, the student's role (and in the case of Reciprocal Teaching programs, the role of classmates) increases until ideally he or she engages in self-questioning during reading without the aid of the teacher.

In light of the earlier discussion of the reading process, several features stand out. First, at the core of these programs are activities to train students to identify the important connections in the text. For instance, the four key components of Reciprocal Teaching programs are making predictions, seeking explanations when content is unclear, summarizing by identifying the relations between multiple events and facts, and self-questioning while reading. Similarly, in Reading Recovery programs, students are continuously encouraged to assess their understanding of the content and to resolve any confusion using text cues and strategies such as rereading. These core activities provide participants with opportunities to develop the higher-order cognitive skills needed for reading comprehension, such as standards of referential and causal/logical coherence, reading strategies (e.g., summarizing), metacognitive knowledge (e.g., knowing when a forward inference is warranted), effective attention allocation, and inferential skills. Although these skills are not directly taught in the programs, examples by the teachers (and sometimes by classmates) and feedback on the questions generated by the students presumably foster their development.

Second, these effective reading programs devote an enormous amount of time to the reading of a particular text. It is quite common to devote an entire class hour to understanding a few paragraphs, with the result that original content repeatedly is processed. Furthermore, the motivation and social control provided by the interaction with the teacher and classmates ensures that a large portion of available attention is devoted to the reading task. As a result, the limitations that the student's attentional capacity would ordinarily impose are greatly reduced. Information is processed repeatedly, in conjunction with many other pieces of information, and thus many meaningful connections can be forged.

Third, the interactive nature of these programs reduces the limiting effect of insufficient background knowledge. Because the comprehension process is shared, students can draw on the expertise of the teacher and of classmates in addition to their own to establish coherence. This shared knowledge includes not only facts and events, but also basic skills (e.g., word recognition and definitions, syntactic knowledge) and higher-order cognitive skills (e.g., inferential strategies, metacognition) important to the reading process.

At the secondary school level, few integral reading programs have been developed. The traditional assumption among educators has been that once students typically master basic reading skills during the first few years of schooling, no further instruction in this area is needed because comprehension will inevitably follow. Yet many students enter secondary school with serious deficits in the higher-order cognitive skills and background knowledge needed to understand texts. When remediation of these difficulties does occur at this level, it mostly consists of individual activities or exercises embedded in the instruction of another academic subject. Similar to the reading programs discussed earlier, the most effective of these remediation techniques help students identify the referential and causal/logical connections within the text. Such techniques include questioning and self-questioning exercises (e.g., Pressley, Symons, McDaniel, Snyder, & Turnure, 1988; van den Broek, Tzeng, Risden, Trabasso, & Basche, 1998), summarization and theme-extraction activities (e.g., Alvermann & Moore, 1991), and mnemonic imaging of the information (e.g., Mastropieri & Scruggs, 1991; for reviews, see Pressley & McCormick, 1995; Weinstein & Mayer, 1986). By supplementing instruction in a specific academic subject such as history or biology, these techniques have the benefit of consuming relatively little class time and of improving reading comprehension skills while fostering expertise in a content area.

Fostering Basic Skills. The successful reading instruction and remediation programs discussed above focus on the acquisition of higher-order cognitive skills. Many other current reading programs devote considerable time to teaching students such basic skills as phonological awareness and word decoding (e.g., Torgeson & Hecht, 1996).[11] Such instruction by itself does not generally produce expert readers. Yet a firm grasp of basic skills ensures that students can accurately translate the text into meaningful input to higher-order comprehension processes during reading, and that they can concentrate their attentional capacity on identifying meaningful relations and on creating coherence without diverting attention to the mechanics of reading. For this reason, training in basic skills is sometimes embedded within the reading curricula just described, particularly those administered at the elementary school level (e.g., Clay, 1985).

Evaluating programs: Summary. Many effective reading programs share the goal of developing students' ability to identify meaningful referential and causal/logical relations within text. By encouraging and modeling the standards and strategies for building coherence, by focusing available attention, and by developing content knowledge and inferential skills, these programs address several common sources of failure in reading comprehension. The learning situations created by these programs, of course, differ considerably from spontaneously independent reading with respect to the assistance provided to readers and the amount of time and effort devoted to a text. The hope, however, is that the practiced skills will become internalized and automatic, so that they can be applied spontaneously and effortlessly in future reading situations.

CONCLUDING REMARKS

Understanding the reading process and the possible sources of failure suggests why some current instructional programs are successful as well as how to design new ones that are as effective as possible. The instructional methods described above illustrate both types of implications. These specific implementations are given not only because they have been proven to be effective (in the case of existing methods) or are promising (in the case of new methods), but also because they illustrate how a thorough understanding of the reading process may inform a broad range of educational practices (e.g., direct instruction, interactive programs, text design).

All of these programs have in common their focus on directing the attention of the reader and on facilitating the identification of meaningful relations. As knowledge of the reading process has improved, the central role of these activities has become clearer. Their implications for educational practice are equally clear. The central aim of reading instruction should be to provide readers with the skills and opportunities necessary to identify the individual text elements and to connect them into a coherent mental representation of the text. This is true for elementary education, but it becomes even more relevant in the middle and upper school years.

Although the focus of this chapter has been on fostering comprehension skills in the context of reading, it is important to note that many of these skills (e.g., comprehension strategies, attention-focusing skills, background knowledge) can be learned from other contexts as well.[12] Examples of such contexts are social interactions, television viewing, real-life events, and discussions. Thus, to a considerable degree, "reading instruction" can take place outside the reading context. Indeed, very beginning readers may learn some skills more easily in these other settings, which do not depend on as yet undeveloped basic skills such as decoding. This also means that many skills required for reading can be developed before children are even exposed to text. Learning to read starts well before formal instruction itself.

ACKNOWLEDGMENTS

We would like to thank Michelle Gaddy, Michael Graves, Tracy Linderholm, Barbara Taylor, and Yuhtsuen Tzeng for their comments on an earlier version of this paper. This research was supported by the Guy Bond Endowment and by the Center for Cognitive Sciences at the University of Minnesota through a grant from the National Institute of Child Health and Human Development (HD-07151).

NOTES

1. Access to the representation is required even when the reader has the text available to perform a task. The reason for this is that the representation

includes the reader's interpretation of the text. Thus any task that involves the meaning of the text requires access to the mental representation.

2. Units of analysis other than clauses can be chosen to construct a network. These units can be smaller ones such as propositions or larger ones such as paragraphs. It appears, however, that most readers process texts at a clause level (e.g., McNamara & Kintsch, 1996; Trabasso & Suh, 1993). Regardless of the level of analysis selected, however, the important point here is to illustrate the network nature of the representation.

3. The "activation" of an event can be measured in various ways. One common procedure is to present readers with probe words that describe text events on a computer screen. A reader's task is to say the words aloud as quickly as possible. The faster that a reader does so (compared to saying control words), the more the probed events were activated.

4. Readers of most skill levels and in most circumstances attempt to identify causal and referential relations. Different types of relations (e.g., thematic, moral, hierarchical) are possible, and the extent to which they are made depends on the specific goals or tasks of the readers as well as on their knowledge and reading skills (e.g., Graesser, Singer, & Trabasso, 1994). These inferences use as their foundation the referential and causal/logical relations that readers have identified.

5. In cognitive-psychological terms, these two sources are known as semantic and episodic memory, respectively. Semantic memory contains an individual's general knowledge about the world, abstracted from different experiences and built up over one's entire lifetime. A subsection of semantic memory, called procedural memory, contains reading strategies and standards for coherence, to be discussed later. Episodic memory contains information about specific experiences, in this case of having read a specific text. Two terms, *short-term memory* or *working memory*, are used to refer to the reader's attentional capacity.

6. At times, additional processing takes places. For example, comprehenders may pause at transition points during reading (such as the end of a paragraph or of the entire text) to integrate the preceding text. Conversely, good readers may briefly delay processing in anticipation of relevant information in subsequent sentences (van den Broek, 1994).

7. The focus here is on readers' attentional resources as a limiting factor. It should be pointed out, however, that these limitations also serve an important positive function by preventing overload of the cognitive system. Without limitations, readers would fall prey to an inferential explosion (Warren, Nicholas, & Trabasso, 1979), which would likely bring the reading process to a stop.

8. A similar situation occurs with respect to access of the text representation, either during reading or at a later time. Readers can select from among various access strategies, depending on their skills and goals (e.g., to remember all they can, to retell particular elements, to apply the information).

9. These problems are not restricted to beginning readers only. Even advanced comprehenders frequently make "classic" mistakes, such as insensitivity to multiple causality. Arguments about the reduction of violent crime, for example, are often based on single-cause assumptions. Some argue that much violent crime is caused by the proliferation of guns ("guns kill"), whereas others

argue that it is caused by the nature of people ("people kill"). Each position has implications for policy and intervention (i.e., whether to increase gun control or to impose stiffer punishments). Of course, violent crime is likely to be the result of a combination of these two and other causes. Likewise, after the 1987 stock market crash, experts disagreed strongly about what caused the crash and hence about what actions should be taken to prevent a recurrence. Analysis of the different views and recommendations shows that the differences were the result of intentional or unintentional selectivity in determining which multiple causal relations to include in the accounts of the crash and its precipitating events (Shapiro et al., 1995).

10. As stated earlier, making a text more reader-friendly is appropriate if the goal is transmission of information. If the goal is to help readers develop strategies for comprehending user-unfriendly texts, then revision is either not desired or should be done in a controlled fashion, leaving the gaps and breaks that are the target of strategy instruction in place.

11. The role of phonological codes in reading is not limited to Indo-German languages such as English. Recent research has shown that even languages that have been thought of as logographic (i.e., nonphonological) rely strongly on phonological components. Examples are Chinese (Perfetti & Zhang, 1996) and Maya (Coe, 1992). Indeed, Coe (1992) shows how the erroneous belief that Maya contained no phonological components delayed deciphering of this language for many decades.

12. Other abilities, such as decoding skills and reading-specific attention-allocation skills, are more exclusively developed in reading contexts.

REFERENCES

Adams, M. J. (1990). *Beginning to read: Thinking and learning about print.* Cambridge, MA: MIT Press.

Adams, M. J., & Bruck, M. (1995). Resolving the "great debate." *American Educator, 19*(7), 10–20.

Alvermann, D. E., & Moore, D. W. (1991). Secondary school reading. In R. Barr, M. L., Kamil, P. B. Mosenthal, & P. D. Pearson (Eds.), *Handbook of reading research,* (Vol. 2; pp. 951–983). New York: Longman.

Beck, I. L., McKeown, M. G., Sinatra, G. M., & Loxterman, J. A. (1991). Revising social studies text from a text-processing perspective: Evidence of improved comprehensibility. *Reading Research Quarterly, 26*(3), 251–276.

Bloom, C. P., Fletcher, C. R., van den Broek, P., Reitz, L., & Shapiro, B. P. (1990). An on-line assessment of causal reasoning during comprehension. *Memory and Cognition, 18*(1), 65–71.

Bourg, T., & Stephenson, S. (1997). Comprehending characters' emotions: The role of event categories and causal connectivity. In P. W. van den Broek, P. J. Bauer, & T. Bourg (Eds.), *Developmental spans in event comprehension and representation: Bridging fictional and actual events* (pp. 295–319). Mahwah, NJ: Erlbaum.

Britton, B. K., & Graesser, A. C. (1996). *Models of understanding text.* Mahwah, NJ: Erlbaum.

Britton, B. K., & Gulgoz, S. (1991). Using Kintsch's computational model to improve instructional text: Effects of repairing inference calls on recall and cognitive structures. *Journal of Educational Psychology, 83*(3), 329–345.

Casteel, M. A. (1993). Effects of inference necessity and reading goal on children's inferential generation. *Developmental Psychology, 29*(2), 346–357.

Chi, M. T. H., Feltovich, P. J., & Glaser, R. (1981). Categorization and representation of physics problems by experts and novices. *Cognitive Sciences, 5,* 121–152.

Clay, M. M. (1985). *The early detection of reading difficulties: A diagnostic survey with recovery procedure.* Portsmouth, NJ: Heinemann.

Clay, M. M. (1991). *Becoming literate: The construction of inner control.* Portsmouth, NJ: Heinemann.

Coe, M. D. (1992). *Breaking the Maya code.* New York: Thames & Hudson.

Daneman, M, & Carpenter, P. A. (1980). Individual differences in working memory and reading. *Journal of Verbal Learning and Verbal Behavior, 19*(4), 450–466.

Dempster, F. N. (1981). Memory span: Sources of individual and developmental differences. *Psychological Bulletin, 89*(1), 63–100.

Dempster, F. N., & Rohwer, W. D. (1983). Age differences and modality effects in immediate and final recall. *Child Development, 54*(1), 30–41.

Dixon, P., LeFevre, J., & Twilley, L. C. (1988). Word knowledge and working memory as predictors of reading skill. *Journal of Educational Psychology, 80*(4), 465–472.

Ericsson, K. A., & Kintsch, W. (1995). Long-term working memory. *Psychological Review, 102*(2), 211–245.

Fletcher, C. R. (1986). Strategies for the allocation of short-term memory during comprehension. *Journal of Memory and Language, 25*(1), 43–58.

Fletcher, C. R., & Bloom, C. P. (1988). Causal reasoning in the comprehension of simple narrative texts. *Journal of Memory and Language, 27*(3), 235–244.

Gernsbacher, M. A. (1990). *Language comprehension as structure building.* Hillsdale, NJ: Erlbaum.

Gernsbacher, M. A. (1994). *Handbook of psycholinguistics.* San Diego, CA: Academic.

Goldman, S. R. (1985). Inferential reasoning in and about narrative texts. In A. C. Graesser & J. B. Black (Eds.), *The psychology of questions* (pp. 247–276). Hillsdale, NJ: Erlbaum.

Goldman, S. R., & Saul, E. U. (1990). Flexibility in text processing: A strategy competition model. *Learning and Individual Differences, 2*(2), 181–219.

Goldman, S. R., & Varma, S. (1995). CAPping the construction-integration model of discourse comprehension. In C. A. Weaver, S. Mannes, & C. R. Fletcher (Eds.), *Discourse comprehension: Essays in honor of Walter Kintsch* (pp. 337–358). Hillsdale, NJ: Erlbaum.

Goldman, S. R., & Varnhagen, C. K. (1986). Memory for embedded and sequential story structures. *Journal of Memory and Language, 25*(4), 401–418.

Goodman, K. S. (1989). Whole-language research: Foundations and development. *Elementary School Journal, 90*(2), 207–221.

Graesser, A. C., & Clark, L. F. (1985). *The structures and procedures of implicit knowledge.* Norwood, NJ: Ablex.

Graesser, A. C., Singer, M., & Trabasso, T. (1994). Constructing inferences during narrative text comprehension. *Psychological Review, 101*(3), 371–395.

Graves, M., Slater, W. H., Roen, D., Redd-Boyd, T., Duin, A. H., Furniss, D. W., & Hazeltine, P. (1988). Some characteristics of memorable expository writing: Effects of revisions by writers with different backgrounds. *Research in the Teaching of English, 22*(3), 242–265.

Horiba, Y., van den Broek, P., & Fletcher, C. R. (1993). Second-language readers' memory for narrative texts: Evidence for structure-preserving top-down processing. *Language Learning, 43*(2), 345–372.

Jussim, L. (1989). Teacher expectations: Self-fulfilling prophecies, perceptual biases, and accuracy. *Journal of Personality and Social Psychology, 57*(3), 469–480.

Just, M. A., & Carpenter, P. A. (1992). A capacity theory of comprehension: Individual differences in working memory. *Psychological Review, 99*(1), 122–149.

Kail, R. (1991). Developmental change in speed of processing during childhood and adolescence. *Psychological Bulletin, 109*(3), 490–501.

Kim, S., van Dusen, L., Freudenthal, D., & Williams, D. (1992, January). *Understanding of elaborative processing in text comprehension: Text-provided elaboration versus self-generated elaboration.* Paper presented at the annual Winter Text Conference, Jackson Hole, WY.

Kintsch, W. (1988). The role of knowledge in discourse comprehension: A construction-integration model. *Psychological Review, 95*(2), 163–182.

Kintsch, W., & van Dijk, T. A. (1978). Toward a model of text comprehension and production. *Psychological Review, 85*(5), 363–394.

Klatzky, R. L. (1980). *Human memory: Structures and processes* (2nd ed.). San Francisco: Freeman.

Landau, S., Lorch, E. P., & Milich, R. (1992). Visual attention to and comprehension of television in attention-deficit hyperactivity disordered and normal boys. *Child Development, 63*(4), 928–937.

Langston, M. C., & Trabasso, T. (1998). Identifying causal connections and modeling integration of narrative discourse. In H. van Oostendorp & S. R. Goldman (Eds.), *The construction of mental representations during reading* (pp 29–69). Mahwah, NJ: Erlbaum.

Lee-Sammons, W. H., & Whitney, P. (1991). Reading perspectives and memory for text: An individual differences analysis. *Journal of Experimental Psychology: Learning, Memory, and Cognition, 17*(6), 1074–1081.

Lorch, E., Milich, R., Polley, R., van den Broek, P., Baer, S., Hooks K., Hartung, C., & Welsh, R. (1995). *Comprehension of televised stories in attention deficit disordered and normal boys: Effects of diffuse attention.* Unpublished manuscript.

Lorch, R. F., Jr., Lorch, E. P., & Klusewitz, M. A. (1993). College students' conditional knowledge about reading. *Journal of Educational Psychology, 85*(2), 239–252.

Madon, S., Jussim, L., & Eccles, J. (1997). In search of the powerful self-fulfilling prophecy. *Journal of Personality and Social Psychology, 72*(4), 791–809.

Mastropieri, M., & Scruggs, T. E. (1991). *Teaching students ways to remember: Strategies for learning mnemonically.* Cambridge, MA: Brookline.

Mayer, R. E. (1975). Forward transfer of different reading strategies evoked by testlike events in mathematics text. *Journal of Educational Psychology, 67*(2), 165–169.

McKoon, G., & Ratcliff, R. (1980). Priming in item recognition: The organization of propositions in memory for text. *Journal of Verbal Learning and Verbal Behavior, 19*(4), 369–386.

McNamara, D. S., & Kintsch, W. (1996). Learning from texts: Effects of prior knowledge and text coherence. *Discourse Processes, 22*(3), 247–288.

Miller, J. R., & Kintsch, W. (1980). Readability and recall of short prose passages: A theoretical analysis. *Journal of Experimental Psychology: Human Learning and Memory, 6*(4), 335–354.

Miller, P., & Seier, W. (1994). Strategy utilization deficiencies in children: When, where, and why. In H. Reese (Ed.), *Advances in child development and behavior,* (Vol. 25; pp. 107–156). New York: Academic.

Oakhill, J. (1994). Individual differences in children's text comprehension. In M. A. Gernsbacher (Ed.), *Handbook of psycholinguistics* (pp. 821–848). New York: Academic.

O'Brien, E. J. (1987). Antecedent search processes and the structure of text. *Journal of Experimental Psychology: Learning, Memory, and Cognition, 13*(2), 278–290.

O'Brien, E. J., & Albrecht, J. E. (1991). The role of context in accessing antecedents in text. *Journal of Experimental Psychology: Learning, Memory, and Cognition, 17*(1), 94–102.

O'Brien, E. J., & Myers, J. L. (1987). The role of causal connections in the retrieval of text. *Memory and Cognition, 15*(5), 419–427.

Palincsar, A. S., & Brown, A. L. (1984). Reciprocal teaching of comprehension-fostering and comprehension-monitoring activities. *Cognition and Instruction, 1*(2), 117–175.

Patel, V. L., Arocha, J. F., & Kaufman, D. R. (1994). Diagnostic reasoning and medical expertise. In D. Medin (Ed.), *The psychology of learning and motivation* (Vol 30; pp. 187–251). New York: Academic.

Perfetti, C. A. (1994). Psycholinguistics and reading ability. In M. A. Gernsbacher (Ed.), *Handbook of psycholinguistics* (pp. 849–894). New York: Academic.

Perfetti, C. A., & Zhang, S. (1996). What it means to read. In M. F. Graves, P. van den Broek, & B. M. Taylor (Eds.), *The first R: Every child's right to read* (pp. 37–61). New York: Teachers College Press.

Pressley, M., & Afflerbach, P. (1995). *Verbal protocols of reading: The nature of constructively responsive reading.* Hillsdale, NJ: Erlbaum.

Pressley, M., El-Dinary, P. B., Gaskins, I. W., Schuder, T., Bergman, J. L., Almaasi, J., & Brown, R. (1992). Beyond direct explanation: Transactional instruction of reading comprehension strategies. *Elementary School Journal, 92*(5), 513–555.

Pressley, M., & McCormick, C. B. (1995). *Advanced educational psychology for educators, researchers, and policymakers.* New York: HarperCollins.

Pressley, M., Symons, S., McDaniel, M. A., Snyder, B. L., & Turnure, J. E. (1988). Elaborative interrogation facilitates acquisition of confusing facts. *Journal of Educational Psychology, 80*(3), 268–278.

Rayner, K., & Pollatsek, A. (1989). *The psychology of reading.* Englewood Cliffs, NJ: Prentice-Hall.

Schank, R. C., & Abelson, R. P. (1977). *Scripts, plans, goals, and understanding: An inquiry into human knowledge structures.* Hillsdale, NJ: Erlbaum.

Schultz, T. R. (1982). Rules of causal attribution. *Monographs of the Society for Research in Child Development, 47*(1, Serial No. 194).

Shapiro, B. P., van den Broek, P., & Fletcher, C. R. (1995). Using story-based causal diagrams to analyze disagreements about complex events. *Discourse Processes, 20*(1), 51–77.

Siegler, R. S. (1995). Children's thinking: How does change occur? In W. Schneider & F. Weinert (Eds.), *Memory performance and competencies: Issues in growth and development* (pp. 407–430). Mahwah, NJ: Erlbaum.

Singer, M. (1994). Discourse inference processes. In M. A. Gernsbacher (Ed.), *Handbook of psycholinguistics* (pp. 479–515). San Diego: Academic.

Singer, M., & Ritchot, K. F. M. (1996). The role of working memory capacity and knowledge access in text inference processing. *Memory and Cognition, 24*(6), 733–743.

Stahl, S. A., & Miller, P. D. (1989). Whole language and language experience approaches for beginning reading: A quantitative research synthesis. *Review of Educational Research, 59*(1), 87–116.

Sticht, T. G., & James, J. H. (1984). Listening and reading. In P. D. Pearson (Ed.), *Handbook of reading research,* Part 2. New York: Longman.

Thompson, J. G., & Myers, N. A. (1985). Inferences and recall at ages four and seven. *Child Development, 56*(5), 1134–1144.

Torgeson, J. K., & Hecht, S. A. (1996). What it means to learn to read. In M. F. Graves, P. van den Broek, & B. M. Taylor (Eds.), *The first R: Every child's right to read* (pp. 133–159). New York: Teachers College Press.

Trabasso, T., Secco, T., & van den Broek, P. W. (1984). Causal cohesion and story coherence. In H. Mandl, N. L. Stein, & T. Trabasso (Eds.), *Learning and comprehension of text* (pp. 83–111). Hillsdale, NJ: Erlbaum.

Trabasso, T., & Sperry, L. L. (1985). Causal relatedness and importance of story events. *Journal of Memory and Language, 24*(5), 595–611.

Trabasso, T., & Suh, S. (1993). Understanding text: Achieving explanatory coherence through on-line inferences and mental operations in working memory. *Discourse Processes, 16*(1–2), 3–34.

Trabasso, T., & van den Broek, P. (1985). Causal thinking and the representation of narrative events. *Journal of Memory and Language, 24*(5), 612–630.

Trabasso, T., van den Broek, P. W., & Liu, L. (1988). A model for generating questions that assess and promote comprehension. *Questioning Exchange, 2*(1), 25–38.

van den Broek, P. (1988). The effects of causal relations and hierarchical position on the importance of story statements. *Journal of Memory and Language, 27* (1), 1–22.

van den Broek, P. (1989a). Causal reasoning and inference making in judging the importance of story statements. *Child Development, 60*(2), 286–297.

van den Broek, P. (1989b). The effects of causal structure on the comprehension of narratives: Implications for education. *Reading Psychology: An International Quarterly, 10*(1), 19–44.

van den Broek, P. W. (1990). The causal inference maker: Towards a process model of inference generation in text comprehension. In D. A. Balota, G. B. Flores d'Arcais, & K. Rayner (Eds.), *Comprehension processes in reading* (pp. 423–445). Hillsdale, NJ: Erlbaum.

van den Broek, P. W. (1994). Comprehension and memory of narrative texts: Inferences and coherence. In M. A. Gernsbacher (Ed.), *Handbook of psycholinguistics* (pp. 539–588). San Diego: Academic.

van den Broek, P. W. (1997). Discovering the cement of the universe: The development of event comprehension from childhood to adulthood. In P. W. van den Broek, P. J. Bauer, & T. Bourg (Eds.), *Developmental spans in event comprehension and representation* (pp. 321–342). Mahwah, NJ: Erlbaum.

van den Broek, P. W., Linderholm, T., Gaddy, M., Mischinski, M., Crittenden, A., & Samuels, J. (1998). *Comparison of the effects of principled revisions on adult readers' comprehension and recall of easy and difficult narrative texts.* Unpublished manuscript.

van den Broek, P. W., & Lorch, R. F., Jr. (1993). Network representations of causal relations in memory for narrative texts: Evidence from primed recognition. *Discourse Processes, 16*(1–2), 75–98.

van den Broek, P., Lorch, R. F., Jr., Linderholm, T., & Gustafson, M. (1998). *The effect of reading goals on inference generation during reading expository texts.* Unpublished manuscript.

van den Broek, P., Lorch, E. P., & Thurlow, R. (1996). Children's and adults' memory for television stories: The role of causal factors, story-grammar categories, and hierarchical level. *Child Development, 67*(6), 3010–3028.

van den Broek, P. W., Risden, K., Fletcher, C. R., & Thurlow, R. (1996). A "landscape" view of reading: Fluctuating patterns of activation and the construction of a stable memory representation. In B. K. Britton & A. C. Graesser (Eds.), *Models of understanding text* (pp. 165–187). Mahwah, NJ: Erlbaum.

van den Broek, P. W., Risden, K., & Husebye-Hartman, E. (1995). The role of readers' standards for coherence in the generation of inferences during reading. In R. F. Lorch, Jr., & E. J. O'Brien (Eds.), *Sources of coherence in reading* (pp. 353–373). Hillsdale, NJ: Erlbaum.

van den Broek, P. W., Rohleder, L., & Narváez, D. (1996). Causal inferences in the comprehension of literary texts. In R. J. Kreuz & M. S. MacNealy (Eds.), *Empirical approaches to literature and aesthetics* (pp. 179–220). Norwood, NJ: Ablex.

van den Broek, P. W., & Thurlow, R. (1990, November) *Reinstatements and elaborative inferences during the reading of narratives.* Paper presented at meeting of Psychonomic Society, New Orleans.

van den Broek, P., Tzeng, Y., Risden, K., Trabasso, T. & Basche, P. (1998). *Developmental differences in the effects of questioning on reading comprehension.* Unpublished manuscript.

van den Broek, P., Young, M., Tzeng, Y., & Linderholm, T. (1998). The landscape model of reading: Inferences and the on-line construction of a memory representation. In H. van Oostendorp & S. R. Goldman (Eds.), *The construction of mental representations during reading.* (pp. 71–98). Mahwah, NJ: Erlbaum.

van Oostendorp, H. (1991). Inferences and integrations made by readers of script-based texts. *Journal of Research in Reading, 14*(1), 3–20.

Vonk, W., & Noordman, L. G. (1990). On the control of inferences in text understanding. In D. A. Balota, G. B. Flores d'Arcais, & K. Rayner (Eds.), *Comprehension processes in reading* (pp. 447–463). Hillsdale, NJ: Erlbaum.

Vurpillot, E. (1968). The development of scanning strategies and their relation to visual differentiation. *Journal of Experimental Child Psychology, 6*(4), 632–650.

Warren, W. H., Nicholas, D. W., & Trabasso, T. (1979). Event chains and inferences in understanding narratives. In R. O. Freedle (Ed.), *New directions in discourse processing* (pp. 23–52). Norwood, NJ: Ablex.

Weinstein, C. F., & Mayer, R. F. (1986). The teaching of learning strategies. In M. C. Wittrock (Ed.). *Handbook of research on teaching* (3rd ed.; pp. 315–327). New York: Macmillan.

Whitney, P., Ritchie, B. G., & Clark, M. B. (1991). Working-memory capacity and the use of elaborative inferences in text comprehension. *Discourse Processes, 14*(2), 133–145.

Yuill, N., & Oakhill, J. (1988). Effects of inference awareness training on poor reading comprehension. *Applied Cognitive Psychology, 2*(1), 33–45.

Zwaan, R. A., & Brown, C. M. (1996). The influence of language proficiency and comprehension skill on situation-model construction. *Discourse Processes, 21* (3), 289–327.

2

Comprehension Instruction in Elementary School: A Quarter-Century of Research Progress

MICHAEL PRESSLEY

The 1997 Bond Lecture, which is the basis for this chapter, was not my first fall trip to Minneapolis or the University of Minnesota. A quarter-century ago, in the autumn of 1973, I began doctoral studies at the Institute of Child Development at Minnesota. Consequently, I feel a strong intellectual connection to the University of Minnesota. Back in 1973 there was much happening on the Minnesota campus that directly connects to the work I review in this chapter. With a few examples, I argue in this chapter that reading as a field was greatly advanced by the work that went on at Minnesota in the 1970s. After presenting those examples, I review the research progress relevant to the development of comprehension through instruction, building to a set of conclusions about instruction that makes sense for the development of comprehension abilities in elementary school students.

MINNESOTA CONCEPTUALIZATIONS OF READING IN THE 1970S

Instruction that promotes comprehension skills occurs over a number of years. It is necessary to impart basic word-recognition skills as well as higher-order (i.e., self-regulative) comprehension processes (e.g., relating text to prior knowledge, making predictions based on prior knowledge, constructing mental images, generating on-line summaries of text understanding, and monitoring when summary construction is challenging). Notably, in the 1970s, there was work at Minnesota on issues related both to basic word recognition and to self-regulation of higher-order cognitive processes.

Basic Word-Recognition Processes

Samuels (1970) documented in elegant and well-controlled experiments that students get less out of print experiences when words are accompanied by illustrations capturing the meaning of the word. Specifically, when pictures accompany words, the pictures permit the children to "recognize" the words without attending to letter- and word-level cues, and hence they fail to attend to the letter-level cues in the words and instead learn them as sight words. This finding was well in advance of a great deal of research which established that attending to semantic-context cues (such as pictures) undermines learning to recognize words based on letter- and word-level cues alone (Nicholson, 1991; Nicholson, Bailey, & McArthur, 1991), a scientific conclusion that flies in the face of recent instructional recommendations emanating from the whole-language literacy educator community (e.g., Weaver, 1994).

Jay Samuels was also involved in research with David LaBerge (e.g., LaBerge & Samuels, 1974) establishing that slow, effortful recognition of words through sounding out and blending did not permit easy comprehension of words. In particular, they advanced the case that word recognition and comprehension compete for the limited cognitive capacity that is working memory (or short-term memory, attention, or consciousness, depending on your conceptual preference). That is, consistent with Miller's (1956) framework, they believed that reading comprehension depends on those 5 ± 2 pieces of information that can be juggled in thought at any one time—but so does word recognition. Thus, when readers are first struggling to recognize a word, much short-term capacity must be dedicated to sounding out the word, with the result that comprehension of words is uncertain. As readers re-encounter a new word, word recognition becomes more automatic; and with automaticity in word recognition, the capacity demands for it decrease, thus freeing up capacity that can be applied to comprehension. What LaBerge and Samuels (1974) established was that not all word recognitions are equal, that some come at a much higher cost in terms of cognitive resources than others, with high-cost, effortful sounding out of words undermining comprehension and automatic word recognition facilitating comprehension.

Vocabulary

Sometime early in my graduate career, I learned about a text being developed by then–Minnesota faculty member, P. David Pearson. He and Dale Johnson were working on *Teaching Reading Vocabulary* (Johnson & Pearson, 1978), which was a comprehensive compendium of the many methods for increasing student vocabulary development. Throughout that volume, and a companion book dedicated to comprehension (Pearson & Johnson, 1978), it was clear Pearson believed that increasing vocabulary development was key in developing reading comprehension. The concluding quote in the vocabulary book came from Samuel Johnson (from *The Idler*, No. 20). It said it all with respect to the importance of vocabulary development in comprehension according to the Johnson and Pearson perspective: "He that reads and grows no wiser seldom suspects his own deficiency but complains of hard words and obscure sentences and asks why books are written which cannot be understood." Although there were certainly others before Johnson and Pearson who conceived of comprehension as depending on vocabulary, they put together in one place all the thinking about how vocabulary could be increased, based on conceptual and empirical analyses of the day, in a way that affected a nation of reading educators.

Strategies Research

By the time I arrived at Minnesota, John Flavell's work on the development of children's memory strategies was already considered classic research. For example, Flavell, Beach, and Chinsky (1966) had established that 5-year-olds were less likely than 10-year-olds to rehearse word lists that they were asked to remember, a finding that inspired many constructive replications that teased out the subtleties of child developmental increases in use of rehearsal strategies. This work on memory development did much to inspire the conclusion that with development children became more cognitively active and, in particular, are more likely to use strategies (see Ornstein, 1978).

Flavell's work went well beyond establishing the developmental difference in strategy use, however. He and his associates, all of whom were Minnesota graduate students at the time, determined that when children did not produce strategies on their own, often they could carry out the strategies if instructed to do so (Keeney, Cannizzo, & Flavell, 1967; Moely, Olsen, Halwes, & Flavell, 1969). This conclusion anticipated work, reviewed later in this chapter, that even when children do not use effective comprehension strategies on their own, they can be taught to use them.

Studies in Which Processing Instruction was Varied. I remember well the very first journal articles I read as a graduate student at Minnesota. The three leadoff articles in the October 1973 *Journal of Verbal Learning and Verbal Behavior* were by James Jenkins and his then student colleagues (Hyde & Jenkins, 1973; Till & Jenkins, 1973; Walsh & Jenkins, 1973). These studies were concerned with memory, establishing definitively that what the head does during a task defines what the head will remember. Thus memory of words proved greater when subjects were asked to process the words meaningfully (e.g., given the word *table,* deciding whether a table is pleasant or not) than when they focused on the physical features of the words (e.g., determining whether *table* has an *e* in it).

When the results of Flavell's and Jenkins's work were considered together, several conclusions emerged: (1) There are different ways to process a set of materials, and how materials are processed affects what the learner learns. (2) Many psychological processes are controllable by the learner. (3) With advancing age, there are improvements in children's control of their processing, such that, at least with respect to some tasks (e.g., list learning), older children are more likely to elect task-appropriate processes than are younger children. In the autumn of 1973, there was a lot of excitement at the University of Minnesota about the research potential of both Flavell's and Jenkins's thinking about strategic processing, with that potential coming to fruition in a number of arenas, including reading comprehension instruction, as I will relate later.

Studies of Imagery and Reading. Although Flavell's and Jenkins's ideas were not studied with respect to reading at Minnesota before I arrived there, they were being explored with respect to reading at other places. In particular, in the autumn of 1973 I became aware of the work of Joel Levin (1973), who had demonstrated that instructions to generate mental images during reading facilitated the comprehension and memory for text of at least some weak grade-4 readers. The grade-4 students who were affected positively by the imagery instructions were ones who had experienced comprehension difficulties in the past, not seeming to construct on their own well-organized representations of ideas in text. That they benefited from the imagery instructions suggested that these students were production-deficient with respect to strategies for organizing the ideas in text but that they were capable of doing so with instruction.

The potential connections between the ideas being explored in the memory literature and Levin's thinking about comprehension as mediated by use of imagery strategy were apparent to me even in my first year of graduate school, as I reflected on both Flavell's and Levin's writings extensively during that period of time. My thinking was helped along during that first year by encounters with two other individuals, special education faculty member Jim Turnure and a researcher in special education then employed at the university, Arthur Taylor. Both were concerned with imagery and related processes, and, in particular, how instruction in such processes could benefit weaker elementary students. For example, with Fred Danner, who was then a graduate student in the Institute of Child Development, Taylor had conducted an impressive study of the striking effects of imagery instructions on the associative learning of children in grades 1 through 6 (Danner & Taylor, 1973). Again, that work could be interpreted as consistent with the conclusion that children could be taught to use a strategy that they did not use spontaneously.

Metamemory and Metacognition

Without a doubt, however, the greatest buzz at the Institute of Child Development when I arrived there in September 1973 was with respect to the construct of metamemory, which is what people know about their memories. This was largely because of a very large study recently completed by Kreutzer, Leonard, and Flavell (published in 1975), which tapped children's understanding of their memories. Children in kindergarten, grade 1, grade 3, and grade 5 were asked 14 questions that tapped their knowledge of memory storage and retrieval. Many of the questions required the children to make a choice—to decide, for instance, whether it was better to dial a telephone number immediately after hearing it or get a drink of water before dialing. Other items were more open-ended, for example, one requiring students to report how to find a jacket that they had lost at school. In general, what Kreutzer and colleagues (1975) discovered was that metamemory improved with increasing age.

As Flavell and his students at the Institute reflected on the metamemory results, there was a sense that metamemory was a potentially very important explanatory construct. One emergent hypothesis was that metamemory might explain why older children were more likely than younger children to use strategies. That is, the older children's use of strategies might be fueled by their understanding that intellectual tasks can be accomplished by cognitive-strategic activities and that task-appropriate, cognitive-strategic actions can improve performance. Such knowledge of memory might be the executive (Newell & Simon, 1972) in the self-regulation of strategies and cognitive activities.

Even in the autumn of 1973, metamemory was being thought of as only one possible "meta," however. I recall discussions of meta-attention, metaperception, and metalinguistics from that era, with the overarching construct referred to as metacognition. Metacognition was being seen as the controlling part of the cognitive system, the homunculus that just had to be there but had eluded analytical study up until that point (e.g., Newell & Simon, 1972). The thinking about the importance of metacognition in executive functioning and self-regulation would anticipate much such thinking with respect to the self-regulation of comprehension, taken up later in this chapter.

Summary

When I began graduate school at Minnesota in 1973, important basic research was occurring at the University that set the stage for a revolution in the study of reading in general and reading comprehension in particular. There was awareness that semantic-context cues accompanying a word in print could transform a reading task into a guessing game based on the nonprint cues (e.g., as when Samuels's [1970] prereaders named the pictures rather than read the words accompanying the pictures; Smith [1971]). It was also clear, based on LaBerge and Samuels's (1974) work, that learning to recognize words is a gradual process, with slow, effortful sounding out of words only eventually giving way to automatic word recognition as readers acquired increasing experience with individual words. An especially relevant insight was that comprehension of words is undermined to the extent that word recognition is slow and effortful rather than automatic and effortless (LaBerge & Samuels, 1974).

Cognitive psychologists were thinking much about strategies. Particularly important, Jenkins and his colleagues established that what a learner acquires from an experience depends on how the learner processed the experience. Other researchers had determined that it often was possible to teach strategies to children that affected their processing in ways that improved academic performance (see Brown, 1978, for a summary). Most relevant was that some reading strategies, such as mentally imagining the ideas expressed in a text, were being explored in studies with children. That such instructional studies were successful provided evidence that children were not being as strategic as they might be. A hypothesis then emerging in Flavell's group at the Institute of Child Development was that failures to use strategies that could mediate demanding cognitive tasks might represent metacognitive failure. That is, before learners use a strategy appropriately, they need to know much about where and when to use the strategy as well as how to adapt it to various task situations.

I reviewed these insights from a quarter-century ago to make the case that the intellectual foundations for modern comprehension instruction are very deep. I also reviewed them because I have been struck that there are many contemporary reading researchers and teachers who do not know the distinguished intellectual lineage of the strategies they are teaching. Indeed, the ideas just reviewed went far in defining the research on reading in general, and comprehension instruction in particular, that occurred in the two decades following my first days of graduate school.

THE COGNITIVE EXPERIMENTAL PSYCHOLOGY OF READING

Since the early 1970s, there has been a plethora of experimental research on reading and reading instruction. Much of this work has been revealing about instruction that improves comprehension. I review briefly in this section work that I believe has been especially important.

Word Recognition

Skilled readers are adept at sounding out words, sometimes on a letter-by-letter basis but also through recognition of common letter sequences (e.g., prefixes, suffixes, base words; Ehri, 1991, 1992). Once it is sounded out, the child often recognizes the word just pronounced because many words in the books encountered by beginning readers are ones that have been in their speaking vocabularies for several years. Within the constraints of the working memory system (LaBerge & Samuels, 1974), the logical conclusion is that if children can recognize words in the books they are reading, they will understand them (Gough & Tunmer, 1986).

In fact, that seems to be the case, with Maureen Lovett and her colleagues at Toronto's Hospital for Sick Children providing important data related to this point. The students in Lovett's work were so far behind in reading that they had been referred to the hospital because school officials and parents suspected biological dyslexia. Rather than rushing to the conclusion that such children have a biological difference that makes it impossible for them to learn to read, Lovett and her colleagues tried to teach the students to read through intensive instruction. Lovett, Ransby, Hardwick, Johns, and Donaldson (1989) succeeded in improving the decoding of very weak readers from the ages 9 to 13 by teaching the students to (1) associate letters and sounds, (2) use their knowledge of letter–sound associations to analyze words into compenent sounds, and (3) blend component sounds to produce words. As a function of receiving the word-recognition instruction, there was improved reading comprehension relative to participants in a control condition, as assessed by a standardized test. Lovett and colleagues (1994) succeeded again in teaching young readers who were experiencing great difficulties in learning to recognize words to do so, again teaching them to analyze words phonologically and blend the sounds in them. Again, there was improved performance on a standardized comprehension measure relative to a control condition. The Lovett studies were especially impressive because of the degree of experimental control in them, including controls to eliminate the possibility that treatment effects were nothing more than placebo effects. Moreover, her results are very credible because they have been accompanied by other demonstrations of the potency of systematic word-recognition instruction in promoting reading skills in students experiencing difficulties when they are beginning to read (see also Vellutino et al., 1996).

Being able to recognize words, however, is not enough (LaBerge & Samuel, 1974). Comprehension is facilitated to the extent that word recognition occurs with ease. Thus, instruction that increases the automaticity of word recognition should promote comprehension. A problem with this line of argument is that training children to read words faster and more certainly has not always produced improved comprehension (e.g., Fleisher, Jenkins, & Pany, 1979; Yuill & Oakhill, 1988).

Nonetheless, a recent analysis involving especially thorough training of word recognition produced data more consistent with the conclusion that learning words to the point of automaticity improves reading comprehension. Tan and Nicholson (1997) studied 7- to 10-year-old weaker readers. In the critical training condition of the study, participants practiced recognizing target words until they could read each word without hesitation. This training condition included only brief training about the meaning of the target words. In contrast, in the control condition, training consisted of discussions between the experimenter and the student about the meanings of target words, although the students did not see the words (i.e., the experimenter read the words to the students). Thus the control condition was heavily oriented toward developing participants' understanding of the word, with no attention to the development of recognition of it.

Following training, the participants read a passage containing the target words, with 12 comprehension questions following the reading. The trained participants answered more comprehension questions than did control participants, even though in the control condition, readers developed understanding of the target words better than readers in the training condition. See Breznitz (1997a, 1997b) for another set of analyses confirming that more rapid decoding improves comprehension, probably by freeing up more short-term capacity for comprehension.

In summary, experimental psychologists interested in reading have provided a great deal of data consistent with the conclusion that word-recognition skills can be improved in ways that promote understanding of what is read. Words cannot be understood or their meanings combined with those of other words if they are not first recognized.

Knowledge of Vocabulary

Good readers have extensive vocabularies (e.g., Anderson & Freebody, 1981). Moreover, experimental psychologists have proven successful in demonstrating that this is a causal connection—that having a more extensive vocabulary promotes comprehension skill (Beck, Perfetti, & Mc-Keown, 1982; McKeown, Beck, Omanson, & Perfetti, 1983; McKeown, Beck, Omanson, & Pople, 1985). Beck and colleagues' (1982) study is a well-known example. In that investigation, grade-4 children were taught 104 new vocabulary words over a period of 5 months, with the students encountering the words often as part of the intervention and using the words in multiple ways as part of instruction. At the end of the study, comprehension tended to be better for students receiving the vocabulary intervention compared to those who had not, including an analysis of pretest-to-posttest gain scores on a standardized comprehension test.

Comprehension Strategies Instruction

My first published research study focused on teaching grade-3 students to use mental imagery when they read (Pressley, 1976). That the imagery instruction improved factual memory of prose was consistent with the hypotheses that (1) 8-year-olds do not use imagery strategies on their own, or at least not to the extent they could, and (2) 8-year-olds could mediate their processing of text using mental imagery.

Many studies evaluating the potency of particular comprehension strategies followed that one, with most very similar in design. In one condition, students would be taught a strategy that the investigator believed might enhance comprehension. Control participants would not be taught the strategy. The participants would then read some text and be tested on it. A strategy was considered to mediate comprehension if performance on the test was superior for the students receiving the strategy instruction.

A number of strategies proved potent in such experiments, including generation of questions during reading, constructing mental images representing the ideas in text, analyzing stories into their components (e.g., setting, characters, problems, attempts at resolution of problems, resolution), and summarizing (for reviews, see Pearson & Fielding, 1991; Pressley, Johnson, Symons, McGoldrick, & Kurita, 1989). A limitation of these studies was that they only involved teaching of single strategies, even though skilled reading involves articulation of a number of strategies in interaction (Pressley & Afflerbach, 1995). Experimental psychologists responded with studies involving the instruction of multiple comprehension strategies.

Teaching of Multiple Strategies and the Development of Student Metacognition

In the late 1970s and early 1980s, there were many demonstrations of quantitative relationships between metacognition and effective cognition, and, in particular, between metacognition and effective strategy use, including during reading (Schneider, 1985). These demonstrations were viewed as consistent with Flavell's (e.g., 1977) argument that metacognition is important in regulating strategy use. If that were true, then it made sense to design strategy instruction so as to enhance metacognitive development—to assure that students knew when and where to apply the strategies they were learning and the benefits produced by use of strategies. In fact, such metacognitive embellishment of strategies instruction did result in more certain, appropriate use of strategies (Pressley, Borkowski, & O'Sullivan, 1984, 1985). One of the most prominent of the efforts for teaching multiple comprehension strategies with metacognitive embellishment was *reciprocal teaching* (Palincsar & Brown, 1984).

Four comprehension strategies were at the heart of reciprocal teaching (i.e., prediction, questioning, seeking clarification when confused, summarization), with students taught in small groups over a fairly short period of time (e.g., 20 lessons) to use these strategies as they read text. The approach involved a particular sequence of events that was repeated a number of times. After a portion of text was read, the student leader of the group, a role that rotated among reading group members, posed a question to the other members of the group. The group members attempted to respond. Then the student leader proposed a summary of the passage just read. The other students in the group were invited to point out confusing parts of the text and to seek clarifications about those parts by posing questions. The group members were also invited to make predictions about upcoming text, with a great deal of flexible discussion of text and issues in text occurring with this framework.

Palincsar and Brown (1984) believed that students learned how and when to use the strategies that were taught (i.e., prediction, summarization, seeking clarification, questioning) through the student-led group lessons. That is, during the group lessons it was apparent that making predictions makes sense before reading a segment of text, posing questions and seeking clarification should be carried out as reading proceeds, and attempts at summarization should occur after a text has been read.

Across all the studies of reciprocal teaching (Rosenshine & Meister, 1984), there were consistent, striking effects on cognitive-process measures, such as those tapping summarization and self-questioning skills. With respect to standardized comprehension, however, the effects were less striking, with an average effect size of 0.3 standard deviations. Reciprocal teaching was more successful when there was more direct teaching of the four comprehension strategies than when there was not.

Palincsar and Brown were not the only ones in the early 1980s giving hard thought to how instruction in multiple strategies might be embellished. Roehler and Duffy (1984) hypothesized that instruction in comprehension strategies should begin with teacher explanations of strategies and mental modeling of their use (i.e., showing students how to apply strategies by thinking aloud; Duffy & Roehler, 1989). Then student practice of the strategies in the context of real reading could occur. Such practice could be monitored by the teacher, with additional explanations and modeling provided as needed, explanations and modeling that could be rich in metacognitive information, such as when and where to use the strategies being taught and how to adapt them to new situations. Feedback and instruction could be reduced as students became more and more independent (i. e., instruction could be scaffolded). Cuing and prompting of strategy use should continue, according to Roehler and Duffy's thinking, until students autonomously apply the strategies they are learning.

The Roehler and Duffy (1984) thinking influenced a number of educators to attempt strategies instruction in their settings. In the late 1980s and early 1990s my research took a dramatic turn away from true experimentation in order to document what instruction in multiple-comprehension strategies looks like in schools. This ended up documenting strategies instruction as conceived by Roehler and Duffy (1984), for they had influenced the educators in all three of the settings I studied. That work is reviewed in the next section of this chapter, following a summary of the experimental research that I think is critical for elementary reading educators to keep in mind as they reflect on how to increase comprehension skills in their students.

Summary

The Minnesota research and thinking of the early 1970s in part stimulated a great deal of experimental research on reading. Much was learned in the past 25 years about how to teach word-recognition skills and the criticality of word-recognition instruction in the development of skilled reading, that is, reading that occurs with high comprehension. That vocabulary knowledge matters to comprehension also was established in true experiments, experiments in which teaching of vocabulary was validated as effective in promoting students' abilities to understand text. Perhaps the most salient hypothesis with respect to comprehension, however, was that it could be increased by teaching comprehension strategies to students. In fact, there were many confirmations that teaching students to carry out individual strategies could affect what they acquired from text. These successes led to thinking that multiple comprehension strategies might be taught profitably, if the teaching was metacognitively embellished. Palincsar and Brown (1984) felt that metacognitive understandings might be internalized from practicing use of strategies with small groups of other children. Roehler and Duffy (1984) were much more inclined toward more direct and more extensive teaching, with their perspective going far to impact the educators designing comprehension instruction in schools, the work taken up next.

SCHOOL-BASED INSTRUCTION
OF MULTIPLE COMPREHENSION STRATEGIES

By the end of the 1980s I was aware of educator efforts to carry out instruction in comprehension strategies based on the research of the past several decades. In visiting schools where instruction in strategies was occurring, however, it struck me that it was not being operationalized in any way resembling the type of instruction used in the true experiments validating instruction in comprehension strategies (Pressley et al., 1994, 1995). Even so, often the instruction seemed to be going well, and there were indicators that the students were using the strategies (e.g., school district quasi-experimental validations documented superior achievement in schools deploying strategies instruction). I wanted to understand such instruction and determine whether it was really as effective as it seemed.

However, true experimental methods, which had predominated in the basic research on strategies instruction, were entirely mismatched to the task of understanding the instruction as it occurred in classrooms (Pressley et al., 1995). Thus I turned to qualitative methods (e. g., Lincoln & Guba, 1985; Strauss & Corbin, 1990), including intensive case studies involving long-term observations and interviews of teachers who were teaching comprehension strategies. These qualitative investigations succeeded in producing detailed understanding of the many components comprising strategies instruction in three instructional programs that seemed to be successful (Pressley, El-Dinary, Gaskins, Schuder, Bergman, Almasi, & Brown, 1992).

A striking finding in this work was that strategies instruction was very similar in the three settings that were studied. What was it like?

- Students were taught to use a small repertoire of strategies (e.g., predicting, generating questions, checking back, imagery, summarization).
- Consistent with Roehler and Duffy's (1984) perspective, there was extensive direct explanation and modeling of strategies. Such explanations occurred during both small- and large-group instruction as well as during one-to-one tutoring and reinstruction. Initial explanations and modeling are more complete than later explanations and modeling, although the teachers were emphatic that explanations and modeling should continue for a long time after introduction of strategies. Strategies were introduced slowly, one or a few at a time, with repertoires built up over an academic year or more.
- There was extensive student practice of strategies, with teacher guidance and feedback in response to student needs during such practice. The students did not learn the strategies quickly. Facile use of strategies occurred across a wide range of tasks and materials only after extensive practice in adapting strategies to a wide range of situations and text types.
- Strategies teaching and student applications of strategies occurred across the curriculum.
- Flexibility in strategy use was emphasized, with teachers often pointing out how different students might apply strategies in different ways to the same content.
- Students were often required to model overtly their use of strategies and explain how they were attempting to understand the texts they were reading.
- The teachers provided extensive commentary to students about when and where to apply the strategies they were learning as well as information about the learning benefits produced by use of strategies. (That is, instruction was metacognitively rich.) The teachers prompted use of strategies when students did not use them on their own, with the prompts often in the form of questions suggesting additional strategic processing or possible ways to extend or expand an interpretation. The teachers did not prompt students to use particular strategies but rather tended to prompt them to think about what they could do at this point of a reading.

- When children read in small groups, use of strategies often drove their interpretive discussion of text. Thus students might report on the images they formed as they read, the points that seemed confusing, and their personal summaries.
- Although cognitive in their orientation, the teachers explicitly reinforced student efforts and successes in applying strategies and accomplishing difficult academic tasks.

What had occurred in the settings I studied was that educators with years of field experience were aware of the research literature on comprehension strategies. They selected from that literature the strategies and methods that made the most sense to them in light of their years of experience. The leaders in all three of the settings I studied were aware of Roehler and Duffy's (1984) work on direct explanation and found compelling their rationale for heavy doses of mental modeling during instruction and much subsequent guided practice for students of the strategies they were learning.

As illuminating as the qualitative studies were, the question remained for me of whether such strategies instruction was effective enough that its advantages could be demonstrated in a well-controlled comparison. The 3 years of qualitative work permitted the design of a study that was informative with respect to this issue.

Classroom Experiment

Brown, Pressley, Van Meter and Schuder (1996) undertook a year-long quasi-experimental investigation of the effects of the types of strategies instruction described in the last section. Five grade-2 classrooms receiving instruction in comprehension strategies were matched with grade-2 classrooms taught by teachers who were well regarded as language arts teachers but who were not using a strategies instruction approach. In each classroom, a group of readers who were low achieving at the beginning of grade 2 were identified; the reading of these students was studied intensely.

In the fall of the year, the weak students in the strategies-instruction classrooms and the weak readers in the control classrooms did not differ on standardized measures of reading comprehension and word-attack skills. By the spring, there were clear differences on these measures favoring the strategies-instructed students. In addition, there were differences favoring the strategies-instructed students on other measures (e.g., strategies-instructed students made more diverse and richer interpretations of what they read than did controls). Brown and colleagues (1996) were also able to demonstrate that strategies-instructed students learned more during daily lessons than did control participants (i.e., when given the same lesson in class, the strategies-instructed students remembered more of the content later). In short, although the control students improved over the course of the year (i.e., the control condition was not a "straw person" condition by any means), the strategies-instructed students improved significantly more.

Other Demonstrations of Effective Multiple-Strategies Instruction

In addition to the Brown and colleagues (1996) study at the grade-2 level, there have been at least two true experimental evaluations of strategies instruction consistent with the teaching described earlier in this section. Cathy Collins (1991) improved comprehension in grades 5/6 students by providing a semester (3 days a week) of lessons in comprehension strategies. Her students were taught to predict, seek clarification when uncertain, look for patterns and principles in arguments presented in text, analyze decision-making that occurs during text processing, problem solve (including the use of backward reasoning and visualization), summarize, adapt ideas in text (including rearranging parts of ideas in text), and negotiate interpretations of texts in groups. Although the strategies-instructed students did not differ from controls before the intervention with respect to standardized comprehension performance, there was a difference of 3 standard deviations between treated and control conditions on the posttest, a very large effect for the treatment.

Valerie Anderson (1992; see also Anderson & Roit, 1993) conducted a 3-month experimental investigation of the effects of instruction in multiple comprehension strategies on reading-disabled students in grades 6 through 11. Students were taught comprehension strategies in small groups, with nine groups of strategies-instructed students and seven control groups. Although both strategies-instructed and control students made gains on standardized comprehension measures from before to after the study, the gains were greater in the trained group than in the control condition. Anderson (1992) also collected a variety of qualitative data supporting the conclusion that reading for meaning improved in the strategies-instructed condition: For example, strategies instruction increased student willingness to read difficult material and attempt to understand it. Strategies-instructed students were more likely to collaborate with classmates to discover meanings in text. The strategies-instructed students also reacted to and elaborated text more than did the control participants.

Summary

At least from grade 2 on, weaker readers benefit from instruction about how to use multiple comprehension strategies. Such instruction is long term. It involves extensive teacher explanations and modeling, with this input from the teacher the start of a constructivist learning process (Pressley, Harris, & Marks, 1992). That is, the explanations and modeling encourage students to try to use strategies, and as they do, the students construct detailed understandings for themselves about how the strategy works, the benefits it produces, and how it can be used in a variety of situations. There is nothing passive about the instruction in multiple strategies that I have been studying.

I look forward to additional study of such instruction. I have made the case elsewhere (see Pressley & Afflerbach, 1995) that such instruction stimulates young readers to begin to read in the same way that exceptionally mature readers process text. That is, very mature readers predict ideas that might be encountered in a text, ask questions as they read, reread when confused, construct images depicting the relations expressed in text, and attempt to summarize what they have read. Despite the salient success of instruction in multiple comprehension strategies, I will conclude this chapter with a reminder that the research literature of the past 25 years includes evidence to support more than instruction in comprehension strategies as a means for improving student comprehension abilities.

WHAT SHOULD INSTRUCTION AIMED AT IMPROVING STUDENT COMPREHENSION SKILLS BE THE INSTRUCTION OF?

I have many reservations about the research reviewed here. One is that so much more work has focused on weaker students compared to more typical or gifted readers. Another is that most of the experiments are short term, a few months to a school year at most, while school-based interventions and instructional practices typically have their effects over years. Even so, I think there is enough evidence to argue for a variety of instructional practices to promote reading comprehension:

- Make certain that students make good progress in development of word-recognition skills; provide systematic, explicit instruction in sounding out words for those students who have difficulties with word recognition.
- Have students read many easy and instructional-level books in order to encourage automatic word recognition.

- Teach vocabulary.
- Teach students to use a small repertoire of comprehension strategies, beginning with teacher explanations and modeling of strategies use and continuing with long-term student practice of the
  strategies in a variety of situations and with a variety of texts.

The scientific community has made great progress is learning how
good readers decode and understand text; they have also made great
progress in the last 25 years in demonstrating the potency of teaching
students to use the processes that good readers use. I am thrilled by this
progress. As it turns out, however, there are those who continue to argue
against direct teaching of reading skills, believing that children's literacy
development is best stimulated by immersion in literacy experiences
alone. Moreover, in the same 25 years when so much scientific progress
was made, the whole-language position was developed and came to pre-
dominate in the language arts marketplace. I am hopeful that during the
second quarter-century of my career, the scientific community studying
reading will be as successful in the schoolplace as it has been in the marketplace of academic ideas during the first quarter century of my career.

REFERENCES

Anderson, R. C. & Freebody, P. (1981). Vocabulary knowledge. In J. T. Gutherie
(Ed.), *Comprehension and teaching: Research reviews.* Newark, DE: International
Reading Association.

Anderson, V. (1992). A teacher development project in transactional strategy instruction for teachers of severely reading-disabled adolescents. *Teaching &
Teacher Education, 8,* 391–403.

Anderson, V. and Roit, M. (1993). Planning and implementing collaborative strategy instruction for delayed readers in grades 6–10. *Elementary School Journal,
94,* 121–137.

Beck, I. L., Perfetti, C. A., & McKeown, M. G. (1982). Effects of long-term vocabulary instruction on lexical access and reading comprehension. *Journal of
Educational Psychology, 74,* 506–521.

Breznitz, Z. (1997a). Effects of accelerated reading rate on memory for text among
dyslexic readers. *Journal of Educational Psychology, 89,* 289–297.

Breznitz, Z. (1997b). Enhancing the reading of dyslexic children by reading acceleration and auditory masking. *Journal of Educational Psychology, 89,* 103–
113.

Brown, A. L. (1978). Knowing when, where, and how to remember: A problem
of metacognition. In R. Glaser (Ed.), *Advances in instructional psychology, Vol. 1.*
Hillsdale, NJ: Erlbaum.

Brown, R., Pressley, M., Van Meter, P., & Schuder, T. (1996). A quasi-experimental validation of transactional strategies instruction with low-achieving second grade readers. *Journal of Educational Psychology, 88*, 18–37.

Collins, C. (1991). Reading instruction that increases thinking abilities. *Journal of Reading, 34*, 510–516.

Danner, F. W., & Taylor, A. M. (1973). Integrated pictures and relational imagery training in children's learning. *Journal of Experimental Child Psychology, 16*, 47–54.

Duffy, G. G., & Roehler, L. R. (1989). Why strategy instruction is so difficult and what we need to do about it. In C. B. McCormick, G. Miller, & M. Pressley (Eds.), *Cognitive strategy research: From basic research to educational applications* (pp. 133–154). New York: Springer-Verlag.

Ehri, L. C. (1991). Development of the ability to read words. In R. Barr, M. L. Kamil, P. B. Mosenthal, & P. D. Pearson (Eds.), *Handbook of reading research* (Vol. 2; pp. 383–417). New York: Longman.

Ehri, L. C. (1992). Reconceptualizing the development of sight word reading and its relationship to recoding. In P. B. Gough, L. C. Ehri, & R. Treiman (Eds.), *Reading acquisition* (pp. 107–143). Hillsdale, NJ: Erlbaum.

Flavell, J. H. (1977). *Cognitive development.* Englewood Cliffs, NJ: Prentice-Hall.

Flavell, J. H., Beach, D. H., & Chinsky, J. M. (1966). Spontaneous verbal rehearsal in a memory task as a function of age. *Child Development, 37*, 283–299.

Fleisher, L. S., Jenkins, J. R., & Pany, D. (1979). Effects on poor readers' comprehension of training in rapid decoding. *Reading Research Quarterly, 15*, 30–48.

Gough, P. B. & Tunmer, W. E. (1986). Decoding, reading, and reading disability. *Remedial and Special Education, 7*, 6–10.

Hyde, T. S., & Jenkins, J. J. (1973). Recall for words as a function of semantic, graphic, and syntactic orienting tasks. *Journal of Verbal Learning and Verbal Behavior, 12*, 471–480.

Johnson, D. D., & Pearson, P. D. (1978). *Teaching reading vocabulary.* New York: Holt, Rinehart & Winston.

Keeney, F. J., Cannizzo, S. R., & Flavell, J. H. (1967). Spontaneous and induced verbal rehearsal in a recall task. *Child Development, 38*, 953–966.

Kreutzer, M. A., Leonard, C., & Flavell, J. H. (1975). An interview study of children's knowledge about memory. *Monographs of the Society for Research in Child Development, 40* (Serial No. 159).

LaBerge, D., & Samuels, S. J. (1974). Toward a theory of automatic information processing in reading. *Cognitive Psychology, 6*, 293–323.

Levin, J. R. (1973). Inducing comprehension in poor readers: A test of a recent model. *Journal of Educational Psychology, 65*, 19–24.

Lincoln, Y. S., & Guba, E. G. (1985). *Naturalistic inquiry.* Newbury Park, CA: Sage.

Lovett, M. W., Borden, S. L., Deluca, T., Lacarenza, L., Benson, N. J., and Brackstone, D. (1994). Treating the core deficits of developmental dyslexia: Evidence of transfer of learning after phonologically- and strategy-based reading training programs. *Developmental Psychology, 30*, 805–822.

Lovett, M. W., Ransby, M. J., Hardwick, N., Johns, M. S., & Donaldson, S. A. (1989). Can dyslexia be treated? Treatment-specific and generalized treatment effects in dyslexic children's response to remediation. *Brain and Language, 37,* 90–121.

McKeown, M. G., Beck, I. L., Omanson, R. C., & Perfetti, C. A. (1983). The effects of long-term vocabulary instruction on reading comprehension: A replication. *Journal of Reading Behavior, 15,* 3–18.

McKeown, M. G., Beck, I. L., Omanson, R. C., & Pople, M. T. (1985). Some effects of the nature and frequency of vocabulary instruction on the knowledge and use of words. *Reading Research Quarterly, 20,* 522–535.

Miller, G. A. (1956). The magical number seven, plus-or-minus two: Some limits on our capacity for processing information. *Psychological Review, 63,* 81–97.

Moely, B. E., Olson, F. A., Halwes, T. G., & Flavell, J. H. (1969). Production deficiency in young children's clustered recall. *Developmental Psychology, 1,* 26–34.

Newell, A., & Simon, H. A. (1972). *Human problem solving.* Englewood Cliffs, NJ: Prentice-Hall.

Nicholson, T. (1991). Do children read words better in context or in lists? A classic study revisited. *Journal of Educational Psychology, 83,* 444–450.

Nicholson, T., Bailey, J., & McArthur, J. (1991). Context cues in reading: The gap between research and popular opinion. *Journal of Reading: Writing and Learning Disabilities, 7,* 33–41.

Ornstein, P. A. (Ed.) (1978). *Memory development in children.* Hillsdale, NJ: Erlbaum.

Palincsar, A. S., & Brown, A. L. (1984). Reciprocal teaching of comprehension-fostering and monitoring activities. *Cognition and Instruction, 1,* 117–175.

Pearson, P. D., & Fielding, L. (1991). Comprehension instructrion. In R. Barr, M. L. Kamil, P. B. Mosenthal, & P. D. Pearson (Eds.), *Handbook of reading research* (Vol. 2; pp. 815–860). New York: Longman.

Pearson, P. D., & Johnson, D. D. (1978). *Teaching reading comprehension.* New York: Holt, Rinehart & Winston.

Pressley, G. M. (1976). Mental imagery helps eight-year-olds remember what they read. *Journal of Educational Psychology, 68,* 355–359.

Pressley, M., & Afflerbach, P. (1995). *Verbal protocols of reading: The nature of constructively responsive reading.* Hillsdale, NJ: Erlbaum.

Pressley, M., Almasi, J., Schuder, T., Bergman, J., Hite, S., El-Dinary, P. B., & Brown, R. (1994). Transactional instruction of comprehension strategies: The Montgomery County MD SAIL Program. *Reading and Writing Quarterly, 10,* 5–19.

Pressley, M., Borkowski, J. G., & O'Sullivan, J. T. (1984). Memory strategy instruction is made of this: Metamemory and durable strategy use. *Educational Psychologist, 19,* 94–107.

Pressley, M., Borkowski, J. G., & O'Sullivan, J. T. (1985). Children's metamemory and the teaching of memory strategies. In D. L. Forrest-Pressley, G. E. MacKinnin, & T. G. Waller (Eds.), *Metacognition, cognition, and human performance.* (pp. 111–153). New York: Academic Press.

Pressley, M., El-Dinary, P. B., Brown, R., Schuder, T., Bergman, J. L., York, M., Gaskins, I. W., & Faculties and Administration of Benchmark School and the Montgomery County MD SAIL/SIA Programs. (1995). A transactional strategies instruction Christmas carol. In A. McKeough, J. Lupart, & A. Marini

(Eds.) *Teaching for transfer: Fostering generalization in learning.* (pp. 177–213). Hillsdale, NJ: Erlbaum.

Pressley, M., El-Dinary, P. B., Gaskins, I., Schuder, T., Bergman, J., Almasi, L., & Brown, R. (1992). Beyond direct explanation: Transactional instruction of reading comprehension strategies. *Elementary School Journal, 92,* 511–554.

Pressley, M., Harris, K. R., & Marks, M. B. (1992). But good strategy instructors are constructivists!! *Educational Psychology Review, 4,* 1–32.

Pressley, M., Johnson, C. J., Symons, S., McGoldrick, J. A., & Kurita, J. A. (1989). Strategies that improve memory and comprehension of text. *Elementary School Journal, 90,* 3–32.

Roehler, L. R., & Duffy, G. G. (1984). Direct explanation of comprehension processes. In G. G. Duffy, L. R. Roehler, & J. Mason (Eds.), *Comprehension instruction: Perspectives and suggestions* (pp. 265–280). New York: Longman.

Rosenshine, B., & Meister, C. (1984). Reciprocal teaching: A review of nineteen experimental studies. *Review of Educational Research, 64,* 479–530.

Samuels, S. J. (1970). Effects of pictures on learning to read, comprehension, and attitudes. *Review of Educational Research, 40,* 397–407.

Schneider, W. (1985). Developmental trends in the metamemory-memory behavior relationship: An integrative review. In D. L. Forrest-Pressley, G. E. MacKinnon, & T. G. Waller (Eds.), *Metacognition, cognition, and human performance* (Vol. 1; pp. 57–109). Orlando, FL: Academic Press.

Smith, F. (1971). *Understanding reading: A psycholinguistic analysis of reading and learning to read.* New York: Holt, Rinehart & Winston.

Strauss, A., & Corbin, J. (1990). *Basics of qualitative research: Grounded theory procedures and techniques.* Newbury Park, CA: Sage.

Tan, A., & Nicholson, T. (1997). Flashcards revisited: Training poor readers to read words faster improves their comprehension of text. *Journal of Educational Psychology, 89,* 276–288.

Till, R. E., & Jenkins, J. J. (1973). The effects of cued orienting tasks on the free recall of words. *Journal of Verbal Learning and Verbal Behavior, 12,* 489–498.

Vellutino, F. R., Scanlon, D. M., Sipay, E. R., Small, S. G., Pratt, A., Chen, R., & Denckla, M. B. (1996). Cognitive profiles of difficult-to-remediate and readily remediated poor readers: Early intervention as a vehicle for distinguishing between cognitive and experiential deficits as a basic cause of specific reading disability. *Journal of Educational Psychology, 88,* 601–638.

Walsh, D. A., & Jenkins, J. K. (1973). Effects of orienting tasks on free recall in incidental learning: "Difficulty," "effort," and "process" explanations. *Journal of Verbal Learning and Verbal Behavior, 12,* 481–488.

Weaver, C. (1994). *Understanding whole language: From principles to practice.* Portsmouth, NH: Heinemann.

Yuill, N., & Oakhill, J. (1988). Effects of inference awareness training on poor reading comprehension. *Applied Cognitive Psychology, 2,* 33–45.

3

Explicit and Implicit Instruction in Comprehension

JANICE A. DOLE

Thirty years ago, most reading educators believed that comprehension abilities improved through instruction in the numerous skills identified in basal reading programs (N. Smith, 1986). Teachers who used basal reading programs, and most did, judiciously taught a prescribed set of discrete and quite mechanical comprehension skills as part of their basal instruction. Today few teachers, and still fewer researchers, believe that teaching a prescribed and mechanical set of comprehension skills is synonymous with teaching reading comprehension. There is a largely agreed-upon research base to support the position that because comprehension is more than a set of discrete skills, teaching a set of such skills is insufficient for improving comprehension (Anderson, Hiebert, Scott, & Wilkinson, 1984; Rosenshine & Stevens, 1984).

However, the reading field is currently caught between conflicting views of how best to improve students' comprehension abilities. There are many ways to characterize these conflicting views—basals versus whole-language approaches, basals versus literature-based programs, teacher-centered versus student-centered instruction, comprehension versus interpretation, and so forth. In this chapter, I have chosen to focus on one particular way to characterize the problem—explicit versus implicit comprehension instruction.

Some researchers and educators, convinced by numerous studies supporting the use of comprehension strategies, suggest that comprehension instruction should consist of the explicit teaching of various strategies that expert readers use (Pressley & Afflerbach, 1995). Such suggestions are based on the cognitive and metacognitive research of the 1980s (for reviews, see Baker & Brown, 1984; Dole, Duffy, Roehler, & Pearson,

1991; Pressley, Johnson, Symons, McGoldrick, & Kurita, 1989). Other researchers and educators, many of whom advocate a literature-based reading program, support the use of implicit or indirect instruction. Some argue for setting up rich contexts for learning and providing students with choice and purpose for reading (Goodman, 1986). Others argue for instruction through personal responses to and discussions about literature (Eeds & Wells, 1989; Hill, Johnson, & Schlick Noe, 1995). These positions are supported by philosophical movements such as Progressive Education (Hines, 1972) and social construction models of learning (Bakhtin, 1986; Vygotsky, 1978).

In this chapter I discuss these two instructional formats—explicit and implicit instruction in comprehension. First, I provide a historical perspective on each instructional format, discussing psychological theories of learning and philosophies of education that underlie each. I also discuss how these instructional formats are related to broader psychological and philosophical views about teaching and learning. Next, I place various representations of explicit and implicit instruction on a continuum of comprehension models. I conclude with several observations related to comprehension instruction in American schools today.

EXPLICIT COMPREHENSION INSTRUCTION

I begin my discussion on explicit comprehension instruction with early theory and research on reading, theory and research rooted in behaviorism. This discussion may seem like an odd place to start. Certainly, very few people accept the principles of behaviorism today as a basis on which to conceptualize instruction. However, I believe that we cannot make sense out of what is happening today in the comprehension field without an adequate understanding of the roots of that instruction—which lie squarely in behavioral principles as applied to basal reading programs.

While decoding instruction has had a long and distinguished history of attention and debate, comprehension instruction has only recently received much attention. Early in the twentieth century, the accepted model of reading instruction did not include the teaching of comprehension. Psychologists interested in reading believed that reading comprehension *could not be taught and did not need to be taught* (N. Smith, 1986). They believed that students could comprehend through reading just as they comprehended through listening. Reading was considered to be a process of mastering, or "cracking," the code. Once students could decode, then comprehension occurred automatically. In other words, reading was decoding plus oral language comprehension (Gough, 1972). Thus comprehension was something that researchers did not think much about (but see Bartlett, 1932; Thorndike, 1917).

At the same time in the 1920s and 1930s, educational researchers did begin to connect research with instruction by promoting the idea that reading instruction should be based on research principles (N. Smith, 1986). These research principles were derived from the psychology of learning. Because behaviorism was the predominant model of learning during the early to mid-twentieth century, the research used to inform reading instruction was based on behaviorist principles (Driscoll, 1994).

Behaviorist Principles of Instruction

Behaviorist principles were evident in the basal reading programs so common to reading instruction during the mid-twentieth century. For example, instruction was thought to be best presented in a series of *small steps.* Each step was thought to build on the previous one, which had to be "mastered." Indeed, the term *skill mastery* became commonplace in basal programs. Another component of basal instruction rooted in behaviorist principles was the idea of *instructional objectives* (Driscoll, 1994). Basal reading programs, indeed all instruction during the mid-twentieth century, included a set of instructional objectives that described in detail the new behavior that was to occur after instruction. Teachers' manuals of basal programs were replete with instructional objectives for the various skills that were thought to be needed for successful comprehension.

During the 1960s and 1970s, additional research on programmed and computer-assisted instruction incorporated what psychologists thought to be the best components of behavioral principles. These principles came to be associated with the term *direct instruction.* Although there are many definitions of and criteria for direct instruction, Rosenshine and Stevens (1984) targeted three important components that cut across the various definitions. These components include *demonstration, guided practice with feedback,* and *independent practice.* Demonstration consisted of the teacher giving students clear and explicit directions on what to do. Guided practice occurred when teachers guided students through the use of the skill. In this step, teachers and students worked together to practice the skill that had been taught. Lastly, independent practice required students to practice the skill on their own, without teacher or peer help.

From this generic model of direct instruction, as well as from additional behaviorist principles of learning, came a new and different instructional reading program that was to have an enormous impact on models of teaching and instruction as well as on reading. The commercial program DISTAR (Science Research Associates, 1968) was designed to use demonstration, guided practice, and corrective feedback to teach reading to urban minority children (Roehler & Duffy, 1991). Although DISTAR's initial focus was on the teaching and learning of phonics skills, the program's direct instruction method came to include all reading practices. DISTAR practices included precisely scripted lessons in which teachers demonstrated, cued students to correct responses, and provided feedback and "extrinsic reinforcement." With the success of DISTAR in many urban school settings (Becker, 1977), the direct instruction method received support within the educational community.

Despite the success of DISTAR and additional research on the effectiveness of direct instruction, many educators had—and still have—a difficult time accepting the direct instruction model (O'Flahavan & Seidl, 1997). Many educators rejected the rote drill-and-practice approach of the direct instruction model and questioned its utility with average learners and in ill-structured domains such as comprehension. Besides, the direct instruction method has been associated with teacher-centered approaches to instruction. Educators have been concerned that many critically important affective habits of successful reading—like enjoying reading—are left out in direct instruction models. Many think the focus of direct instruction is on small, unimportant skills that are readily observed and recorded. Educators have pointed out that these skills may not be the critical ones for comprehension (Tierney & Cunningham, 1984).

It should be noted that at the same time that DISTAR was entering classrooms as a viable form of reading instruction, research on teaching was amassing an enormous amount of data on what effective instruction looked like (Brophy & Good, 1986). The research focused on effective teaching skills associated with high student achievement. Studies were conducted primarily in the areas of reading and mathematics. This body of research, sometimes referred to as teacher effects research, added strength to behavioral principles as a theoretical framework for instruction.

Cognitive Principles and Comprehension

In the midst of this intellectual activity, a huge paradigm shift in the field of psychology was under way. The shift led researchers away from the dominant behavioral model to a new cognitive model of learning.

This cognitive revolution of the 1970s forced researchers to rethink the comprehension process and comprehension instruction. It was at this time that the relationship between listening and reading became clearer, as researchers came to view comprehension through listening as different in important ways from comprehension through reading (Sticht & James,

1984). Just because readers decoded a text did not mean that they understood it. Additionally, research documented that comprehension was not a passive process in which readers merely absorbed meaning from the text, as was suggested by early behavioral principles. Instead, reading was viewed as an active process in which readers interacted with the text to produce meaning (Rumelhart & Ortony, 1977). Thus, reading came to be viewed as an interactive process in which reader and text together construct meaning.

At about the same time that researchers began to look at the cognitive processes involved in comprehension, a related body of research was being amassed on metacognition. The umbrella term *metacognition* arose from interest in the cognitive processing of experts and novices (for a review, see Chi, Glaser, & Farr, 1988). This interest led to research on what it is that good readers do that may be different from what poor readers do. These good reader/poor reader studies produced a volume of research on the strategic nature of the reading process (Baker & Brown, 1984). Research showed that good readers were strategic readers. They appeared to have a purpose for reading, they monitored their comprehension as they read, and they reflected on their reading. When comprehension broke down, good readers were found to use a variety of strategies to repair their understanding. Further, good readers used various strategies flexibly, and they adapted their strategies to different contexts.

In contrast, poor readers were seen to use few strategies. They did not have available to them the variety of strategies used by good readers. And when they did use a particular strategy, they tended to use it inflexibly and apply it indiscriminately.

However, a host of studies, reviewed by Pressley, Johnson, and colleagues (1989) and Dole and colleagues (1991), were developed to see if lower-achieving readers could learn the strategies used intuitively by good readers. Researchers adapted some components of a direct instruction model to develop effective instruction (Pearson & Gallagher, 1983). These components included *demonstration* and *explanation, guided practice* and *independent practice.* When lower-achieving readers were taught to use strategies, such as determining the most important information and visualizing while reading, their comprehension improved.

During the 1980s many reading researchers traded in the term *direct* instruction for a term that appeared to carry less negative baggage. Based on a body of research on teaching strategies for comprehension, researchers coined the term *explicit* instruction to refer to a variety of teacher activities associated with student achievement (Pearson & Gallagher, 1983; Rosenshine & Stevens, 1984). Explicit instruction came to include not only telling students what they would be learning, but also giving them the procedural and conditional knowledge to do so (Paris, Lipson, & Wixson, 1983).

Pearson and Dole (1987) described the difference between the new explicit instruction and the old direct instruction in reading comprehension. They argued that with explicit instruction, teachers directed and students practiced the whole process of comprehension every time they read. Explicit instruction, unlike direct instruction, did not break comprehension down into a set of subskills that were then practiced one by one. Explicit instruction in comprehension focused on practice with the whole of comprehension.

Second, explicit instruction did not imply mastery of comprehension. In traditional direct instruction models, students practiced until they mastered a given skill; then they moved on to a new one. With explicit instruction, there is no assumption that comprehension is ever mastered. Instead, the assumption is that comprehension ability will always vary with the background knowledge and strategic ability of the reader. Third, with explicit instruction there is no assumption that there is one right answer. In fact, there could be more than one answer to and interpretation of a given comprehension question.

Cognitive Theory and Classroom Practice

Despite the proliferation of studies in the 1980s verifying the effectiveness of explicit strategy instruction, the research did not appear to have much impact on reading instruction in American classrooms. I agree with El-Dinary, Pressley, and Schuder's (1992) argument that strategy instruction was simply too different from teachers' prevailing notions about skills instruction.

Thus teachers went on teaching the skills in their basal reading programs. I believe they did so for many reasons. One was that most teachers were not aware of the growing body of research on the comprehension process and comprehension instruction. The research had not reached them, nor had textbook publishers yet incorporated the new research into their basal reading programs (Dole, Rogers, & Osborn, 1987). Second, many teachers did not know what else to do. At that time, most of them reported that they relied heavily on their basal programs for their reading instruction (Durkin, 1983; Mason & Osborn, 1982). Third, many teachers believed that since basal reading programs were written by the people they considered to be the experts, the skills listed must indeed be those that needed to be taught (Shannon, 1989).

IMPLICIT COMPREHENSION INSTRUCTION

Unlike explicit instruction, implicit instruction has a long tradition rooted more in philosophy than in psychology. During the early 1900s, a popular movement known as Progressive Education led educators to focus on children and their experiences rather than teachers and the curriculum. Influenced by Dewey's (1913, 1916) philosophy, educators believed that children needed real and direct experiences interacting with their world rather than contrived experiences constructed by teachers. Also critical to children's learning were *choice, interest,* and *purpose.* Children must have a choice in what they do, and they will learn when they have an interest in and purpose for learning. Thus, according to Progressives, real-world activities should be used for instruction (Hines, 1972), for example, writing a letter to grandparents and mailing it, or constructing a birdhouse.

Edelsky, Altwerger, and Flores (1991) pointed out that the Progressive Education movement can be understood best against the sociocultural backdrop of the early 1900s. At that time, schools focused on rote learning and memorization, and children were forced into long and arduous labor in factories. Progressives advocated a reversal of instructional methods to counter what was considered by many at that time as outmoded and oppressive views of child development. The Progressive Education movement and its child-centered approach to instruction withered and reemerged several times during the twentieth century, most recently in the Open Education movement of the 1960s.

Whole Language

During the late 1970s and early 1980s, a new orientation to reading instruction, known as *whole language,* took shape. Based on philosophical principles of child-centered instruction as well as psycholinguistic theory and research conducted during the 1970s (Goodman, 1986), whole language was to dramatically change the nature of reading instruction in many American classrooms. Whole language also helped shatter basal programs' dominance in elementary reading classrooms. This is a particularly interesting event, since the huge body of research in cognitive psychology and reading impacted on teachers and classrooms so little.

I believe that it is also interesting that a major premise of whole language has been the use of implicit, as opposed to explicit, instruction. As a matter of fact, many would argue that the rigidity of programs like DISTAR led to a backlash resulting in the more implicit instruction represented by whole language. This argument is consistent with a sociocultural interpretation of the Progressive Education movement as well.

In part, whole language is based on first-language acquisition theory, which describes and explains how children learn oral language (Garcia & Pearson, 1990). Advocates of whole language argue that children learn to read just as they learn to speak and listen. Thus, they see literacy as an extension of oral language development. According to whole-language adherents, just as oral language development is a natural process, so too is literacy development a natural process (Goodman, 1986). Whole-language advocates do not separate reading and writing, nor do they separate these abilities from speaking and listening. They see all four of the language arts as interrelated, and therefore they propose that the teaching of language arts should be integrated.

Whole-language enthusiasts argue that instruction in literacy, both reading and writing, should occur in rich contexts—as does oral language. Advocates point out that oral language development occurs because there is a need for it; that is, individuals have a purpose for and value communicating with others. Thus literacy instruction should be purposeful as well. Students should read for authentic reasons—for example, to find out more information or to enjoy a book. Such purposes are in marked contrast to reading for the teacher or for a grade. Whole-language classrooms provide numerous opportunities for children to read good literature—whole texts rather than excerpts—and also provide a rich context for reading. Students should also write for authentic reasons. Authentic writing tasks include writing for real audiences and real purposes—for example, to send a letter to grandparents or to create a brochure.

Whole language, like implicit instruction in general, places the teacher in the role of facilitator, rather than guide or expert. The teacher's role is to provide the rich context, which includes lots of books to read, time to read and write, and real purposes for reading and writing. Sometimes teachers *demonstrate* how they read and what they do as they read (Newman, 1985; F. Smith, 1981). But demonstrations come at "teachable moments" when a teacher notices that students are having a particular problem. Demonstrations cannot be planned ahead of time because they should occur as needed. Comprehension instruction, if it occurs at all, should not follow a predetermined curriculum.

What impact has whole language had on classroom practice? I believe the effects are difficult to determine since whole language has been interpreted differently by different people. This is one reason that many proponents include misconceptions about whole language in their definitions of it (Edelsky et al., 1991; Weaver, 1990). In part as a result of this, teachers changed their instruction in many different ways. This became a problem when two "whole-language" teachers could create very different-looking classrooms with very different kinds of instruction.

However, I believe there have been three critical changes in American comprehension instruction prompted by whole language. First, because basal reading programs had been criticized so heavily for their "deskilling" of teachers and their poor-quality literature (Davison & Kantor, 1982; Goodman, 1988; Shannon, 1989), many teachers and school districts abandoned basal programs entirely (although this is changing quite rapidly even as I write). Second, many teachers developed their reading programs around individual picture books and sets of novels for older students. Thus students stopped reading basal stories and started reading high-quality children's and adolescent literature. Third, I believe that as teachers moved away from basals, many of them gave up teaching comprehension skills. Some teachers may have misinterpreted whole language to mean that there should be no instruction at all. I think that whole language was interpreted by many as practice in reading and writing. And as teachers abandoned the basals, they also threw out the guided reading lesson as well as the teaching of comprehension skills. As a result, many teachers simply did not know what to teach. The result of all this has been a fragmentation of teachers' understandings about and teaching of comprehension in American classrooms.

Literary Response Theory and Practice

Whole-language advocates did, in fact, present an alternative comprehension curriculum that, I think, just not did catch on. This curriculum, sometimes called "literary response" or "reader response" (Beach, 1993; Beach & Hynds, 1991), is in many ways consistent with cognitive views about the comprehension process. Both view meaning not as residing in the text but as arising from an interaction (Rumelhart & Ortony, 1977), or transaction (Rosenblatt, 1978), between the reader and the text. Both put different weights at different times on the reader and the text, and both allow many alternative, but plausible, interpretations of a text based on characteristics of the reader.

The focus of much of the literary response research has been on readers and the different social, personal, cultural, and idiosyncratic responses they make to texts. Reader response researchers have looked at how readers respond emotionally to texts; connect texts to their own experiences, attitudes and beliefs; and interpret and evaluate texts (for a review, see Beach & Hynds, 1991). They have also focused on particular stances that readers take and how those stances affect responses (Langer, 1992; Rosenblatt, 1978).

Over the last 10 years or so, many researchers and teachers wanting to develop a literature-based reading program have moved to a literary response perspective on the teaching of reading. A literary response perspective suggests different kinds of classroom instruction in reading than do cognitive or whole-language perspectives. Further, literary response perspectives lead to a form of implicit instruction that stands in contrast to most of the traditional comprehension instruction.

Literary response theory has taken shape in the form of literature circles or study groups (Eeds & Wells, 1989; Peterson & Eeds, 1990). In these groups, students read and respond to literature. In reader response discussion groups, teachers and students talk about a commonly read novel, focusing on students' *personal* and *social* reactions to the literature. Teachers and students ask questions such as "What is your impression of Phillip so far?" "What mood or feeling did the novel leave with you?" Teachers also ask Socratic questions such as "What would be an example?" "What are you implying by that?" and "Why do you think that is true?" (Hirsch, 1997). Unlike in basal reading programs, teachers do not ask students convergent questions to which they themselves already know the answer.

Reader response theorists and literature study group proponents would argue that all instruction in comprehension should be implicit. Karolides (1997) describes it well:

> It is probable that the learning-to-read factors attended to . . . are multiple. The teacher leads them [the students] to consider their comments, to reconsider and develop their reading through the interactive discussion that she promotes. She leads them back to the text to confirm their assertions and to amplify them. She encourages them to relate to the context of the setting and character. The students are learning to be attentive to multiple voices, to reflect on subtleties expressed in the text. *These skills, with practice, will become a part of the internal processing of texts.* (p. 25; emphases added)

Thus, it is clear that no direct or explicit teaching occurs in reader response activities. However, advocates expect that, over time and with practice, students will internalize the reader response–type processing of texts that occurs as part of the literature study groups. Thus, literature circles represent a good example of implicit comprehension instruction.

THE CURRENT COMPREHENSION SCENE

So, given the history of explicit and implicit comprehension instruction in this century and given the newest developments in theory and practice, what can be said of comprehension instruction as it occurs in the late 1990s? I know of no very recent surveys of how teachers currently teach reading comprehension in American classrooms. One of the problems with such a survey is that instruction is changing so fast. Resarchers run the risk of shooting at a fast-moving target to get a handle on what is happening in American classrooms today. Nevertheless, I think I can make several comments about explicit and implicit comprehension instruction as we close out the twentieth century.

- *Despite a significant body of research in the 1980s suggesting the effectiveness of strategy instruction, especially for lower-achieving readers, strategy instruction has not been implemented in many American classrooms.* As Pressley and his colleagues described well (Pressley, Goodchild, Fleet, Zajchowski, & Evans, 1989), strategy instruction is a difficult conceptual leap for teachers who have been used to teaching skills. It appeared that although teachers had been somewhat successful at teaching strategies when they were taught how to do so, they did not seem to be able to sustain that teaching over time (Duffy & Roehler, 1989). In addition, strategy instruction requires using an explicit teaching model that may make many teachers uncomfortable, especially in an era of acceptance of implicit instruction.

I do know of one large-scale program that has managed to incorporate instruction in comprehension strategy into a full-fledged curriculum. Keene and Zimmerman (1997) describe a project funded by a nonprofit business and public education coalition in Denver, Colorado. Using the strategies identified by Dole and colleagues (1991) and Pressley, Johnson and colleagues (1989), teachers have developed and successfully implemented a reading and writing curriculum based on comprehension strategies. Developed over a period of more than 10 years of experience, the program serves as a model of what teachers can do using an explicit strategy instructional model.

There is other good news related to teaching strategies as well. In a recent paper, Rosenshine (1997) discussed the extent to which cognitive strategy instruction has been implemented in recent basal reading programs. To his surprise, and mine, he found that cognitive strategy instruction was alive and well in current basal programs. Developers of basal programs have paid attention to the research on comprehension strategies and now include these strategies as part of their instructional program.

To what extent teachers who use these programs have actually changed their instruction to be more explicit and strategic, though, is unknown. Teachers have a history of selective and flexible use of basal reading programs (Dole & Osborn, 1991), and I imagine this is still the case. But there is no research on the extent to which teachers are faithful to the teaching of comprehension strategies found in the most recent basal programs. Further, while there is some research comparing effective strategy instruction with traditional basal instruction (Dole, Brown, & Trathen, 1996), I know of no studies comparing the teaching of these new strategies in basals with the teaching of traditional comprehension skills in basals. Thus I can make the assumption that the new basal instruction is better than the old, and that assumption fits well with current research. But it remains an empirical question.

- *Many teachers who have abandoned basal reading programs have also abandoned comprehension instruction.* I realize this is a strong statement, but my own observations bear it out. I believe that when teachers rejected the basal reading program, they also rejected the directed or guided reading lesson,—which is so basic to teaching comprehension. Thus some teachers do not know the most basic framework for comprehension instruction—build or activate prior knowledge, promote interest and engagement in a selection, ask questions, reflect on what has been read. I have had many experiences where administrators and teachers have asked me, "What is guided reading?"

It is hard to tell whether teachers did not have this basic knowledge to begin with or whether they had the knowledge and rejected it along with the basal reading program. Certainly, advocates of reader response perspectives—as well as whole-language perspectives (Shannon, 1989)—have promoted the idea of rejecting all the activities in basal programs because they "basalize and trivialize" children's literature (Karnowski, 1997, p. 308). Instead, teachers are told to "trust the literature, the students and yourself" (Karnowski, 1997, p. 311).

The use of literature in the form of content-area trade books, big books, and little books in classrooms has seemed to increase students' motivation to read (Guthrie et al., 1996; Guthrie & Wigfield, 1997; Neuman & Roskos, 1997). Many teachers understand the importance of motivation to read, and they have watched their students' motivation increase with the amount and quality of the tradebooks they have in their classrooms (Morrow, 1992).

Nevertheless, it has been my observation that many teachers appear as though they simply do not know what to do other than have their students read. This may be part of a belief system held by some teachers, especially as they interpret whole language. In a survey I recently conducted, one teacher responded to a question about what was important to teach in order to improve reading abilities: "just have the kids practice reading and practice writing." But I do not believe this is a universal understanding of teachers. Many teachers just do not know what to do.

• *Many teachers want to learn more effective ways of instructing.* This point is a personal observation that is corroborated, I believe, by recent trends in the publishing industry. Many teachers are purchasing, reading, and sharing a new genre of books on the literacy process (see, e.g., Hill et al., 1995; Karolides, 1997; Peterson & Eeds, 1990; Routman, 1994: Short, Harste, & Burke, 1996). It is likely that this genre of books was spawned by the highly popular books written by Graves (1983), Calkins (1986), and Atwell (1987). The books are being used in workshops throughout the country and are being read by many elementary and secondary teachers. They are written in a nonacademic style and tone. They are written through the eyes of teachers struggling to find ways to engage their students with text and to have them become readers and writers.

Interestingly, there are no chapters on comprehension instruction in most of these books. Almost all of these books advocate some form of implicit comprehension instruction based on whole-language or reader response perspectives, rather than the explicit teaching of strategies (but see Keene & Zimmerman, 1997).

• *Some teachers want easy answers in the increasingly complex world of teaching and learning.* I say this with some misgivings because I do not want to disparage teachers and their efforts. But I find some teachers who are unwilling to take on the admittedly complex job of fully analyzing their thinking about comprehension and comprehension instruction. It is sometimes difficult to convince them that unless they have a conceptual understanding about the reading process itself, their instruction will likely be inadequate.

I believe a lack of understanding of the comprehension process is one reason for the proliferation of tradebooks in classrooms and the emphasis on practice in reading. I believe that whole language has been interpreted by many teachers as using literature instead of basals and practice instead of instruction. So, teachers have been able to reject basals and to provide students with time to practice. At the same time, whole language has also been interpreted as not using the instructional activities in basal programs. Thus many teachers do not teach the guided reading lesson or traditional comprehension skills.

• *Regardless of the theoretical and instructional approach, many advocates of that approach seem to think they have the answer.* Whether the approach is direct or explicit instruction, whole language, or reader response, there are some adherents who cannot seem to look beyond their one approach to embrace multiple approaches to teaching comprehension. Clearly, whole-language advocates were correct in identifying a significant problem of old basal reading programs. Old programs included bland texts accompanied by bland instruction. The texts and instruction failed to promote students' motivation and interest in reading. When there is motivation and interest in reading, comprehension is improved. And clearly the direct and explicit instruction models of reading have been shown to demonstrate improved reading comprehension for many students, especially lower-achieving readers. This research is largely quantitative in nature, and it is certainly robust. Further, an examination of the best of literature discussions will convince educators that there is much merit in developing thoughtful, careful readers who understand the relationships between stories and their own personal lives and experiences. Even though there are only a few research studies supporting this approach (see Eeds & Wells, 1989), the numerous anecdotes of students' responses would indicate that students' comprehension benefited from the instruction they received.

CONCLUSION

The critical question, and the most complex one to answer, is how to teach comprehension in such as a way as to incorporate the best of explicit and implicit instructional models. But I think this merging of models is problematic. Here is why. While educators, philosophers, and researchers debate the advantages and disadvantages of explicit and implicit instruction, teachers view the debate as pendulum swings rather than significant discussions. Constant changes and different recommended methodologies appear to reinforce many teachers' existing conceptions that theory and research tell them nothing. Therefore, for many practitioners, education continues to be a series of pendulum-swinging fads. And, if the description of trends in this chapter is at all accurate, the field *has* moved from one pendulum swing to the other.

Despite the climate of this current educational milieu, there are researchers and practitioners who are managing to find an appropriate balance between explicit and implicit instruction that is necessary for improving comprehension abilities. I use the term *balance* cautiously because it is fast becoming trite as an educational term. Nevertheless, I can point to reasonable researchers and practitioners who are able to combine explicit and implicit instruction into a coherent, comprehensive program. Recent examples include work by McMahon and Raphael (1997), Guthrie and colleagues (1996), Baumann and Ivey (1997), and Gaskins and Gaskins (1997). Examination of these programs suggests that they incorporate the best components of comprehension instruction by including explicit teaching embedded within a print-rich context that allows students to make sense of, and enjoy, what they read. Perhaps these models of comprehension instruction will some day be understood and embraced by many more American teachers and, in the end, reasonableness will win out.

REFERENCES

Anderson, R. C., Hiebert, E. H., Scott, J. A., & Wilkinson, I. A. G. (1985). *Becoming a nation of readers: The report of the Commission of Reading.* Washington, DC: National Academy of Education.

Atwell, N. (1987). *In the middle: Writing, reading, and learning with adolescents.* Portsmouth, NH: Heinemann.

Baker, L., & Brown, A. L. (1984). Metacognitive skills and reading. In P. D. Pearson, R. Barr, M. L. Kamil, & P. Mosenthal (Eds.), *Handbook of reading research* (Vol. 1; pp. 353–394). New York: Longman.

Bakhtin, M. (1986). *Speech genres and other essays.* Austin: University of Texas Press.

Bartlett, F. C. (1932). *Remembering: A study in experimental and social psychology.* Cambridge, UK: Cambridge University Press.

Baumann, J. F., & Ivey, G. (1997). Delicate balances: Striving for curricular and instructional equilibrium in a second-grade, literature/strategy-based classroom. *Reading Research Quarterly, 32,* 244–275.

Beach, R. (1993). *A teacher's introduction to reader-response theories.* Urbana, IL: National Council of Teachers of English.

Beach, R., & Hynds, S. (1991). Research on response to literature. In R. Barr, M. L. Kamil, P. Mosenthal, & P. D. Pearson (Eds.), *Handbook of reading research* (Vol. 2; pp. 453–489). White Plains, NY: Longman.

Becker, W. C. (1977). Teaching reading and language to the disadvantaged—What we have learned from the field. *Harvard Educational Review, 47,* 518–543.

Brophy, J. E., & Good, T. L. (1986). Teacher behavior and student achievement. In M. C. Wittrock (Ed.), *Handbook of research on teaching* (pp. 328–375). New York: Macmillan.

Calkins, L. M. (1986). *The art of teaching writing.* Portsmouth, NH: Heinemann.

Chi, M. T. H., Glaser, R., & Farr, M. J. (Eds.) (1988). *The nature of expertise.* Hillsdale, NJ: Erlbaum.

Davison, A., & Kantor, R. N. (1982). On the failure of readability formulas to define readable texts: A case study from adaptations. *Reading Research Quarterly, 17,* 187–209.

Dewey, J. (1913). *Interest and effort in education.* Boston: Riverside.

Dewey, J. (1916). *Democracy and education.* New York: Macmillan.

Dole, J. A., Brown, K. J., & Trathen, W. (1996). The effects of strategy instruction on the comprehension performance of at-risk students. *Reading Research Quarterly, 31,* 62–88.

Dole, J. A., Duffy, G. G., Roehler, L. R., & Pearson, P. D. (1991). Moving from the old to the new: Research on reading comprehension instruction. *Review of Educational Research, 61,* 239–264.

Dole, J. A., & Osborn, J. (1991). The selection and use of language arts textbooks. In J. Flood, J. M. Jensen, D. Lapp, & J. R. Squire (Eds.), *Handbook for research on teaching the English language arts* (pp. 521–528). New York: Macmillan.

Dole, J. A., Rogers, T., & Osborn, J. (1987). Improving the selection of basal reading programs: A report of the Textbook Adoption Guidelines Project. *Elementary School Journal, 87,* 283–298,

Driscoll, M. P. (1994). *Psychology of learning for instruction.* Boston: Allyn & Bacon.

Duffy, G. G., & Roehler, L. R. (1989). Why strategy instruction is so difficult and what we need to do about it. In C. B. McCormick, G. Miller, & M. Pressley (Eds.), *Cognitive strategy research: From basic research to educational applications* (pp. 133–154). New York: Springer-Verlag.

Durkin, D. (1983). Is there a match between what elementary teachers do and what basal reader manuals recommend? *Reading Teacher, 37,* 734–744.

Edelsky, C., Altwerger, B., & Flores, B. (1991). *Whole language: What's the difference?* Portsmouth, NH: Heinemann.

Eeds, M., & Wells, D. (1989). Grand conversations: An explanation of meaning construction in literature study groups. *Research in the Teaching of English, 23,* 4–29.

El-Dinary, P. B., Pressley, M., & Schuder, T. (1992). Becoming a strategies teacher: An observational and interview study of three teachers learning transactional strategies instruction. In C. Kinzer & D. Leu (Eds.), *Forty-first yearbook of the National Reading Conference* (pp. 453–462). Chicago: National Reading Conference.

Garcia, G. E., & Pearson, P. D. (1990). *Modifying reading instruction to maximize its effectiveness for all students* (Technical Rep. No. 489). Urbana: University of Illinois, Center for the Study of Reading.

Gaskins, I. W., & Gaskins, J. C. (1997). Creating readers who read for meaning and love to read: The Benchmark school reading program. In S. A. Stahl and D. A. Hayes (Eds.), *Instructional models in reading* (pp. 131–159). Hillsdale, NJ: Erlbaum.

Goodman, K. S. (1986). *What's whole in whole language?* Portsmouth, NH: Heinemann.

Goodman, K. S. (1988). Look what they've done to Judy Blume!: The basalization of children's literature. *The New Advocate, 1,* 29–41.

Gough, P. B. (1972). One second of reading. In J. F. Kavanagh & I. G. Mattingly (Eds.), *Language by ear and by eye.* Cambridge, MA: MIT Press.

Graves, D. H. (1983). *Writing: Teachers and children at work.* Portsmouth, NH: Heinemann.

Guthrie, J. T., Van Meter, P., McCann, A. D., Wigfield, A., Bennett, L., Poundstone, C., Rice, M. E., Faibisch, F. M., Hunt, B., & Mitchell, A. M. (1996). Growth in literacy engagement: Changes in motivations and strategies during concept-oriented reading instruction. *Reading Research Quarterly, 31,* 234–240.

Guthrie, J. T., & Wigfield, A. (Eds.). (1997). *Reading engagement: Motivating readers through integrated instruction.* Newark, DE: International Reading Association.

Hill, B. C., Johnson, N.J., & Schlick Noe, K. L. (1995). *Literature circles and response.* Norwood, MA: Christopher-Gordon.

Hines, V. (1972). Progressivism in practice. In J. Squire (Ed.), *A new look at Progressive Education* (pp. 118–165). Washington, DC: Association of Supervision and Curriculum Development.

Hirsch, K. (1997). I can't be like Pippi 'cause I'm afraid to live alone: Third graders' response to novels. In N.J. Karolides (Ed.), *Reader response in elementary classrooms* (pp. 137–154). Mahwah, NJ: Erlbaum.

Karnowski, L. (1997). Reconsidering teachers' roles and procedures: Developing dialoguing skills. In N.J. Karolides (Ed.), *Reader response in elementary classrooms* (pp. 301–313). Mahwah, NJ: Erlbaum.

Karolides, N.J. (Ed.). (1997). *Reader response in elementary classrooms.* Mahwah, NJ: Erlbaum.

Keene, E. O., & Zimmerman, S. (1997). *Mosaic of thought: Teaching comprehension in a reader's workshop.* Portsmouth, NH: Heinemann.

Langer, J. A. (1992). *Literature instruction: A focus on student response.* Urbana, IL: National Council of Teachers of English.

Mason, J., & Osborn, J. (1982). *When do children begin "reading to learn?" A survey of classroom reading instruction practices in grades two through five.* (Technical Rep. No. 261). Urbana: University of Illinois, Center for the Study of Reading.

McMahon, S. I., Raphael, T. E., with Goatley, V. J., & Pardo, L. S. (1997). *The Book Club connection: Literacy learning and classroom talk.* New York: Teachers College Press.

Morrow, L. M. (1992). The impact of a literature-based program on literacy achievement, use of literature, and attitudes of children from minority backgrounds. *Reading Research Quarterly, 27,* 250–275.

Neuman, S. B., & Roskos, K. (1997). Literacy knowledge in practice: Contexts of participation for young writers and readers. *Reading Research Quarterly, 32,* 10–32.

Newman, J. M. (1985). Whole language: Theory in use. Portsmouth, NH: Heinemann.

O'Flahavan, J. F., & Seidl, B. L. (1997). Fostering literature communities in school: A case for sociocultural approaches to reading instruction. In S. A. Stahl & D. A. Hayes (Eds.), *Instructional models in reading* (pp. 203–220). Hillsdale, NJ: Erlbaum.

Paris, S. G., Lipson, M. Y., & Wixson, K. K. (1983). Becoming a strategic reader. *Contemporary Educational Psychology, 8,* 293–316.

Pearson, P. D., & Dole, J. A. (1987). Explicit comprehension instruction: A review of research and a new conceptualization of instruction. *Elementary School Journal, 88* (2), 151–165.

Pearson, P. D., & Gallagher, M. C. (1983). The instruction of reading comprehension. *Contemporary Educational Psychology, 8,* 317–344.

Peterson, R., & Eeds, M. (1990). *Grand conversations: Literature groups in action.* New York: Scholastic.

Pressley, M., & Afflerbach, P. (1995). *Verbal protocols of reading: The nature of constructively responsive reading.* Hillsdale, NJ: Erlbaum.

Pressley, M., Goodchild, F., Fleet, J., Zajchowski, R., & Evans, E. D. (1989). The challenges of strategy instruction. *Elementary School Journal, 89*, 301–342.

Pressley, M., Johnson, C. J. Symons, S., McGoldrick, J., & Kurita, J. (1989). Strategies that improve children's memory and comprehension of text. *Elementary School Journal, 90*, 3–32.

Roehler, L. R., & Duffy, G. G. (1991). Teachers' instructional actions. In R. Barr, M. L. Kamil, P. Mosenthal, & P. D. Pearson (Eds.), *Handbook of reading research* (Vol. 2; pp. 861–883). New York: Longman.

Rosenblatt, L. M. (1978). *The reader, the text, the poem.* Carbondale: Southern Illinois University Press.

Rosenshine, B. (1997, March). *The case for explicit, teacher-led, cognitive strategy instruction.* Paper presented to the American Educational Research Association, Chicago.

Rosenshine, B., & Stevens, R. (1984). Classroom instruction in reading. In P. D. Pearson, R. Barr, M. L. Kamil, & P. Mosenthal (Eds.), *Handbook of reading research* (Vol. 1; pp. 745–798). New York: Longman.

Routman, R. (1994). *Invitations: Changing as teachers and learners, K-12.* Portsmouth, NH: Heinemann.

Rumelhart, D. E. , & Ortony, A. (1977). The representation of knowledge in memory. In R. C. Anderson, R. J. Spiro, & W. E. Montague (Eds.), *Schooling and the acquisition of knowledge.* (pp. 99–36). Hillsdale, NJ: Erlbaum.

Science Research Associates. (1968). *Direct Instruction Systems for Teaching Arithmetic and Reading.* Chicago: Author.

Shannon, P. (1989). *Broken promises: Reading instruction in twentieth century America.* New York: Bergin & Garvey.

Short, K. G., Harste, J. C., & Burke, C. (1996). *Creating classrooms for authors and inquirers.* Portsmouth, NH: Heinemann.

Smith, F. (1981). Demonstrations, engagement and sensitivity: A revised approach to language learning. *Language Arts, 58*, 103–112.

Smith, N. B. (1986). *American reading instruction.* Newark, DE: International Reading Association.

Sticht, T. G., & James, J. H. (1984). Listening and reading. In P. D. Pearson, R. Barr, M. L. Kamil, & P. Mosenthal (Eds.), *Handbook of reading research.* (Vol. 1; pp. 293–317). New York: Longman.

Thorndike, E. L. (1917). Reading as reasoning: A study of mistakes in paragraph reading. *Journal of Educational Psychology, 8*, 323–332.

Tierney, R. J., & Cunningham, J. W. (1984). Research on teaching reading comprehension. In P. D. Pearson, R. Barr, M. L. Kamil, & P. Mosenthal (Eds.), *Handbook of reading research.* (Vol. 1; pp. 609–655). New York: Longman.

Vygotsky, L. S. (1978). *Mind in society.* Cambridge, MA: MIT Press.

Weaver, C. (1990). *Understanding whole language.* Portsmouth, NH: Heinemann.

4

Balancing Literature and Instruction: Lessons from the Book Club Project

TAFFY E. RAPHAEL

During the past decade, our field has seen pendulum swings between traditional instruction and whole language, between use of basal readers and authentic literary texts, and between skills focus and holistic instruction. Further, issues of authenticity and meaning, voice and power, as well as professional development and teacher education, have been added to an already full plate of demands literacy educators. The Book Club research program (McMahon & Raphael, 1997b; Raphael, Pardo, Highfield, & McMahon, 1997) was conducted within this atmosphere.

We had multiple goals:

- Honoring the literature that served as the texts for instruction
- Providing instruction within an integrated literacy curriculum
- Grounding literacy activity in the social interactions among students and between teachers and students
- Emphasizing the relationship between language and thought
- Building a sense of community and ownership among teachers, students, and university-based researchers

In this chapter, I focus on five areas in which we feel we've made some progress. First, we identified and used a powerful theoretical lens to guide us as we created the instructional framework underlying the Book Club program (Gavelek & Raphael, 1996; McMahon & Raphael, 1997a). Second, we developed a curriculum that both honored the literature and provided a focus for literacy instruction (Raphael & Goatley, 1994; Raphael, Pardo, Highfield, & McMahon, 1997). Third, we detailed complex and varying roles teachers and students assume as they engage in literate thought and participate in literacy activities (Au & Raphael, 1998; Raphael & Goatley, 1994). Fourth, we described diverse learners' participation within Book Club (Goatley, Brock, & Raphael, 1995; Raphael & Brock, 1993; Raphael, Brock & Wallace, 1997). And, fifth, we have begun to explore models for teachers learning to teach using Book Club (Florio-Ruane, Raphael, Glazier, McVee, & Wallace, 1997; Raphael, 1997).

LESSON #1: THE POWER OF THEORY TO GUIDE PRACTICE AND OF PRACTICE TO INFORM THEORY

I first began thinking about developing an instructional program based on student-led book clubs when I shared the podium with Dick Allington at a regional conference in Vancouver, British Columbia, in 1989. In his presentation, he noted contrasts between what young children experience in school when they talk about text and the talk among readers outside school settings. As a former classroom teacher, I found that his comments hit home. How often had I asked students to read interesting and engaging text, then followed up by asking them to tell me who the main character was, his or her problem, and how it was solved? How little those conversations had in common with what I would characterize as "real" talk about text. My school focus had been on vocabulary, comprehension, and recalling detail.

How different this was from a recent conversation I had with my sister-in-law, Kate, about Amy Tan's *The Hundred Secret Senses* (1995). In our conversation, we touched on the relationship between the sisters, the degree to which we'd enjoyed the book, and connections between this book, Tan's other books, and Tan's own life and experiences. Never once did Kate ask me, "What is the name of the main character?" "What is her problem?" "Where did this story take place?"

In creating the Book Club line of research, I wanted to introduce students to a love of literature. As Lee Galda (1998) suggests, literature mirrors our own lives and provides a window into distant peoples, times, and places. I wanted students to love talking about books, and I wanted them to develop the literate abilities they would require to feel and be successful. The theory that would guide our work needed to help us organize a context that is conversation-based but with opportunities for teacher instruction. We were drawn to others who were examining "dialogic teaching" (e.g., Almasi, 1995; Alvermann, 1996; Alvermann et al., 1996; Beck, McKeown, Sandora, Kucan, Worthy, 1996; Burbules, 1993; Marshall, Smagorinsky, & Smith, 1995).

Dialogic teaching comes out of a theoretical position captured in a family of theories variously termed Vygotskian, social constructionist, sociocultural, and sociohistorical (see, e.g., Gavelek, 1986; Harré, 1984; Vygotsky, 1986; Wertsch, 1985, 1991). This family of theories shares an emphasis on the social bases for an individual's development. They emphasize that an individual's learning is "mediated" by others who are more knowledgeable than themselves, that these mediators interpret the learners' experiences, helping them label events, activities, and even emotional responses. This made a great deal of sense to those of us developing the Book Club program, but we struggled with determining where mediation might occur, how to balance teacher-directed and student-directed activities, how we could assess students' progress, and how to help teachers teach in ways they themselves had not experienced.

We found a model called the Vygotsky Space (Gavelek & Raphael, 1996; Harré, 1984) particularly helpful as we planned. I like this model because it helps me picture what is meant by dialogic instruction, by the language-based nature of learning, and by learning as a process of internalizing what has been presented in public forums. The model consists of two axes: the public/private and the social/individual (see Figure 4.1).

I begin with the public/private axis. Think of public "spaces" in the classroom as being visible ones. For example, when a teacher is reading aloud to students and stops to comment on how the book is making her feel, this is a public event. When a student sits in the Author's Chair to share a journal entry, this is in the public space. When a teacher reads a child's journal entry or listens to a small group of children talking, this occurs within the public spaces of the classroom. In contrast, when a reader reads silently, the thinking and response occurs within the private space of the classroom. As the child considers what to write in his journal, that thinking happens within the private spaces.

Now let's consider the other axis, the social/individual. This axis gets at the two different functions of school. On the one hand, schools are to guide children as they learn about the conventional knowledge of our culture, conventional ways of interacting, of responding, of connecting to each other and to texts, and so forth. These are the social practices of our culture and the knowledge of our society. As teachers, we have a responsibility to teach these to our students. However, schooling is also the place where we want students to transform what they have learned in new and unique ways. Thus we are constantly working within the tensions of these two goals: the social or conventional ways of doing things and the individual transformations of these same practices.

When we put these two axes together, crossing them as you see in Figure 4.1, we get the Vygotsky Space, which consists of four quadrants.

Figure 4.1. The Vygotsky Space.

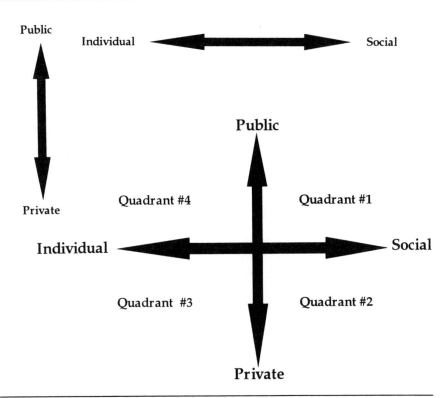

Source: Gavelek & Raphael (1996) p. 186.

In the first quadrant, we have the public and social spaces of the class-room. I see this space as a site for teachers to make public the conventional wisdom of our culture and, in terms of literacy, the knowledge that literate individuals draw upon: skills, strategies, and dispositions. In terms of Book Club, this was the whole-class setting in which conventions for response, comprehension, and so forth could be introduced, modeled, and encouraged. For example, in Mrs. Pardo's fifth-grade urban class-room (Mrs. Pardo was an original member of the Book Club research team) children learned to respond to what they had read by drawing the images that the words in the text had created in their minds. They learned to use effectively text-processing strategies such as predicting, summarizing, and sequencing.

The second quadrant is a site where students have the opportunity to use what they have learned in the public spaces in the same manner and for the same purposes as they were taught. Kathy Highfield's fifth grade students, for example, read literature such as Beatty's *Charlie Ske-daddle* (1987) and, in their reading logs, drew images created in their minds about events such as the farm residents being stalked by a panther. (Ms. Highfield taught in a rural school and was also an original member of the Book Club research team.) They read about Sal in Sharon Creech's *Walk Two Moons* (1995) and wrote responses in their reading logs about their relationship to their friends and families.

The third quadrant encompasses private opportunities for students to transform what they have learned in the public and social spaces, what they have practiced in the private and social spaces. By transforming what they have learned, they create something new and unique that serves their own purposes. Taking a rather simple example, Mandy and Lena, students in Laura Pardo's classroom, had been reading *Behind Rebel Lines* (Reit, 1988). They had also viewed a videotape set during the Civil War and containing a scene in which two main characters were married. They had been listening to another group of peers describe the engagement of a couple in their Book Club book, *Turn Homeward, Hannalee* (Beatty, 1984). In her log, Lena predicted that Emma would marry. She drew a picture of a man and a woman, labeling the picture "Picture & Prediction of Emma and husband." Mandy noticed Lena's two responses. She suggested that Lena had created a new response and called Laura over to see it. Laura applauded Lena's new response format within the small group and later, during community share, had the two girls share what they had created. The new response format transformed two responses to create what the class came to call a "picture-prediction," an image they had of what they thought might happen in a later chapter in a story. This transformation reflects learning in the public and social spaces: learning about different forms of response, learning that as readers we depart from taught forms of response rather than routinely applying them, learning that taking risks with new ideas and new forms of response is valued, and so forth.

However, without the fourth quadrant, we would never have any way of knowing that such transformations occur. In the fourth quadrant, publication of private activity occurs. Publication—through logs or through book club discussions—can reveal not only the fact that students have learned conventional knowledge, but also, as in Mandy's and Lena's case, the transformations that take place. Sometimes transformations become part of the conventional knowledge of the community. For example, many students were quite taken with the idea of a picture-prediction and began to use it. The term held particular meaning for this class and became part of the discourse in the public and social space of their classroom. This cycling among and between the various quadrants becomes the historical basis for learning. That which a learner transforms becomes part of our conventional knowledge, only to be transformed again and again over the life of a community and the life of a learner.

These four quadrants highlight, to me, both the kinds of literacy learning opportunities that are important in literature-based literacy instruction and the different roles that teachers and students play within the process. In Book Club, we established four contexts, or components, that comprised the overall program and provided multiple opportunities for dialogic teaching and for meaningful interactions among students. First, students read daily. Second, they wrote daily, often in journals or reading logs, but also in sustained writing activity related to themes in the literature. Third, students talked about the literature and their response in small, student-led discussion groups, called book clubs (note that lower-case refers to the student-led book clubs, while upper case refers to the Book Club program, which includes all four components). Fourth, there was a whole-class component (i.e., community share) in which instruction and large-group discussions could occur. Community share was a site for explicit teaching and teacher modeling, as well as less teacher-directed roles. Reading and writing were private spaces where students could engage either by appropriating what they had been taught in the public and social space or by transforming learned knowledge in individual ways. Their journals and the book clubs provided a public space where students' thinking could be made visible to their peers and the teacher.

In short, one of the initial lessons we learned from this line of research was the value of having a clear theoretical lens and a viable conceptual model to help us identify program components as well as to construct the curriculum and develop ways to evaluate our own and our students' progress.

LESSON #2: A CURRICULUM TO BALANCE RESPECT FOR THE LITERATURE WITH LITERACY INSTRUCTION

When we were creating the Book Club program, literature-based instruction was becoming increasingly popular. However, the instructional approaches varied from child-centered approaches where student choice and free reading were emphasized to relatively traditional teacher-directed use of literature, or what Goodman (1988) has characterized as "basalizing" the literature. We were committed to a curriculum that both

Figure 4.2. A balanced literacy curriculum.

Comprehension	*Composition*	*Literary Aspects*	*Language Conventions*
Background Knowledge: prediction	Process: planning drafting revising	Literary Elements: theme plot character setting	Sound/Symbol Grammar Syntax Interaction
Text Processing: summarizing sequencing identifying importance	Writing as a Tool Writing from Sources On-Demand Writing	Response to Literature: personal creative critical	
Monitoring: clarifying planning			

honored the literature and provided space for teachers to teach the conventional knowledge about text processing (i.e., vocabulary, comprehension, and monitoring) and our language system itself (at the letter, word, text, and interaction levels). Based on extensive research within our field (Raphael & Brock, 1997), we identified four areas of the curriculum that we emphasized in the Book Club program—comprehension, composition, literary aspects, and language conventions (see Figure 4.2). We learned that it was crucial to define what we meant by a "balanced" approach, since over the past few years this term has become very ambiguous and "acts as a lightning rod for larger issues . . . from techniques for developmentally appropriate skills teaching to control of classrooms" (Freppon & Dahl, 1998, p. 247).

Comprehension

Reviews of research underscore the importance of instruction in comprehension (e.g., Dole, Duffy, Roehler, & Pearson, 1991; Duffy, Roehler, & Mason, 1984; Pearson, 1986; Pearson & Fielding, 1991). Further, current research continues to emphasize related areas, including *vocabulary instruction* (e.g., Watts, 1995), *strategy instruction* (e.g., Baumann & Bergeron, 1993; Block, 1993; Danoff, Harris & Graham, 1993; Dole, Brown, & Trathen, 1996; Lysynchuk, Pressley, & Vye, 1990; Wood, Winne, & Carney, 1995), and *monitoring* (e.g., Baumann, Seifert-Kessell, & Jones, 1992; Beck et al., 1996; Dreher & Sammons, 1994).

Reading comprehension instruction takes the mystery out of the reading process, helping students assume control. It provides them with the means to gather information, connect ideas, identify important issues, and monitor their success. Today, comprehension instruction includes ways to recall text details, as well as how to critically analyze and meaningfully engage with a wide range of texts (e.g., A. Brown, 1992; Guthrie et al., 1996). One elementary student who participated in Questioning the Author—an intervention designed to improve text understanding (Beck et al., 1996)—describes what he sees as advantages of learning to question, thinking critically, and talking about what he reads:

> Me and Alvis, we always get in something. We always disagree with each other. Then we read on and start disagreeing with ourselves. Then we find out about our disagreement and why we were wrong. We disagree with ourselves if we're wrong. (p. 409)

We found Dole and colleagues' division of comprehension strategies into a few broad categories (Dole, Duffy, Roehler, & Pearson, 1991) to be very helpful for organizing the strategies taught within Book Club. We focused on vocabulary instruction, text-processing strategies such as inferencing and sequencing, and monitoring strategies.

Composition

The composition curricular component is based on research documenting important relationships between reading and writing. These relationships have been described for the past two decades (e.g., Au, Carroll, & Scheu, 1997; Dyson, 1992; Graves & Hansen, 1983; Hiebert, 1991; Spivey & Calfee, in press; Teale, 1987). Within the writing component, we determined to include two different kinds of writing activities to support students' understanding, interpretation, and talk about text. First, we drew from existing research studies and reviews (e.g., Denyer & Florio-Ruane, 1998; Lensmire, 1994; Patthey-Chavez & Clare, 1996; Power, 1995; Sperling, 1991; Stotsky, 1995) to create ways to engage students in *sustained writing about issues and topics* that related to the texts they read during Book Club. For example, students created essays about racism after reading three novels by Mildred Taylor. They wrote about the implications of living forever after reading about the lives of the Tuck family in Natalie Babbitt's *Tuck Everlasting* (1975).

Second, we identified ways students could use writing as *a tool to promote critical and higher-order thinking* about the texts they were reading. We encouraged such analysis through reflections, dialogue, journals, and notebooks (e.g., Barone, 1990; Dekker, 1991; Newell, 1994). We also encouraged students to gather information from multiple sources, synthesize the information, and present it to peers (e.g., Dixson-Krauss, 1995; Dyson, 1992; Many, Fyfe, Lewis, & Mitchell, 1996; Rosaen, 1990; Schroder, 1996). For example, students in Laura Pardo's and Kathy High-field's fifth-grade classrooms wrote extensive reports about aspects of the Civil War during a two-week research phase prior to reading historical fiction set during that era in the subsequent 3-week Book Club phase. Such activities required students to sift through texts written from different perspectives and ask themselves questions such as "What is the author trying to tell me in this paper?" or "What does this particular author want me to think about my topic?"

Literary Aspects

To honor the literature, the curriculum focused on teaching students both to understand the structure of literary texts (e.g., plot, theme, characterization) and to respond in various ways to the literature (i.e., personal, creative, and critical response). Many studies demonstrate links between reading instruction and learning about literature, encouraging or teaching readers' response to the literature, and understanding the variation in teachers' roles (see Eeds & Wells, 1989; Goatley, Brock, & Raphael, 1995; McGee, 1992; McMahon & Raphael, 1997b; Roser & Martinez, 1995; Sipe, 1998).

Julianne demonstrates a range of responses in her reading log entry from April 28, after completing 10 pages in Beatty's *Turn Homeward, Hannalee* (1984) (see Figure 4.3). In one entry she writes about her feelings in response to the students' capture by the northern troops. In a second, she draws her image of two of the main characters as the older one, Rosellen, comforts the younger one, Hannalee, by putting her hand on Hannalee's shoulder. In a third entry, she considers ways that Rosellen and Hannalee are similar to and different from each other. This one entry illustrates the emphasis in Book Club on both personal response and understanding how authors craft stories. It reveals Julianne's ability to identify key events within the plot and appreciate the character development by the author.

Language Conventions

The fourth curricular area includes all aspects of how our written and oral language work, from the level of sound/symbol relationships to grammatical structures to knowing how to interact within small and large groups to talk about text. We know from research how much students can benefit from explicit instruction in particular language conventions

Figure 4.3. Julianne's log entry.

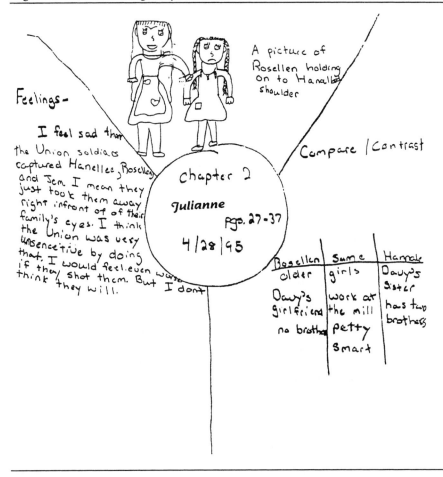

to help them spell (e.g., K. Brown, Sinatra & Wagstaff, 1996; Morris, Blanton, Blanton, & Perney, 1995), decode (e.g., Cunningham, 1992; Gaskins, Gaskins, Anderson, & Schommer, 1995), and write (e.g., Englert, Raphael, Anderson, Stevens, & Anthony, 1991).

Research also suggests that when we make explicit our expectations about interacting *using* language, it helps students learn *how to interact around text* (e.g., Anderson, Chin, Waggoner, & Nguyen, 1998; O'Flahavan, 1989). Talking about text, researchers have found, is both complex and challenging, with a continued need to explore how factors such as gender, classroom status, and so forth influence students' participation

Figure 4.4. Ignoring a curricular area.

Comprehension	Composition	Literary Aspects	Language Conventions
Background Knowledge: prediction	Process: planning drafting revising	Literary Elements: theme plot character setting	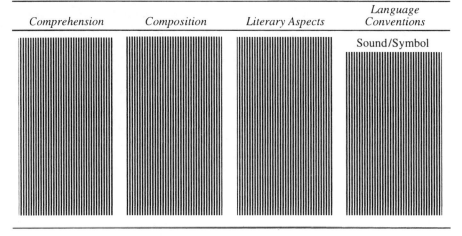 Grammar Syntax Interaction
Text Processing: summarizing sequencing identifying importance	Writing as a Tool Writing from Sources On-Demand Writing	Response to Literature: personal creative critical	
Monitoring: clarifying planning			

Figure 4.5. Overemphasizing a curricular area.

Comprehension	Composition	Literary Aspects	Language Conventions
			Sound/Symbol

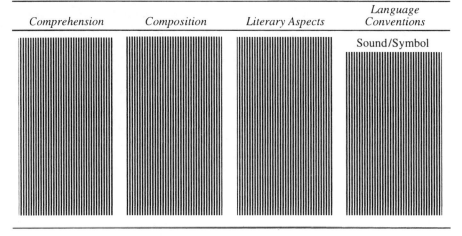

(see Alvermann et al., 1996; Evans, 1996; Freedman, 1993; Williams & Colomb, 1993).

While some current debates pit areas of the curriculum against each other (e.g., phonics first in contrast to a more integrated curriculum), we based our work in an assumption that such choices are arbitrary and short-change students. We believe that it is pointless to exclude particular knowledge from the literacy curriculum (e.g., not encouraging attention to phonemes, as shown in Figure 4.4). However, it is just as pointless to base a curriculum on a single aspect of the curriculum (as shown in Figure 4.5).

Figure 4.6. Teachers' roles.

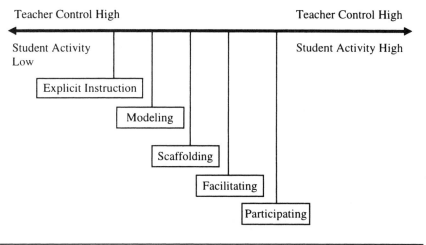

Source: Adapted from Au & Raphael (1998) p. 125.
Copyright © 1998 by Christopher-Gordon Publishers. Used by permission.

LESSON #3: UNDERSTANDING THE COMPLEXITIES
OF TEACHERS' ROLES

Our third lesson related to our developing understandings of the complex and varying roles teachers and students assume as they engage in literate thought and participate in literacy activities (e.g., Au & Raphael, 1998; Raphael, 1998; Raphael & Goatley, 1994). Their roles varied in terms of how much control teachers exercised over topic and turn-taking (see Figure 4.6).

Explicit Instruction

Book Club teachers used explicit teaching during minilessons within community share as they assumed a traditional teacher role by formally transmitting this knowledge. An advantage to explicit teaching stems from being able to impart information to students efficiently. The disadvantages can be traced to promoting a passive attitude toward learning by not encouraging students actively to construct their own understandings. However, when confined to relatively brief (e.g., 10-minute) minilessons, explicit instruction provides a useful way to introduce skills and strategies. Explicit instruction occurs within the social and public quadrant of the Vygotsky Space and is probably the interaction pattern that is most commonly found across classrooms and grade levels.

For example, Raphael (1998) describes a lesson taught by Laura Pardo early in a unit where students are researching causes of the Civil War, prior to reading historical fiction set during that era. A whole-class lesson involved introducing students to criteria for judging inquiry questions. Laura uses an interactive lecture format, where she controls the topic under discussion (inquiry questions and criteria for judging their quality) and the turn-taking. She invites students to participate by asking them fairly pointed questions about the quality of each of a series of questions she displays on the overhead projector.

In her role as explicit instructor, Laura uses classroom talk to develop a particular area of knowledge—in this case, creating inquiry questions. She is responsive to students' comments and engages them as contributors to the classroom talk, but she does not permit the talk to move away from the central focus. Through this talk, she establishes three criteria that will guide her students throughout the inquiry unit as they develop, and then conduct research to answer their questions: The questions must (1) require depth of response, (2) lead to new knowledge generation, and (3) raise other questions. The degree to which they learned what was taught will be reflected in the quality of questions they generate.

"Modeling" Talk During Teacher Read-Aloud

A second role teachers assume is to model otherwise invisible cognitive processes. For example, teachers share their own written responses to literature, so students can see how a mature reader responds to a novel. Teachers demonstrate their enjoyment of and involvement with books when they read aloud to the class. They share their own tastes and preferences as readers, for professional and recreational purposes, so that students know that reading goes beyond the walls of the classroom. This can happen during classroom literacy events such as teacher read-alouds and sustained silent reading, both of which can be thought of as events that occur within the public and social quadrant of the Vygotsky Space. Observations of Laura Pardo reading aloud Hunt's *Across Five Aprils* (1964) revealed how Laura used the read aloud to (1) highlight colloquial expression and dialect, (2) clarify potentially confusing sections of text, (3) highlight clues to characterization, and (4) elicit predictions.

When modeling, the teacher often simply thinks-aloud, sharing her thoughts or asking rhetorical questions of her students. The point is to make her thinking visible for students, helping them see how they may use strategies and skills they have learned as they read new texts on their own.

"Scaffolding" Talk: Building Background Knowledge

A third role parallels a scaffold, providing temporary and adjustable support to students engaging in literate behavior. During literature discussions, teachers ask questions to promote deeper levels of discussion than students may be capable of achieving on their own and to prepare them to conduct literature discussions independent of the teacher.

The example that follows illustrates how Laura scaffolded her students' understanding of the term *civil* when applied to the American Civil War (Raphael, 1998). Students were confused about where the war was being fought and had suggested it might have included another country. In response to a student who suggested that one of the reasons the war was fought was over land, Thea suggested someone was trying to "take over the country." Thea was possibly influenced by having studied the American Revolution and assumed similar causes contributed to the Civil War. Laura scaffolds through questions, through directing a student whom she knows understands the difference, and through directing students attention to a map that is available on one of the classroom bulletin boards. (Note that in presenting the dialogue here and later in the chapter, certain conventions were used to convey the phrasing and tone: /= 1-second pause; [=overlapping speech; placement of the [indicates where the overlap in speech occurred.)

Thea: They were fighting over the land so they could take over the country.
Laura: Well, what country did this war take place in?
Meg: The United States.

.
.
.

Laura: The United States. They were all the same country.
Student: (inaudible, but apparently about other countries' involvement in the war)
Laura: No, this was just the United States. Meg, it might be helpful if you tell us, Meg looked up the word, civil. She asked me if I knew what "civil" meant and I asked her to please look that up.
Meg: The events happening within a community or country.
Laura: Okay, when something happens within the same community or country. It is not a war when one country fights another. It is a fight within the same country. This is an important thing to know. We were not fighting anyone other than ourselves. (Writes on chart: war within the same coun-

try) And the person that I went to first (referring to the first comment in
the first column), said, it was the north and the south were the two sides.
The north was fighting the south. Look on that map up there, above Katrina's head. Tell me what color it looks like the north is up there. (pp.
151–152)

Laura asks Katrina to indicate the blue areas of the map, representing
northern states, then asks the class to look at the yellow areas, indicating
the Great Plains states where pioneers were crossing (a reference to their
previous unit of study in social studies) and the war had not yet arrived.
She ends by asking Katrina to point to the gray area of the map, which
illustrated the southern states. Laura ends this segment by saying, "So,
this is the same / / same country. Civil means same country. North was
fighting South."

By scaffolding, building upon what the students already knew—
Meg's understanding of the term, *civil*; students' knowledge of the North,
South, and Great Plains—she was able to help them understand the na-
ture of a Civil War and how that contrasted with wars between countries.

Facilitating Talk Within Large-Group Settings

Teachers may also be facilitators, helping large groups of students interact
by directing the flow of conversation. The teacher helps smooth the way
but does not engage in lengthy interactions with students. For example,
if students are participating in a literature discussion, the teacher may ask
the group to think about connections between the novel and their own
lives. Or if a child attempts to read a challenging text, the teacher may
have the child engage in partner reading with a peer who is a capable
reader. Teachers may facilitate whole-class or large-group discussions simply by orchestrating turn-taking among a large number of participants.

Participating in Group Discussions

The fifth form of instruction is participating, in which the teacher engages
in the same activities as the students. For example, teachers may participate in literature discussions, sharing their own ideas with students but
not dominating the discussion. During sustained silent reading, teachers
read books of their own choosing, just as students do. Teachers do not
summarize at the end of the segment of conversation or highlight the
ideas they deem to be important. In effect, their contributions are no
more, but no less, important and influential than those of the students.

These examples of teacher-led classroom talk reflect the variety such talk can take, in terms of focus as well as the way in which teachers and students interact. Such talk provides an important vehicle for students' literacy and content-area learning, learning that serves as the foundation for their ability to participate with their peers in meaningful talk about text. When teachers use the public and social settings of community share and reading aloud well, there is opportunity for all students to develop key strategies for participating in Book Club.

LESSON #4: DIVERSE LEARNERS PARTICIPATING IN BOOK CLUBS

A question I am frequently asked is whether Book Club is appropriate for students who traditionally would be removed from the classroom for special support, through special education or in English-as-a-Second-Language resource rooms. We have found, through several studies, powerful evidence that students across age and abilities level can benefit from participating with their peers in Book Club (see Brock, 1997; Goatley, 1997; Goatley et al., 1995; Raphael & Brock, 1993; Raphael, Wallace, Pardo, & Choo, 1996; Scherer, 1997). While not a panacea for helping students accelerate their learning, students find that peers provide important support for their comprehension and interpretation of text, and that the literate activities within the Book Club framework help develop their ownership over literacy.

Raphael, Brock, and Wallace (1997) describe three cases of diverse learners' ability to participate in Book Club classrooms and the active way in which these learners contribute to each group's sense-making. One case study involves Lenny, a child who had spent his first four grades in special education classrooms for reading instruction. In fifth grade, his teacher and parents decided to have him remain with his peers in the regular classroom. Lenny was an active member of his book club group, willing to engage in discussion, read at home each evening to prepare for the next day's Book Club, and engage in the daily classroom reading, writing, and talk about books. In the following example, Lenny and his peers read and discussed a storybook biography, *Christopher Columbus* (Goodnough & Dodson, 1991). A student in the group had asked why no one believed Columbus when he said the earth wasn't flat. Following the question, there are two competing topics on the floor, as Lenny tries to address the question and other students attempt to share their reading log entries. Lenny pursues his point, drawing on the text to support his position. Phillip attempts to share the picture he had drawn in his log, but Mandy responds to Lenny:

Lenny: See, it's right, it says it right. Right here (pointing to a section of text).
Phillip: I drew a picture. I don't got it done. // Well, I predict that Christopher
Mandy: They, they did. They said only some people believed that the world
    was round.

Like Phillip, Julianne attempts to share her log entry, ignoring both Mandy and Lenny, but Lenny pursues his focus.

Lenny: See. See, right here. The most
Julianne: I got, I got a character map too.
Lenny: Educated people knew that the earth was round, not all . . .
Julianne: I said (inaudible), he likes to sail, he has demands, he's persuasive, the
    queen gives his demands, wife died . . .

Lenny continues to make the case that since neither the king nor queen was educated, they didn't support Christopher Columbus. He uses this argument to answer the original question on the floor—why people hadn't believed Columbus. He apparently, with Mandy's continued support, gains consensus as suggested by the end of this segment.

Lenny: . . . Only the king and queen don't know, so how do you
Mandy: . . . and a lot of people didn't know.
Lenny: I know. Only the people who had education knew.
Julianne: Like Christopher Columbus.
Lenny: Yeah. (pp. 188–189)

Lenny demonstrates that he understands the text and can utilize it effectively to make a point. Further, he shows his capacity to hold his own with the rest of the students and to make his own text-based inferences about the reason for the king and queen's initial lack of support.

A second example of diverse learners' potential to contribute and push the thinking of their regular education peers come from a book club where the students discuss Paterson's *Park's Quest* (1988) (Goatley et al., 1995). Interestingly, it is Jason, one of the regular education students, who struggles to make sense of the text. In his log entry, he has bold scribbles over the words, "Chapter 13, 6-3-92 things that could happen like: If Park figured out if he had a sister" (p. 368). His discomfort comes through in his opening comment during book club, "This is boring . . . This is a boring book. I like *Hatchet*" (p. 369). When challenged by his peers, he insists that his only problem is boredom with the book. After some conversation, Jason starts framing a question that may be the base of his confusion; Mei jumps in as if she knows his question already.

Jason: I got a, I got a question. How could, uh, Thanh and u,
Mei: Oh, yeah. That's my question

Some interruptions occur, and Jason finishes his question, "be brothers and sisters. I don't get it." Jean, Stark, and Mei—all students who traditionally would have been attending pull-out programs rather than participating with the regular education classmates—try to help Jason make sense of the text.

Jean: 'Cause they got,
Jason: Because, [because Frank got a divorce and . . . married Park's mother.
Stark: [Oh, I got it.
Jean: [Because they got married and then divorced.
Mei: [From his, from his mother because, because he, [he,
Jean: [Park's (dad) married his, her mother.
Mei: If she, if she said that she had a wife already.
Jason: [I don't get it. Sorry. I don't get it.
Stark: [Noo. What I think had happened is when um,
Jean: When Park's (dad) got divorced he married that lady.
Stark: No, not married. He was two-timing his friends. If you get what I mean.
Mei: Don't they get it? Like, like when you come to the war in Vietnam he was mar, married one of the um, [Vietnamese lady and they come over here.
Stark: [Or no. He was just like,
Mei: And his wife find out that he had another wife in Vietnam and then,
Andy: How would she find out?
Jean: He told her.
Mei: He find out because like some, something has happened like he was having baby and then she was sending letters to them, something like,
Stark: And then the letters went to the wrong place.
Jason: Na uh, she,
Stark: No he went home and,
Jason: Now I get it. Now I get it. Alright, so////
Jason: Park, Park you know, Park's dad is Park Broughton the fourth um, married, a, um, now I get it, married a, um, Vietnam girl, in Vietnam. That, now I get it. Now I get it. (pp. 190–191)

Jason's peers help him sort out his confusions. Notably, they technically were not supposed to be able to understand this text more easily than Jason. Moreover, we consistently found that students who were reluctant to speak in whole-class or teacher-directed situations were forthcoming about confusions among their peers (Brock, 1997; Raphael, Brock, & Wallace, 1997).

Diverse students benefit from opportunities to engage in complex thinking, reflected during peer-led discussions. They make valuable contributions to ongoing conversations—including challenging the thinking of their "regular education" peers. Lenny's involvement and persistence changed what was available to talk about and learn. His conversational involvement played a central role in terms of the content discussed (i.e., the queen, Columbus) and ways in which literary arguments are constructed. He transformed what he had experienced in whole-group discussions and applied it within the small-group context. He knew he needed to (1) bid for a turn to get the floor, (2) be persistent in keeping the floor to build his argument while still being polite in the group, (3) draw on support available to build an argument, and (4) work to convince his peers with the supporting points available. Such abilities are rarely focused on in skill-oriented programs.

In Jason's case, because the students had the opportunity to engage in talk and make their thinking public, his confusions could be identified. Because Stark understood what was happening in the story, he could support his peer's learning. The opportunity to engage in meaningful talk about text benefits both diverse learners and their regular education peers in terms of both the "content" of conversation and ways of effectively engaging in talk.

LESSON #5: TEACHERS LEARNING TO TEACH WITH BOOK CLUB

I close with a comment about teachers' learning to teach within a Book Club model. Many of the teachers with whom I have worked have commented that it is hard to teach in ways that they themselves have never experienced. As a field, we have long argued that to teach writing, it is important for teachers to write. Yet in arguing for more conversation-based models of reading instruction, we have tended to assume that to teach reading, we must simply be readers. What my colleagues and I have learned is that to teach through talk about text, it is helpful to participate actively in literary discussions ourselves, using books that are thematically related and that deal with complex and challenging issues.

Our current work is beginning to explore models of teacher learning about conversation-based instruction. My colleague Susan Florio-Ruane and I have been participating in and studying teacher learning within a Literary Circle (Florio-Ruane et al., 1997; Raphael, 1997). In our reading and discussions, we have taken up the theme of understanding literacy as a cultural practice and ourselves as cultural beings. We are reading ethnic autobiographies, books written by diverse authors including James McBride, Maya Angelou, Jill Ker Conway, and others who share their personal, intellectual, and scholarly journeys as they cross cultural boundaries in and out of school. Through this model, teachers are experiencing Book Club themselves. They are developing units based on a range of themes and multicultural literature, implementing the units in their own classrooms and sharing what they have learned within the group. We hope to be able to share what we have learned to support teachers who wish to engage in dialogic instruction and learn to do so within their school contexts as well as through more formal courses offered in university settings.

CONCLUDING COMMENTS

What are the lessons we've learned from our Book Club project line of work? Quality literacy instruction happens within meaningful contexts, where students are engaged with compelling texts and respond in personally relevant ways. Students must be actively engaged in reading, writing, and talking about text for meaning construction to occur. Teachers cannot teach effectively without knowledge of a repertoire of instructional strategies and a working knowledge of the literacy curriculum. Finally, instruction involves dynamic and shifting conceptions of teachers' and students' roles within any instructional encounter.

ACKNOWLEDGMENTS

Parts of this chapter are modifications of other chapters. I wish to acknowledge and thank Cindy Brock, my co-author on the National Reading Conference plenary address, which appears in the 1997 yearbook; Kathy Au, my co-author on a chapter that appears in our edited volume published by Christopher-Gordon; and Cindy Brock and Susan Wallace, co-authors of a chapter to appear in a book edited by Paratore and McCormack published by the International Reading Association. Finally, some sections are drawn from a chapter that I wrote for a volume edited by Fran Lehr and Jean Osborne for Guilford Press. Each of these prior papers is cited in the related section of this chapter.

REFERENCES

Almasi, J. F. (1995). The nature of fourth graders' sociocognitive conflicts in peer-led and teacher-led discussions of literature. *Reading Research Quarterly, 30*(3), 314–351.

Alvermann, D. E. (1996). Peer-led discussions: Whose interests are served? *Journal of Adolescent and Adult Literacy, 39*(4), 282–289.

Alvermann, D. E., Young, J. P., Weaver, D., Hinchman, K. A., Moore, D. W., Phelps, S. F., Thrash, E. C., & Zalewski, P. (1996). Middle and high school students' perceptions of how they experience text-based discussions: A multicase study. *Reading Research Quarterly, 31*(3), 244–267.

Anderson, R. C., Chin, C., Waggoner, M., & Nguyen, K. (1998). Intellectually stimulating story discussions. In F. Lehr & J. Osborn (Eds.), *Literacy for all: Issues in teaching and learning* (pp. 170–186). New York: Guilford.

Au, K. H., Carroll, J. H., & Scheu, J. R. (1997). *Balanced literacy instruction: A teacher's resource book.* Norwood, MA: Christopher-Gordon.

Au, K. H., & Raphael, T. E. (1998). Curriculum and teaching in literature-based programs. In T. E. Raphael & K. H. Au (Eds.), *Literature-based instruction: Reshaping the curriculum* (pp. 123–148). Norwood, MA: Christopher-Gordon.

Babbitt, N. (1975). *Tuck Everlasting.* New York: Farrer, Straus, & Giroux.

Barone, D. (1990). The written responses of young children: Beyond comprehension to story understanding. *The New Advocate, 3*(1), 49–56.

Baumann, J. F., & Bergeron, B. S. (1993). Story map instruction using children's literature: Effects on first graders' comprehension of central narrative elements. *Journal of Reading Behavior: A Journal of Literacy, 25*(4), 407–437.

Baumann, J. F., Seifert-Kessell, N., & Jones, L. A. (1992). Effect of think-aloud instruction on elementary students' comprehension monitoring abilities. *Journal of Reading Behavior: A Journal of Literacy, 24*(2), 143–172.

Beatty, P. (1987). *Charley Skedaddle.* New York: Troll.

Beatty, P. (1984). *Turn homeward, Hannalee.* New York: Troll.

Beck, I. L., McKeown, M. G., Sandora, C., Kucan, L., & Worthy, J. (1996). Questioning the Author: A yearlong classroom implementation to engage students with text. *Elementary School Journal, 96*(4), 385–414.

Block, C. C. (1993). Strategy instruction in a literature-based reading program. *The Elementary School Journal, 94*(2), 139–151.

Brock, C. H. (1997). Exploring the use of Book Club with second-language learners in mainstream classrooms. In T. E. Raphael, S. I. McMahon, with V. J. Goatley & L. S. Pardo (Eds.), *The Book Club connection: Literacy learning and classroom talk* (pp. 141–158). New York: Teachers College Press.

Brown, A. L. (1992). Design experiments: Theoretical and methodological challenges in creating complex interventions in classroom settings. *The Journal of Learning Sciences, 2,* 141–178.

Brown, K. J., Sinatra, G. M., & Wagstaff, J. M. (1996). Exploring the potential of analogy instruction to support students spelling development. *The Elementary School Journal, 97*(1), 81–99.

Burbules, N. (1993). *Dialogue in teaching: Theory and practice.* New York: Teachers College Press.

Creech, S. (1995). *Walk two moons.* New York: Harper Trophy.

Cunningham, P. M. (1992). What kinds of phonics instruction will we have? In C. Kinzer & D. Leu (Eds.), *Literacy research, theory, and practice: Views from many perspectives* (pp. 17–32). Chicago: National Reading Conference.

Danoff, B., Harris, K. R., & Graham, S. (1993). Incorporating strategy instruction within the writing process in the regular classroom: Effects on the writing of students with and without learning disabilities. *Journal of Reading Behavior: A Journal of Literacy, 25*(3), 295–322.

Dekker, M. M. (1991). Books, reading and response: A teacher-researcher tells a story. *The New Advocate, 4*(1), 37–46.

Denyer, J., & Florio-Ruane, S. (1998). Writing in literature-based programs: Context, communication and curriculum. In T. E. Raphael & K. H. Au (Eds.), *Literature-based instruction: Reshaping the curriculum* (pp. 149–171). Norwood, MA: Christopher-Gordon.

Dixson-Krauss, L. A. (1995). Partner reading and writing: Peer social dialogue and the zone of proximal development. *Journal of Reading Behavior, 27*(1), 45–63.

Dole, J. A., Brown, K. J., & Trathen, W. (1996). The effects of strategy instruction on the comprehension performance of at-risk students. *Reading Research Quarterly, 31*(1), 62–88.

Dole, J. A., Duffy, G. G., Roehler, L. R., & Pearson, P. D. (1991). Moving from the old to the new: Research on reading comprehension instruction. *Review of Educational Research, 61*(2), 239–264.

Dreher, M. J., & Sammons, R. B. (1994). Fifth graders searching for information in a textbook. *Journal of Reading Behavior: A Journal of Literacy, 26*(3), 301–314.

Duffy, G., Roehler, L., & Mason, J. (1984). *Comprehension instruction: Perspectives and suggestions.* New York: Longman.

Dyson, A. H. (1992). *Social worlds of children learning to write.* New York: Teachers College Press.

Eeds, M., & Wells, D. (1989). Grand conversations: An explanation of meaning construction in literature study groups. *Research in the Teaching of English, 23*(1), 4–29.

Englert, C. S., Raphael, T. E., Anderson, L. M., Stevens, D. D., & Anthony, H. M. (1991). Making writing strategies and self-talk visible: Cognitive strategy instruction in writing. *American Educational Research Journal, 28,* 337–372.

Evans, K. S. (1996). Creating spaces for equity? The role of positioning in peer-led discussions. *Language Arts, 73*(3), 194–202.

Florio-Ruane, S., Raphael, T. E., Glazier, J., McVee, M., & Wallace, S. (1997). Discovering culture in discussion of autobiographical literature: Transforming the education of literacy teachers. In C. Kinzer, D. Leu, & K. Hinchman (Eds.), *National Reading Conference Yearbook* (pp. 452–464). Chicago, IL: National Reading Conference.

Freedman, A. (1993). Show and tell? The role of explicit teaching in the learning of new genres. *Research in the Teaching of English, 27*(3), 222–251.

Freppon, P. A., & Dahl, K. L. (1998). Balanced instruction: Insights and considerations. *Reading Research Quarterly, 33*(2), 240–251.

Galda, L. (1998). Literature as mirror and window. In T. E. Raphael & K. H. Au (Eds.), *Literature-based instruction: Transforming the curriculum* (pp. 1–11). Norwood, MA: Christopher-Gordon.

Gaskins, R. W., Gaskins, I. W., Anderson, R. C., & Schommer, M. (1995). The reciprocal relationship between research and development: An example involving a decoding strand for poor readers. *Journal of Reading Behavior: A Journal of Literacy, 27*(3), 337–377.

Gavelek, J. R. (1986). The social context of literacy and schooling: A developmental perspective. In T. E. Raphael (Ed.), *The contexts of school-based literacy* (pp. 3–26). New York: Random House.

Gavelek, J. R., & Raphael, T. E. (1996). Changing talk about text: New roles for teachers and students. *Language Arts, 73*(3), 182–192.

Goatley, V. J. (1997). Talk about text among special education students. In S. I. McMahon, T. E. Raphael, with V. J. Goatley, & L. S. Pardo (Eds.), *The Book Club connection: Literacy learning and classroom talk* (pp. 119–137). New York: Teachers College Press.

Goatley, V. J., Brock, C. H., & Raphael, T. E. (1995). Diverse learners participating in regular education "Book Clubs." *Reading Research Quarterly, 30*(3), 352–380.

Goodman, K. S. (1988). Look what they've done to Judy Blume!: The basalization of children's literature. *The New Advocate, 1*(1), 29–41.

Goodnough, D., & Dodson, B. (1991). *Christopher Columbus.* New York: Troll.

Graves, D. H., & Hansen, J. (1983). The Author's Chair. *Language Arts, 60,* 176–183.

Guthrie, J. T., Van Meter, P., McCann, A. D., Wigfield, A., Bennett, L., Poundstone, C. C., Rice, M. E., Faibisch, F. M., Hunt, B., & Mitchell, A. M. (1996). Growth of literacy engagement: Changes in motivations and strategies during concept-oriented reading instruction. *Reading Research Quarterly, 31*(3), 206–235.

Harré, R. (1984). *Personal being: A theory for individual psychology.* Cambridge, MA: Harvard University Press.

Hiebert, E. H. (1991). The development of word-level strategies in authentic literacy tasks. *Language Arts, 68,* 234–240.

Hunt, I. (1964). *Across five Aprils.* New York: Berkley.

Lensmire, T. (1994). *When children write: Critical re-visions of the writing workshop.* New York: Teachers College Press.

Lysynchuk, L. M., Pressley, M., & Vye, N.J. (1990). Reciprocal teaching improves standardized reading-comprehension performance in poor comprehenders. *The Elementary School Journal, 90*(5), 469–485.

Many, J. E., Fyfe, G. L., Lewis, G., & Mitchell, E. (1996). Traversing the topical landscape: Exploring students' self-directed reading-writing-research processes. *Reading Research Quarterly, 31*(1), 12–35.

Marshall, J. D., Smagorinsky, P., & Smith, M. W. (1995). *The language of interpretation: Patters of discourse in discussions of literature.* Urbana, IL: National Council of Teachers of English.

McGee, L. (1992). Focus on Research: Exploring the literature-based reading revolution. *Language Arts, 69*(7), 529–537.

McMahon, S. I., & Raphael, T. E. (1997a). The Book Club program: Theoretical foundations and components. In S. I. McMahon & T. E. Raphael (Eds.), *The Book Club connection: Literacy learning and classroom talk* (pp. 3–25). New York: Teachers College Press.

McMahon, S. I., Raphael, T. E., with V. J. Goatley, & L. S. Pardo. (Eds.). (1997b).

The Book Club connection: Literacy learning and classroom talk. New York: Teachers College Press.

Morris, D., Blanton, L., Blanton, W. E., & Perney, J. (1995). Spelling instruction and achievement in six classrooms. *The Elementary School Journal, 96*(2), 145–162.

Newell, G. E. (1994). The effects of between-draft responses on students' writing and reasoning about literature. *Written Communication, 11*(3), 311–347.

O'Flahavan, J. F. (1989). *Second graders' social, intellectual, and affective development in varied group discussions about narrative texts: An explanation of participation structures.* Unpublished doctoral dissertation, University of Illinois, Urbana-Champaign.

Paterson, K. (1988). *Park's Quest.* New York: Dutton.

Patthey-Chavez, G. G., & Clare, L. (1996). Task, talk, and text: The influence of instructional conversations on transitional bilingual writers. *Written Communication, 13*(4), 515–563.

Pearson, P. D. (1986). Twenty years of research in reading comprehension. In T. E. Raphael (Ed.), *The contexts of school-based literacy* (pp. 43–62). New York: Random House.

Pearson, P. D., & Fielding, L. (1991). Comprehension Instruction. In R. Barr, M. L. Kamil, P. Mosenthal, & P. D. Pearson (Eds.), *Handbook of Reading Research* (pp. 819–860). New York: Longman.

Power, B. M. (1995). Bearing walls and writing workshops. *Language Arts, 72,* 482–488.

Raphael, T. E. (1997, August). *Autobiography as mirror and window: Understanding cultural influences on literacy development.* Paper presented at the European Conference on Reading. Brussels, Belgium.

Raphael, T. E. (1998). Balanced instruction and the role of classroom talk. In F. Lehr & J. Osborn (Eds.), *Literacy for all: Issues in teaching and learning* (pp. 134–169). New York: Guilford.

Raphael, T. E., & Brock, C. H. (1993). Mei: Learning the literacy culture in an urban elementary school. In D. J. Leu & C. K. Kinzer (Eds.), *Examining central issues in literacy research, theory, and practice* (pp. 179–188). Chicago: National Reading conference.

Raphael, T. E., & Brock, C. H. (1997). Instructional research in literacy: Changing paradigms. In C. Kinzer, K. Hinchman, & D. Leu (Eds.), *Inquiries in literacy: Theory and practice.* (pp. 13–36). Chicago: National Reading Conference.

Raphael, T. E., & Goatley, V. J. (1994). The teacher as "more knowledgeable other:" Changing roles for teaching in alternative reading instruction programs. In C. Kinzer & D. Leu (Eds.), *Multidimensional aspects of literacy research, theory and practice* (pp. 527–536). Chicago, IL: National Reading Conference.

Raphael, T. E., Brock, C. H., & Wallace, S. (1997). Encouraging quality peer talk with diverse students in mainstream classrooms: Learning from and with teachers. In J. R. Paratore & R. McCormack (Eds.), *Peer talk in the classroom: Learning from research* (pp. 176–206). Newark, DE: International Reading Association.

Raphael, T. E., Pardo, L. S., Highfield, K., & McMahon, S. I. (1997). *Book Club: A literature-based curriculum.* Littleton, MA: Small Planet Communication.

Raphael, T. E., Wallace, S. M., Pardo, L. S., & Choo, V. M. (1996, April). Assessing the literacy growth of fifth-grade students: A question of realigning curriculum, instruction, and assessment. Paper presentation at the American Educational Research Association, New York. ERIC Document #400 300.

Reit, S. (1988). *Behind rebel lines.* Orlando, FL: Harcourt Brace.

Rosaen, C. L. (1990). Improving writing opportunities in elementary classrooms. *The Elementary School Journal, 90*(4), 419–434.

Roser, N. L., & Martinez, M. G. (Eds.). (1995). *Book talk and beyond: Children and teachers respond to literature.* Newark, DE: International Reading Association.

Scherer, P. (1997). Book club through a fishbowl: Extensions to early elementary instruction. In S. I. McMahon & T. E. Raphael (Eds.), with V. J. Goatley & L. S. Pardo, *The Book Club connection: Literacy learning and classroom talk* (pp. 250–263). New York: Teachers College Press.

Schroder, G. (1996). The elements of story writing: Using picture books to learn about the elements of chemistry. *Language Arts, 73*(6), 412–418.

Sipe, L. R. (1998). First- and second-grade literary critics: Understanding children's rich response to literature. In T. E. Raphael & K. H. Au (Eds.), *Literature-based instruction: Reshaping the curriculum* (pp. 39–69). Norwood, MA: Christopher-Gordon.

Sperling, M. (1991). Dialogues of deliberation. *Written Communication, 8*(2), 131–162.

Spivey, N. N., & Calfee, R. C. (in press). The reading-writing connection, viewed historically. In N. Nelson & R. C. Calfee (Eds.), *Reading-writing connection: Ninety-seventh yearbook of the National Society for the Study of Education* (Part II). Chicago: University of Chicago Press.

Stotsky, S. (1995). The uses and limitations of personal or personalized writing in writing theory, research, and instruction. *Reading Research Quarterly, 30*(4), 758–776.

Tan, A. (1995). *The hundred secret senses.* New York: Putnam.

Teale, W. H. (1987). Emergent literacy: Reading and writing development in early childhood. In J. Readence & S. Baldwin (Eds.), *Research in literacy: Emerging perspectives: Yearbook of the national reading conference.* (pp. 45–74). Chicago: National Reading Conference.

Vygotsky, L. S. (1986). *Thought and language* (A. Kozulin, Trans.). Cambridge, MA: MIT Press.

Watts, S. (1995). Vocabulary instruction during reading lessons in six classrooms. *Journal of Reading Behavior, 27,* 399–424.

Wertsch, J. V. (1985). *Vygotsky and the social formation of mind.* Cambridge, MA: Harvard University Press.

Wertsch, J. V. (1991). *Voices of the mind.* New York: Oxford University Press.

Williams, J. M., & Colomb, G. G. (1993). The case for explicit teaching: Why what you don't know won't help you. *Research in the Teaching of English, 27*(3), 252–264.

Wood, E., Winne, P. H., & Carney, P. A. (1995). Evaluating the effects of training high school students to use summarization when training includes analogically similar information. *JRB: A Journal of Literacy, 27*(4), 605–626.

5

Building Student Capacity to Work Productively During Peer-Assisted Reading Activities

LYNN S. FUCHS
DOUGLAS FUCHS

The learning and social behavior profiles of public school classrooms are becoming increasingly diverse as more children enter school at risk for failure (Hodgkinson, 1995; Stallings, 1995) and as the reform policies of detracking (Braddock et al., 1992) and full inclusion of students with disabilities (D. Fuchs & Fuchs, 1994) are implemented. This heterogeneity strains the capacity of conventional instructional methods to address all students' learning needs. With conventionally designed lessons, presentations typically address a particular skill or strategy geared to meet the needs of a small group of students who function near the middle of the class (L. Fuchs, Fuchs, Phillips, & Simmons, 1993).

One promising alternative to conventional instructional methods is collaborative learning arrangements, whereby children work together to support each other's learning. Research demonstrates that in the elementary grades, children's development of reading competence can improve when they work collaboratively on structured learning activities (Greenwood, Delquadri, & Hall, 1989; Rosenshine & Meister, 1994; Stevens, Madden, Slavin, & Farnish, 1987). With collaborative learning, different groups of children can operate on varying levels of curricula, using alternative instructional procedures. In these ways, teachers can create many simultaneous "lessons" to address the full range of learning needs in classrooms.

Two of the most thoroughly researched collaborative learning methods in the area of reading are Cooperative Integrated Reading and Composition (CIRC; Stevens et al., 1987) and Reciprocal Teaching (RT; Palincsar & Brown, 1984). CIRC teachers conduct daily small-group basal instruction along with weekly direct instruction reading lessons in comprehension-fostering and metacognitive strategies. For these direct instruction lessons, teachers use special CIRC materials. Students work in mixed-ability learning teams to master the basal and direct instruction lesson content, using stimulus materials related to the basal text, which teams of teachers develop. Collaborative activities include oral reading in pairs, decoding, work on story structure, prediction, and story summary activities. A cooperative reward structure is used, whereby groups are responsible for individual student learning, and teams receive certificates and other rewards.

With RT, students read a passage of expository material, paragraph by paragraph. While reading, they learn and practice four comprehension strategies: generating questions, summarizing, clarifying word meanings and confusing text, and predicting subsequent paragraphs. In the early stages of RT, the teacher models these strategies; then students practice the strategies on the next section of the text as the teacher tailors feedback to each student through modeling, coaching, hints, and explanations. The teacher also invites students to react to peers' statements by elaborating or commenting, suggesting other questions, requesting clarifications, and helping to resolve misunderstandings. In the course of this guided practice, the teacher gradually shifts responsibility to the students for mediating discussions, as the teacher observes and helps as needed. At this point, sessions become dialogues among the students as they support each other and alternate between prompting the use of a strategy, applying and verbalizing that strategy, and commenting on the application.

Despite the availability of these impressive, well-developed, and tested methods, we were reluctant to adopt either approach as we struggled to help teachers make their primary- and intermediate-grade classrooms more responsive to a wide range of children. Our reluctance stemmed from feasibility and usability concerns. With respect to CIRC, a substantial commitment is demanded from teachers in terms of the percentage of their allocated reading instruction time. In addition, CIRC requires schools to invest considerable effort in creating and duplicating materials. RT, on the other hand, may be inappropriate for younger elementary-age children, where effects are unclear (Rosenshine & Meister, 1994). Moreover, for two reasons, the approach can be difficult for teachers to master. First, RT's strategic comprehension behaviors are unfamiliar to many teachers (Pressley, 1997). Second, the techniques required to help children develop responsibility for and competence in engaging peers' strategic behavior can be challenging.

For these reasons, we initially were attracted to a third validated form of collaborative learning, Class-Wide Peer Tutoring (CWPT; Greenwood et al., 1989), which better meets several feasibility and adoptability criteria. CWPT requires no materials development and only minimal duplication at the beginning of the school year; it occurs only three times a week, for 40 minutes per session, as a supplement to any instructional approach the teacher uses; and it is simple for teachers and students to learn. With CWPT, children work in pairs; one child reads aloud for 5 minutes while the partner identifies and corrects errors; the partner asks who, what, why, where, and when questions for 5 minutes; then students switch roles and repeat activities.

We did, however, question whether the CWPT activities might be enriched, and effectiveness thereby enhanced, without detracting from ease of implementation. Therefore, in 1989, we set out to develop and research a set of collaborative learning methods that would (1) be appropriate for children throughout the primary and intermediate grades, (2) incorporate the richness represented in CIRC and RT, and (3) benefit from the strong feasibility associated with CWPT.

In our initial work, we incorporated the CWPT structure. However, we substituted the CWPT activities with a potentially richer set of activities. Our first experiment tested CWPT against this modified and potentially enriched CWPT. Since 1989, we have built and researched a modified CWPT structure in reading, known as Peer-Assisted Learning Strategies (PALS). In this chapter, we describe the research program we have undertaken over the past 8 years to develop and test the program.

In this description of the PALS research base, we highlight three investigations that illustrate three types of studies in this research program. The first study represents our early work, in which, as we developed PALS, we contrasted the contribution of alternative components. The second study is one of several experimental evaluations of PALS's effectiveness, conducted once major components of the treatment had been specified. In the third study, we illustrate more recent fine-tuning efforts with an examination of how student training in providing elaborated help added to treatment effectiveness.

THE CONTRIBUTION OF ALTERNATIVE COMPONENTS

In the first major PALS experiment (Simmons, Fuchs, Fuchs, Hodge, & Mathes, 1994), conducted in 1990–1991, we focused on two dimensions of the PALS treatment: what activities to include and whether tutoring should be reciprocal. Our research questions were: (1) Does an enriched, but more complicated, set of peer-mediated activities support greater student learning than does the more simple set of CWPT activities? (2) Does role reciprocity, whereby both students serve as tutor and tutee in each session, enhance learning?

Why Examine Instructional Complexity?

CWPT comprises two primary components: (1) organizational procedures that provide structure for scheduling, pairing students, arranging the physical environment, and monitoring student participation, and (2) content-specific activities (i.e., sustained reading and answering who, what, where, when, and why questions). CWPT's organizational structure is elegant; we decided to maintain it. As already discussed, however, we were less certain about the CWPT activities. Although the simplicity of the CWPT activities has merit within increasingly demanding instructional contexts, a number of approaches promote reading fluency and comprehension in more strategic, although more complex, ways. Given the potentially greater efficacy of these validated approaches over those of CWPT, we decided to contrast CWPT activities to more complex activities, while maintaining the same CWPT organizational structure in both treatments.

The three more complex activities we incorporated were repeated reading, paragraph summaries, and prediction activities. Based on LaBerge and Samuels's (1974) theory of automaticity, *repeated reading* is designed to enhance reading fluency so that the cognitive demands of decoding and word recognition are reduced, thereby permitting readers to allocate greater cognitive resources to comprehension. In previous work, repeated reading has increased the number of words read correctly per minute, decreased word-recognition errors, and improved comprehension (Herman, 1985; O'Shea, Sindelar, & O'Shea, 1987; Samuels, 1979). For peer mediation, we operationalized repeated reading in the following way. The reader read a passage for 1 minute (the teacher signaled the beginning and end of the minute for the whole class) while the peer tutor recorded errors. The tutor corrected and provided feedback on errors, using a standard correction procedure, then tallied 1 point for each correctly read sentence. This sequence recurred twice, with readers rereading the same text three times.

The second activity, *paragraph summary,* was a modification of the paragraph-restatement strategy developed and tested by Jenkins, Heliotis, Haynes, and Beck (1986). Generating summaries can be difficult: Students cannot adequately summarize typical fifth-grade material until well into high school and junior college; poor readers have not yet mastered this activity (Brown & Day, 1983). Paragraph summarization requires readers (1) to monitor comprehension and make conscious judgments in the selection and reduction of textual information (Hidi & Anderson, 1986); (2) to allocate attention to the major content and check whether they have understood it (Palincsar & Brown, 1984); and (3) as an application of the generative-process model of reading, to elaborate on the information provided in text (Doctorow, Wittrock, & Marks, 1978). In these ways, paragraph summary reflects cognitive and metacognitive processes, and overt practice in generating summaries should promote those processes. In light of the difficulties children experience in this area, primary- and intermediate-grade children might benefit from practice in formulating summaries. In fact, research demonstrates that practice in paragraph summaries that require identification of main ideas can enhance reading comprehension (Baumann, 1984; Bean & Steenwyk, 1984; Paris, Cross, & Lipson, 1984; Rinehart, Stahl, & Erickson, 1986). In this study, with paragraph summary, the first reader read a paragraph aloud while the tutor identified and corrected errors. Then the reader stopped to identify who or what the paragraph was mostly about and the most important thing that happened. The tutor prompted corrections as necessary.

The third activity, *prediction relay,* extends paragraph summary to half-pages of text and requires formulation and checking of predictions. As described by Palincsar and Brown (1984), expert readers proceed automatically through text until an event alerts them to a comprehension failure, which then prompts debugging activities. One common triggering event is the realization that an expectation about the text has not been confirmed. This premise, of course, assumes that expert readers automatically formulate and check predictions as they read. Research documents, however, that young and poor readers have difficulty evaluating text for internal consistency and compatibility with known facts (Englert & Hiebert, 1984; Markman, 1981). And the ability to interpret what will occur next in text develops slowly (Collins & Smith, 1982). In this study, prediction relay was designed to help children develop and automatize the strategic behavior of formulating and checking predictions about the text they read by practicing that strategy in an overt manner. With prediction relay, the reader made a prediction about the upcoming half-page, which the tutor acknowledged as plausible or requested to be corrected; read that text aloud while the tutor identified and made corrections; (dis)confirmed the prediction while the tutor checked and prompted corrections; and proceeded on to subsequent half-pages in the same way.

Why Assess the Contribution of Role Reciprocity?

According to role theory, academic gains effected with peer and cross-age tutoring may be attributable to the enactment of a role that produces changes in behavior, attitudes, and self-perceptions (Allen, 1976). Most peer tutoring occurs with stronger students acting as tutors, and weaker students, as tutees. Nevertheless, some research suggests the potential for reciprocal tutoring (Top & Osguthorpe, 1987; Wiegmann, Dansereau, & Patterson, 1992). Moreover, as a generative model of learning (Wittrock, 1989) suggests, a tutorial role requires students to engage in active monitoring to identify and correct errors and to elaborate on information in their explanations. These activities may be beneficial to lower-performing students. Despite this potential, Osguthorpe and Scruggs's literature review (1986) concluded that the effects of role reciprocity had not been adequately studied.

Major Study Features

Participants were 31 general educators in grades 2–5. In these classes, where treatments were implemented classwide, we identified 118 children as target research participants. They were in the lower-performing half of each class; 58 had been identified as having a learning disability, 27 were low performers never referred to special education, and 33 performed in the average range. Twenty-three classrooms were assigned randomly to CWPT or to more complex collaborative activities. Half the classrooms in each condition were assigned randomly to a role-reciprocity condition. Eight teachers and their targeted students constituted the control condition, in which the same amount of total reading instruction occurred without collaborative learning. Tutoring took place three times each week for 14 weeks.

Immediately before and after treatment, we administered the Comprehensive Reading Assessment Battery (CRAB; L. Fuchs, Fuchs, & Hamlett, 1989) to each target child. Using four folktales (Brown & Smiley, 1977), two at each administration, the CRAB produces five scores: average number of words read aloud correctly in 3 minutes, average number of questions answered correctly, number of words and number of content words written on a recall of the passage, and number of maze (or multiple-choice cloze) items restored correctly. Treatment fidelity, measured four times in each classroom with direct observation, revealed strong implementation across conditions and time: The mean percentage of correctly implemented components for the four tutoring conditions ranged from 89.78% to 94.54%. We analyzed the database using classroom as the unit of analysis and student type as a dependent variable within classrooms. We found no significant interactions between treatment and type of students, indicating that effects applied across learning-disabled, low-performing, and average-performing children.

Effects on Reading Fluency

Students in all tutoring conditions made significantly greater growth on reading fluency than those in the control condition; effect sizes ranged from .29 to .41 standard deviations. There were, however, no significant differences between tutoring groups. One explanation for this lack of difference is that all tutoring conditions provided considerable opportunity for students to read and receive corrections in a carefully structured manner. Therefore potential differences among conditions may have been obscured by a more potent commonality: increased opportunity to read and receive systematic feedback.

In addition, the lack of difference on reading fluency between more and less complex activities may be attributable to the nature of our repeated reading treatment. The efficacy of repeated reading has been documented in short-term treatments (O'Shea et al., 1987) with controlled passages that maximize common words (Samuels, 1979). By contrast, our repeated-reading treatment lasted a relatively long time and used uncontrolled basal text or library material.

We also found no differences between students who served in one or both tutoring roles. According to role theory (Bierman & Furman, 1981; Cohen, 1984), the opportunity to act as tutor may increase self-perceptions of competence enough to improve academic performance. Yet the relation between academic learning time and achievement suggests the benefits of increased opportunity to read, which was afforded students who participated only as tutees. Moreover, although Wittrock's (1989) model of generative learning postulates that constructing explanations may enhance children's own understanding, the role of tutoring during reading-aloud provides few opportunities for tutors to elaborate. In any case, the absence of differences between role conditions, when combined with findings of greater learning for both conditions over that of a control group, indicated that reading fluency was enhanced with either configuration. Given the complexity associated with the repeated-reading condition, we opted to adopt sustained, rather than repeated, reading.

Effects on Comprehension

Only students who participated in the reciprocal, complex activities improved more than control students on comprehension measures; the average effect size was .65. With respect to reciprocity, we speculated that, in contrast to the reading-aloud activities, paragraph-summary and prediction activities did afford children greater opportunity to benefit from the tutoring role. Via the status associated with the tutoring role or via the actual metacognitive and cognitive demands associated with that role (i.e., monitoring partners' construction of main idea statements and checking the plausibility and actuality of partners' predictions), lower-performing children made greater gains than comparable students who only had opportunities to serve as tutees. This finding, which lends support to role theory and a generative model of learning, led us to adopt role reciprocity.

Comprehension findings also supported the efficacy of the more complex tutoring activities, at least in combination with role reciprocity. As discussed, prior work supports overt practice in strategic comprehension activities such as paragraph summaries (Baumann, 1984; Bean & Steenwyk, 1984; Hare & Borchardt, 1984; Jenkins et al., 1986; Rinehart et al., 1986) and prediction activities (e.g., Palincsar & Brown, 1984; Rosenshine & Meister, 1994). We therefore decided to incorporate the summary and prediction activities into PALS.

ESTIMATING OVERALL TREATMENT EFFECTS

Over several years, we cumulatively tested the contribution of contrasting components and finally arrived at a PALS treatment for which the component parts appeared effective and which teachers found workable in typical classrooms. In the next phase of our research program, therefore, we assessed the overall efficacy of the treatment. In this chapter we describe the PALS treatment tested in that series of studies; then we illustrate this phase with one large investigation (D. Fuchs, Fuchs, Mathes, & Simmons, 1997).

The PALS Treatment

Each week, teachers incorporate three 35-minute PALS sessions into their allocated reading time, implementing PALS with all children in their classes. Teachers begin by conducting seven lessons on how to implement PALS; each lesson lasts 45 to 60 minutes and incorporates teacher presentations, student recitation of information and application of principles, and teacher feedback on student implementation (for manual, see Fuchs, Fuchs, Mathes, & Simmons, 1996).

During PALS, every student in the class is paired; each pair includes a higher- and lower-performing student. The teacher determines dyads by ranking the class on reading competence, doing a median split, and pairing the highest performer from the top half with the highest performer from the bottom half and so on. Although tutoring roles are reciprocal, the higher-performing student reads first for each activity to serve as a model for the lower-performing student. Both students read from material appropriate for the lower reader, which typically is literature the teacher selects at the appropriate difficulty level.

Pairs are assigned to one of two teams for which they earn points. Points are awarded for completing reading activities correctly and demonstrating good tutoring. Each pair keeps track of points on a consecutively numbered scorecard, which represents joint effort and achievement. Each time a student earns a point, the tutor slashes the next number. In addition, as teachers lead PALS sessions, they circulate and award points to reward cooperative behavior and correct tutoring methods. At the end of the week, each pair reports the last number slashed as the pair's total; the teacher sums each team's points; and the class applauds the winning team. Every 4 weeks, the teacher formulates new pairs and team assignments. Thus the motivational system combines competitive (team versus team) and cooperative (combined effort of the pair) structures.

In every session, the first PALS activity is partner reading. Each student reads connected text aloud for 5 minutes, for a total of 10 minutes. The higher-performing student reads first; the lower-performing student rereads the same material. After both students read, the lower-performing student retells for 2 minutes the sequence of what occurred. Students earn 1 point for each correctly read sentence and 10 points for the retell.

The second PALS activity, designed to develop comprehension through summarization and main idea identification, is paragraph shrinking. Continuing to read subsequent sections of text, students orally read one paragraph at a time, stopping to identify its main idea. Tutors guide the identification of the main idea by asking readers to identify who or what the paragraph is mainly about and the most important thing about the who or what. Readers then put these two pieces of information together in 10 or fewer words. For each summary, students earn 1 point for correctly identifying the who or what; 1 point for correctly stating the most important thing; and 1 point for using no more than 10 words. Students continue to monitor and correct reading errors, but points are no longer awarded for reading sentences correctly. After 5 minutes, students switch roles.

The last activity, prediction relay, extends paragraph shrinking to larger chunks of text and requires students to formulate and check predictions. The activity comprises four steps: The reader (1) makes a prediction about what will be learned on the next half-page, (2) reads the half-page aloud while the tutor corrects errors, (3) (dis)confirms the prediction, and

(4) summarizes the main idea. Students earn 1 point for each viable prediction; 1 point for reading each half-page; 1 point for accurately (dis)-
confirming each prediction; and 1 point for each summary component
(the who or what, what mainly happened, and 10 or fewer words). After
5 minutes, students switch roles.

Study Methods and Findings

We assigned 12 schools, stratified on achievement and family income, to
experimental and control groups. At grades 2–6, 20 teachers implemented PALS; 20 did not. PALS teachers implemented the treatment
class-wide. However, we identified three students in each class as research
participants: one with an identified learning disability in reading (LD),
one low achiever never referred for special education (LA), and one average achiever (AA). We tested each research participant with the CRAB
before and after treatment, which lasted 15 weeks. Fidelity data, collected
three times with observation, revealed strong implementation. Instructional plan sheets revealed that PALS and no-PALS teachers allocated
comparable time to reading instruction.

We analyzed the achievement data using treatment, trial, and student type (LD, LA, AA) as factors (classroom was the unit of analysis; trial
was a repeated measure; student type was a dependent measure within
classrooms). We found significant treatment by trial interactions on all
CRAB scores, indicating that, compared to conventional instruction, PALS
students grew more on fluency, accuracy, and comprehension. Moreover,
we found the three-way interaction was not statistically significant; so,
treatment effects were not mediated by the students' initial achievement
status. Aggregated across the three types of students, effect sizes were .22,
.55, and .56, respectively on the scores of CRAB words read correctly,
questions answered corrrectly, and maze blanks restored correctly.

These effects compare favorably with more complicated versions of
collaborative learning. As reported by Slavin (1994), the median effect
size for 52 studies of cooperative learning treatments that lasted more
than 4 weeks was .32, a figure identical to the one reported for RT by
Rosenshine and Meister (1994). Also, in PALS work we have estimated
effects for different types of learners (in subsequent studies, effect sizes
for high achievers were larger than for LD, LA, or AA students).

PALS's effectiveness may reside both in its specific activities and in its
overall organization. In terms of substance, the PALS activities encourage
students to practice overtly strategies shown to strengthen reading comprehension when implemented regularly on instructional-level text. With
respect to organization, PALS provides highly structured, reciprocal, one-

to-one interaction, which (1) permits all students frequent opportunity to respond, (2) facilitates immediate corrective feedback, (3) increases academic engaged time, and (4) offers social support and encouragement, with all students sharing the esteem associated with the tutoring role. Moreover, with the PALS scorecard system, students work cooperatively with partners but compete in teams to earn points. This keeps students working in a focused, productive, and constructive manner.

PALS also offers implementation advantages. PALS materials are concrete, specific, and user-friendly, important criteria if new practices are to be implemented (see McLaughlin, 1991, cited in Gersten, Vaughn, Deshler, & Schiller, 1995). A comprehensive manual, written for teachers, guides implementation. And teachers do not need to develop additional materials or devote more time to reading instruction. Further, PALS can complement whole-language as well as phonics instruction because PALS enhances, rather than providing a radical substitute for, teachers' ongoing reading practices.

FINE-TUNING THE PALS COMPONENTS

In developing PALS, we have struggled with an appropriate balance between effectiveness and ease of implementation. For this reason, we have constantly tested the limits of what might work against what teachers are willing and capable of doing within the constraints of typical classrooms. In the past several years, therefore, we have continued to fine-tune activities, whereby we have examined methods for extending PALS's effectiveness.

The last study we describe is a recent fine-tuning effort (L. Fuchs, Fuchs, Kazdan, & Allen, 1999). Our purpose was to enhance students' capacity to respond constructively to partners' difficulties. Our interest in this topic arose for two reasons. First, observations of students implementing PALS raised concern that, despite PALS's effectiveness, students failed to identify many partners' errors. Moreover, the PALS correction procedures, along with its point structure, encouraged students to make corrections as quickly as possible—usually by providing partners with correct answers.

These impressions were worrisome in light of related research in mathematics. This literature indicates that appropriate response to classmates' difficulties can be important: Students' mathematics learning increases when children provide elaborated help (Nattiv, 1994; Swing & Peterson, 1982; Webb & Farivar, 1994), whereby students prompt classmates to construct their own correct responses rather than simply provide them with answers. Moreover, research indicates that, when encouraged to provide elaborated help but not explicitly taught methods for accomplishing that, students tend to provide confusing explanations (Cooper & Cooper, 1984; Michaels & Bruce, 1991; Palincsar & Brown, 1989) and rely on lectures and demonstrations while providing few opportunities for peers to apply information (L. Fuchs, Fuchs, Bentz, Phillips, & Hamlett, 1994; Webb, Troper, & Fall, 1995). Students do not develop effective interactional styles as a natural consequence of participating in collaborative learning activities (Kohler & Greenwood, 1990). Despite these findings in math, no established collaborative reading program has incorporated explicit methods to help students respond effectively when peers experience difficulty or confusion.

In 1996–1997, we addressed this void. For each PALS activity, we developed explicit methods among which tutors could select to help partners construct correct responses. In Table 5.1, for each PALS activity, we contrast the standard PALS correction procedure with the elaborated, or help-giving, strategies we developed and taught children. In this section, we describe the help-giving PALS treatment, which incorporated these elaborated correction strategies. Then we provide an overview of the study in which we tested the utility of these strategies.

Modified Help-Giving PALS Treatment

Modified help-giving PALS incorporated the same dyadic structure, the same activities (partner reading, paragraph shrinking, and prediction relay), and the same scorecards and team structure. The major difference between PALS and help-giving PALS (HG-PALS) was that rather than teaching the standard PALS correction procedure for each activity, HG-PALS teachers taught students specific strategies for helping partners figure out correct responses on their own. For each PALS activity, from two to four strategies were covered (see Table 5. 1).

The first lesson began with a discussion about watching readers carefully to determine when they need help. Teachers showed a videotape of a PALS dyad as one student experienced difficulty. The teachers led a discussion of what the nature of the student's problem might be. Then, for each strategy, teachers showed a videoclip illustrating the tutor relying on the target strategy to provide help. Teachers then led a discussion about how the tutor's help illustrated the target strategy. After all strategies for that PALS activity had been illustrated and discussed, teachers showed a video of the same tutor providing multiple helping strategies and led a discussion in which students commented on the various strategies. This was followed with a PALS session, after which students de-

Table 5.1. PALS and modified PALS helping methods.

Activity	Condition	
	Help-Giving PALS Strategies	Standard PALS Correction Method
Partner Reading (Helping reader figure out words)	*Step 1:* Coach says, "Stop, you missed that word. Can you figure it out?" Reader figures out word within 4 seconds.	*Step 1:* Coach says, "Stop, you missed that word. Can you figure it out?" Reader figures out word within 4 seconds.
	Step 2: Coach says, "Good. Read that sentence again." OR	*Step 2:* Coach says, "Good. Read that sentence again." OR
	Step 1: Coach says, "Stop, you missed that word. Can you figure it out?"	*Step 1:* Coach says, "Stop, you missed that word. Can you figure it out?"
	Step 2: Coach counts to 4, then helps reader by:	*Step 2:* Coach counts to 4, then tells the word.
	Helping reader use context	
	Helping reader use the vowel sound(s)	
	Saying the word very slowly for the reader	
	Covering up the word and slowly uncovering each part, while asking reader to say each part	
	If, after two strategies, reader is still unable to figure out word, coach gives word and goes on.	
	Step 3: Coach asks, "What word?" Reader says word.	*Step 3:* Coach asks, "What word?" Reader says word.
	Step 4: Coach says, "Good. Read that sentence again."	*Step 4:* Coach says, "Good. Read that sentence again."

scribed the help they provided and classified their help according to the strategies.

We were concerned that the point structure, which encouraged students to work efficiently, might discourage students from using elaborated helping strategies, because helping interrupted text reading for

Table 5.1. *(continued)*

Activity	Condition	
	Help-Giving PALS Strategies	Standard PALS Correction Method
Paragraph Shrinking (Helping reader figure out: 1. who/what paragraph is about and 2. what mainly happened)	*Step 1:* Coach says, "That's not quite right."	*Step 1:* Coach says, "That's not quite right. Skim the paragraph and try again."
	Step 2: Coach offers to help by: Asking reader questions that begin with *who, what, when, where, why,* or *how*	*Step 2:* Reader skims paragraph and tries to answer the missed question. Coach decides to give points or give answer.
	Asking reader to reread first and last sentences in the paragraph; choosing a part of the paragraph that gives the main idea and asking reader to reread it	
	If, after two strategies, the reader is still unable to answer question, coach gives answer and goes on.	

longer durations than the standard PALS correction methods. We therefore modified the point structure for the HG-PALS condition. Students did not award their own points for successful completion of activities. Rather, teachers awarded all points for good tutoring behavior and specific use of helping strategies. And teachers coded points by writing letters over, instead of slashing, numbers; letters stood for the strategies teachers had observed.

Study Methods and Findings

Twenty-four teachers and their students participated in this study; 15 taught grades 2 or 3 (primary grades); 9 taught grade 4 (intermediate grade). Stratifying by grade, we randomly assigned classrooms to experimental or control groups. Within the experimental group, we randomly assigned half the classrooms at each grade to PALS or HG-PALS. We identified three types of learners as our research participants: students with persistent and serious reading and behavior problems (referred to as "at risk"), average-achieving students, and high-achieving students.

Teachers implemented treatments three times a week for 17 weeks. Fidelity was strong in each condition. We pre- and posttested on the reading comprehension subtest of the Stanford Diagnostic Reading Test (SDRT). After all PALS lessons had been conducted, we observed student interactions during PALS and HG-PALS to index (1) the percentage of errors for which corrections were provided and (2) the percentage of corrections for which HG-PALS strategies were employed. Pre- to posttreatment change scores on the SDRT were analyzed using treatment and student type as factors (classroom was treated as the unit of analysis, with student type treated as a dependent measure within classrooms). Student interaction data were aggregated by classroom.

Effects, which were not mediated by students' initial achievement status, revealed the following. In grade 4, compared to standard PALS, HG-PALS students corrected more errors (86% versus 54%) and relied more on HG-PALS helping strategies (97% versus 39%). Along with greater responsiveness, fourth-grade HG-PALS students made differential reading progress (average gains of 6.11, 2.89 and -.22 points on the SDRT, respectively, for HG-PALS, standard PALS, and contrast). Effect sizes favoring the HG-PALS students were .72 compared to standard PALS and .98 compared to the control group.

At the primary grades, however, findings diverged sharply. Compared to HG-PALS and control students, *standard PALS* students made greater reading progress; average gains were 6.60, 1.60, and 2.47 points for standard PALS, HG-PALS, and control groups, respectively. And, to partially explain findings, student interaction data revealed that younger children did not take much advantage of the HG-PALS helping strategies. Rather, primary-grade HG-PALS treatment participants corrected only 60% of errors (versus 25% in standard PALS), and they relied on the HG-PALS helping strategies only 39% of the time (versus 0% in standard PALS).

Therefore the success of the elaborated helping strategies was mediated by students' grade. Older students appeared more capable of learning the HG-PALS helping strategies or integrating those methods into their everyday PALS use. This hypothesis is corroborated by the striking differences, even within the standard PALS condition, between younger and older children's percentages of corrections (25% versus 54%) and use of the modified helping strategies (0% versus 39%). Moreover, older children who had *no* training in the HG-PALS methods appeared to incorporate *some* HG-PALS elaborated strategies; younger children did not. These findings suggest that younger children may not be developmentally ready to master or incorporate use of relatively complex helping strategies.

In addition, from the perspective of developmental reading stages, the standard PALS corrections methods may have been more appropriate and effective for primary-grade children. Developmental models of reading (Chall, 1983; LaBerge & Samuels, 1974; Perfetti & Lesgold, 1979) assume that reading entails component skills, each of which is sufficient for a time, but then new skills must be achieved for reading competence to increase. These components begin with letter–sound recognition and proceed sequentially to decoding, fluency, comprehension, and the ability to integrate and synthesize material (Potter & Wamre, 1990). The simpler, standard PALS correction procedures largely encourage tutors to provide answers; the standard PALS point structure encourages children to proceed quickly through text. These features may have supported more sustained reading and practice (with fewer interruptions compared to the HG-PALS elaborated correcting)—appropriate activites for children who are still acquiring reading fluency and accuracy and who operate on simple text structures that require simple comprehension strategies (Englert & Hiebert, 1984). In this way, the standard PALS correction methods may have better supported development.

In terms of ease of implementation, it is also important to note that the HG-PALS treatment took at least six additional lessons before student mastery of PALS occurred. In addition, across grade levels, teacher satisfaction with HG-PALS was more variable and lower than for standard PALS. In light of these findings, we recommend that primary-grade teachers implement standard PALS. At the intermediate grades, teachers should select the PALS version they consider to meet the needs of their students along with their own implementation concerns.

CONCLUSIONS AND QUALIFICATIONS

Despite evidence of PALS efficacy and apparent ease of implementation, qualifications are necessary. First, our work reveals that, despite significant effects across types of learners, subsets of children do not profit from PALS. In the D. Fuchs, Fuchs, Mathes, & Simmons (1997) study, for example, 20% of LD children failed to show adequate growth. These four children were the poorest readers among those with LD in PALS; three of these four children were also described as disruptive. Clearly, some children require more intensive or different reading methods. This underscores the importance of monitoring students' reading progress to permit schools to identify, throughout the school year, children who require program modifications (L. Fuchs, 1997).

Second, in every PALS study, teachers have been provided with technical assistance, whereby research assistants scheduled and watched teachers implementing PALS lessons. Also, research assistants met with teachers every 2 weeks to help solve implementation problems. This, of course, provided opportunities for research staff to correct teachers' misconceptions quickly and insure implementation. Although teachers have consistently rated the PALS methods as highly feasible, it remains unclear what level of technical support is required to insure accurate implementation. An independent replication at other locations revealed the necessity for technical support: Vadasy, Jenkins, Antil, Phillips, and Pool (1997) demonstrated that with simple access to the manual, few teachers implement PALS. And, among those who do implement, few do so with fidelity. Other implementations, however, suggest that a 1-day workshop along with minimal encouragement may be sufficient to insure strong PALS implementation (Grimes, 1997; Raines, 1997). This issue needs to be evaluated systematically.

A third consideration is PALS's omission of nonreaders. In second through sixth grade, where PALS effectiveness has been demonstrated, some children cannot participate in PALS because the activities require some minimal level of reading capacity. Because of this problem, and because we wished to examine PALS's potential to supplement first-grade reading programs, we have developed and studied a beginning readers' PALS treatment (Mathes, Howard, Allen, & Fuchs, 1998). These PALS activities incorporate focus on identifying sounds, segmenting, blending, and decoding words, as well as story sharing using simple library books. Early evaluations (Mathes et al., 1998; D. Fuchs, Fuchs, & Thompson, 1997) are promising. Nevertheless, additional work investigating optimal combinations of activities and organizational structures is required.

ACKNOWLEDGMENTS

Support for the research described in this chapter was provided by Grants #G008730253, #H023E90020, #H023C40001, and #H324V980001 from the Office of Special Education Programs in the U.S. Department of Education and Core Grant HD 15052 from the National Institute of Child Health and Development to Vanderbilt University. The content in this chapter does not reflect the positions or policies of these funding agencies, and no official endorsement by them should be inferred. Inquiries should be sent to: Lynn S. Fuchs, Box 328 Peabody, Vanderbilt University, Nashville, TN 37203.

REFERENCES

Allen, V. (1976). *Children as teachers: Theory and research on tutoring.* New York: Academic.

Baumann, J. F. (1984). The effectiveness of a direct instruction paradigm for teaching main idea comprehension. *Reading Research Quarterly, 16,* 32–35.

Bean, T. W., & Steenwyk, F. L. (1984). The effect of three forms of summarization instruction on sixth graders' summary writing and comprehension. *Journal of Reading Behavior, 16,* 297–307.

Bierman, K., & Furman, W. (1981). Effects of role assignment rationale on attitudes formed during peer tutoring. *Journal of Educational Psychology, 73,* 33–40.

Braddock, J., II, Hawley, W., Hunt, T., Oakes, J., Slavin, R., & Wheelock, A. (1992). *Realizing our nation's diversity as an opportunity: Alternatives to sorting America's children.* Nashville, TN: Vanderbilt Institute for Public Policy Studies, Center for Education and Human Development Policy.

Brown, A. L., & Day, J. D. (1983). Macrorules for summarizing texts: The development of expertise. *Journal of Verbal Learning and Verbal Behavior, 22,* 1–14.

Brown, A. L., & Smiley, S. (1977). Rating the importance of structural units of prose passages: A problem of metacognitive development. *Child Development, 48,* 1–8.

Chall, J. S. (1983). *Stages of reading development.* New York: McGraw-Hill.

Cohen, E. (1984). Talking and working together: Status, interaction, and learning. In P. Peterson, L. Wilkinson, & M. Hallinan (Eds.), *The social context of instruction* (pp. 171–186). New York: Academic.

Collins, J., & Smith, E. E. (1982). Teaching the process of reading comprehension. In D. K. Detterman & R. J. Sternberg (Eds.), *How and how much can intelligence be increased* (p. 173–185). Norwood, NJ: Ablex.

Cooper, C. R., & Cooper, R. G. (1984). Skill in peer learning discourse. In S. A. Kuczaj (Ed.), *Discourse development* (pp. 89–102). New York: Springer-Verlag.

Doctorow, M., Wittrock, M. C., & Marks, C. (1978). Generative processes in reading comprehension. *Journal of Educational Psychology, 70,* 109–118.

Englert, C. S., & Hiebert, E. H. (1984). Children's developing awareness of text structures in expository materials. *Journal of Educational Psychology, 76,* 65–75.

Fuchs, D., & Fuchs, L. S. (1994). Inclusive schools movement and the radicalization of special education reform. *Exceptional Children, 60,* 294–309.

Fuchs, D., Fuchs, L. S., Mathes, P. G., & Simmons, D.C. (1996). *Peer-assisted learning strategies in reading: A manual* (Available from Box 328 Peabody, Vanderbilt University, Nashville, TN 37203).

Fuchs, D., Fuchs, L. S., Mathes, P. G., & Simmons, D.C. (1997). Peer-Assisted Learning Strategies: Making classrooms more responsive to diversity. *American Educational Research Journal, 34,* 174–206.

Fuchs, D., Fuchs, L. S., & Thompson, A. (1997). *Evaluation of first-grade PALS Title I implementation in Nashville*. Manuscript submitted for publication.

Fuchs, L. S. (1997). *Monitoring student progress toward the development of reading competence: Classroom-based assessment methods*. Paper prepared for the Committee on the Prevention of Reading Disabilities of the National Academy of Sciences.

Fuchs, L. S., Fuchs, D., Bentz, J., Phillips, N. B., & Hamlett, C. L. (1994). The nature of student interactions during peer tutoring with and without prior training and experience. *American Educational Research Journal, 31,* 75–103.

Fuchs, L. S., Fuchs, D., & Hamlett, C. L. (1989). Monitoring reading growth using student recalls: Effects of two teacher feedback systems. *Journal of Educational Research, 83,* 103–111.

Fuchs, L. S., Fuchs, D., Kazdan, S., & Allen, S. (1999). Effects of peer-assisted learning strategies in reading with and without training in elaborated help giving. *Elementary School Journal, 99,* 201-220.

Fuchs, L. S., Fuchs, D., Phillips, N. B., & Simmons, D. (1993). Contextual variables affecting instructional adaptation for difficult-to-teach students. *Exceptional Children, 22,* 725–740.

Gersten, R., Vaughn, S., Deshler, D., & Schiller, E. (1995). *What we know (and still don't know) about utilizing research findings to improve practice: Implications for special education*. Unpublished manuscript.

Greenwood, C. R., Delquadri, J. C., & Hall, R. V. (1989). Longitudinal effects of classwide peer tutoring. *Journal of Educational Psychology, 81,* 371–383.

Grimes, J. (1997). Implementing reading PALS in Iowa. Unpublished raw data.

Hare, V. C., & Borchardt, K. M. (1984). Direct instruction of summarization skills. *Reading Research Quarterly, 20,* 62–78.

Herman, P. A. (1985). The effect of repeated reading on reading rate, speech pauses, and word recognition. *Reading Research Quarterly, 22,* 553–565.

Hidi, S., & Anderson, V. (1986). Producing written summaries: Task demands, cognitive operations, and implications for instruction. *Review of Educational Research, 56,* 473–493.

Hodgkinson, H. L. (1995). What should we call people?: Race, class, and the census for 2000. *Phi Delta Kappan, 77,* 173–179.

Jenkins, J. R., Heliotis, J. D., Haynes, M. C., & Beck, K. (1986). Does passive learning account for disabled readers' comprehension deficits in ordinal reading situations? *Learning Disabilities Quarterly, 9,* 69–75.

Kohler, F. W., & Greenwood, C. R. (1990). Effects of collateral peer supportive behaviors within the classwide peer tutoring program. *Journal of Applied Behavior Analysis, 23,* 307–322.

LaBerge, D., & Samuels, S. J. (1974). Toward a theory of automatic information processing in reading. *Cognitive Psychology, 6,* 293–323.

Markman, E. M. (1981). Comprehension monitoring. In W. P. Dickson (Ed.), *Children's oral communication skills* (pp. 61–84). New York: Academic.

Mathes, P. G., Howard, J. K., Allen, S. H., & Fuchs, D. (1998). Peer-assisted learning strategies for first-grade readers: Responding to the needs of diverse learners. *Reading Research Quarterly, 33,* 62–94.

McLaughlin, M. W. (1991). Enabling professional development: What have we learned? In A. Lieberman & L. Miller (Eds.), *Staff development for education in the 90s: New demands, new realities, new perspectives* (pp. 61–82). New York: Teachers College Press.

Michaels, S., & Bruce, C. (1991). *Discourses on the seasons* (Technical Rep.). Champaign: University of Illinois, Reading Research and Education Center.

Nattiv, A. (1994). Helping behavior and math achievement gain of students using cooperative learning. *Elementary School Journal, 94*, 285–297.

Osguthorpe, R. T., & Scruggs, T. E. (1986). Special education students as tutors: A review and analysis. *Remedial and Special Education, 7*, 15–26.

O'Shea, L. J., Sindelar, P. T., & O'Shea, D. J. (1987). The effects of repeated reading and attentional cues on the reading fluency and comprehension of learning disabled readers. *Learning Disabilities Research, 2*, 103–109.

Palincsar, A. M., & Brown, A. L. (1984). Reciprocal teaching of comprehension-fostering and comprehension-monitoring activities. *Cognition and Instruction, 2*, 117–175.

Palincsar, A. S., & Brown, A. L. (1989). Classroom dialogues to promote self-regulated comprehension. In J. Brophy (Ed.), *Advances in research on teaching* (Vol. 1; pp. 35–71). New York: JAI.

Paris, S. G., Cross, D. R., & Lipson, M. Y. (1984). Informed strategies for learning: A program to improve children's reading awareness and comprehension. *Journal of Educational Psychology, 76*, 1239–1252.

Perfetti, C. A., & Lesgold, A. M. (1979). Coding and comprehension in skilled reading and implications for reading instruction. In L. B. Resnick & P. A. Weaver (Eds.), *Theory and practice of early reading* (Vol. 1; pp. 57–83). Hillsdale, NJ: Erlbaum.

Potter, M. L., & Wamre, H. M. (1990). Curriculum-based measurement and developmental reading models: Opportunities for cross validation. *Exceptional Children, 57*, 16–25.

Pressley, M. (1997). *Remarks on reading comprehension.* Notes prepared for the Chesapeake Institute, Washington, DC.

Raines, R. (1997). Implementing reading PALS in Bakersfield, CA. Unpublished raw data.

Rinehart, S. D., Stahl, S. A., & Erickson, L. G. (1986). Some effects of summarization training on reading and studying. *Research Research Quarterly, 21*, 422–438.

Rosenshine, B., & Meister, C. (1994). Reciprocal Teaching: A review of research. *Review of Educational Research, 64*, 479–530.

Samuels, S. J. (1979). The method of repeated readings. *Reading Teacher, 32*, 403–408.

Simmons, D.C., Fuchs, D., Fuchs, L. S., Hodge, J. P., & Mathes, P. G. (1994). Importance of instructional complexity and role reciprocity to classwide peer tutoring. *Learning Disabilities Research and Practice, 9*, 203–212.

Slavin, R. E. (1994). *Cooperative learning: Theory, research, and practice* (2nd ed.). Boston: Allyn & Bacon.

Stallings J. A. (1995). Ensuring teaching and learning in the 21st century. *Educational Researchers, 24*(6), 4–8.

Stevens, R. J., Madden, N. A., Slavin, R. E., & Farnish, A. M. (1987). Cooperative

Integrated Reading and Composition: Two field experiments. *Reading Research Quarterly, 22,* 433–454.

Swing, S. R., & Peterson, P. L. (1982). The relationship of student ability and small group interaction to student achievement. *American Educational Research Journal, 19,* 259–274.

Top, B. I. L., & Osguthorpe, R. T. (1987). Reverse-role tutoring: The effects of handicapped students tutoring regular class students. *Elementary School Journal, 87,* 413–423.

Vadasy, P. F., Jenkins, J. R., Antil, L. R., Phillips, N. B., & Pool, K. (1997). The research-to-practice ball game: Classwide peer tutoring and teacher interest, implementation, and modifications. *Remedial and Special Education, 18,* 143–156.

Webb, N. M., & Farivar, S. (1994). Promoting helping behavior in cooperative small groups in middle school mathematics. *American Educational Research Journal, 31,* 369–395.

Webb, N. M., Troper, J., & Fall, J. R. (1995). Constructive activity and learning in collaborative small groups. *Journal of Educational Psychology, 87,* 406–423.

Wiegmann, D. A., Dansereau, D. F., & Patterson, M. E. (1992). Cooperative learning: Effects of role playing and ability on performance. *Journal of Experimental Education, 60,* 109–116.

Wittrock, M. C. (1989). Generative processes of comprehension. *Educational Psychologist, 24,* 345–376.

6

A Vocabulary Program to Complement and Bolster a Middle-Grade Comprehension Program

MICHAEL F. GRAVES

The importance of vocabulary is daily demonstrated in schools and out. In the classroom, the achieving students possess the most adequate vocabularies. Because of the verbal nature of most classroom activities, knowledge of words and ability to use language are essential to success in these activities. After schooling has ended, adequacy of vocabulary is almost equally essential for achievement in vocations and in society.

These are the words that Walter Petty, Curtis Herold, and Earline Stoll used in introducing a report on *The State of Knowledge About the Teaching of Vocabulary* (1967, p. 7) commissioned by the National Council of Teachers of English more than three decades ago. I concur fully with their belief in the importance of vocabulary, and I begin this chapter with this quotation because it is a well-crafted and powerful testimonial to the importance of words. Unfortunately, Petty and colleagues' conclusion about the profession's knowledge about how to *teach* vocabulary, while perhaps as well-crafted and as powerful as their statement on the importance of vocabulary, was much less positive. Based on their careful and thorough review of the literature on vocabulary instruction available at the time, Petty and colleagues said this: "The teaching profession seems to know little of substance about the teaching of vocabulary" (p. 84).

Today, this situation has changed markedly: We currently know a great deal about vocabulary instruction (Beck & McKeown, 1990; Blachowicz & Fisher, in press; Graves, 1986; Nagy & Scott, in press). Unfortunately, however, vocabulary instruction is currently a somewhat neglected topic in the field (Cassidy & Wenrich, 1997, 1998); and although we have little information about the vocabulary instruction that actually takes place in schools, the information we do have (Ryder & Graves, 1994; Watts, 1995) suggests that much of the vocabulary instruction makes little use of the knowledge base we have built. In this chapter, I first note what is arguably the single most important fact to keep in mind when planning a vocabulary program and then describe a comprehensive vocabulary program that takes into account this fact and much of the other knowledge we have on vocabulary.

Before continuing, I should note directly that I have chosen to include this chapter on vocabulary in a collection focusing on comprehension for two reasons. One is that an appropriately designed vocabulary program can, as the chapter title suggests, complement and bolster a comprehension program. The other is to make the point that focusing on and arguing for the importance of one aspect of the literacy curriculum should not be interpreted as an argument that other areas of the curriculum are unimportant. All too frequently, the literacy education field focuses huge amounts of attention on the currently hot topics—phonemic awareness and phonics seem to fill that role at the present time, while using authentic children's literature seemed to fill it a short time ago—and neglects other important ones. Certainly, phonemic awareness, phonics, and quality literature are important, but their importance does not justify neglecting other valuable areas of the literacy education curriculum. Similarly, an emphasis on comprehension should not mean a deemphasis on vocabulary.

That said, the single most important fact to keep in mind when planning a vocabulary program is this: The vocabulary-learning task is enormous! Estimates of vocabulary size vary greatly, but a very conservative estimate based on a substantial body of recent and rigorous work (R. Anderson & Nagy, 1992; Anglin, 1993; Nagy & Anderson, 1984; White, Graves, & Slater, 1990) is this: The books and other reading materials used by schoolchildren include well over 100,000 different words. The average child enters school with a reading vocabulary of only a handful of words but learns reading vocabulary at a rate of 3,000 to 4,000 words a year, accumulating a reading vocabulary of something like 25,000 words by the time he or she is in eighth grade and one that may be well over 50,000 words by the end of high school.

A FOUR-PART VOCABULARY PROGRAM

A vocabulary program likely to seriously assist students in the enormous word-learning task they face must of course be a powerful and substantial one. Yet at the same time, it must not constitute an inappropriately large part of the curriculum. Students have a lot of other things to do besides learn vocabulary. The program described here has four components: wide reading, teaching individual words, teaching strategies for learning words independently, and fostering word consciousness. In the remainder of this chapter, I deal with each of these in turn, concluding with a suggestion for how much time the total program is likely to consume.

Wide Reading

Wide reading means extensive reading—reading a lot in a variety of materials. Wide reading is, of course, important for a host of reasons, but it is particularly important to vocabulary growth. If students learn to read something like 3,000 to 4,000 words each year, it is clear that most of the words they learn are not taught directly. With a 180-day school year, teaching 3,000 to 4,000 words would require teaching approximately 20 words each and every school day. Obviously, this does not happen. Instead, students learn many of the words that make up their vocabularies from their reading (R. Anderson, 1996). Thus, if we can substantially increase the amount of reading students do, we can markedly increase their vocabularies. Moreover, wide reading will foster automaticity, provide knowledge about a variety of topics and literary forms, and leave students with a habit that will make them lifelong readers.

Unfortunately, many students do very little reading, and some do almost none (R. Anderson, Wilson, & Fielding, 1988). Clearly, students need to be encouraged to do more reading. There are a number of ways to provide such encouragement.

The first step is to get sizeable collections of current and enticing books, magazines, and other reading material into school libraries and into classrooms. Schools must have substantial collections of new, attractive, interesting, and informative books and magazines that are guaranteed to be there because building a collection and systematically maintaining and adding to it are parts of a routine budget. Unfortunately, there are many schools, particularly schools that enroll many poor children, in which both the school library and classroom libraries are markedly inadequate (Allington, Guice, Michelson, Baker, & Li, 1996). This is a real tragedy. Trying to run a reading program without adequate classroom and school libraries is like trying to run a telemarketing business without telephones. It's absurd.

A second step is for teachers to make use of the many sources for identifying good children's books that are now available. *Book Links*, for example, the bimonthly magazine from the American Library Association, features annotated bibliographies, essays, reviews, and recommendations for using literature with children from preschool through eighth grade. *The Reading Teacher* devotes a monthly column to children's books and annually include annotated bibliographies such as Children's Choices and Teachers' Choices, which highlight current titles that children and teachers have found enticing and informative. So, too, do journals like *Language Arts* and *Voices from the Middle*. Compilations of these bibliographies, such as *More Teachers' Favorite Books for Kids* (International Reading Association, 1997) and *More Teens' Favorite Books* (International Reading Association, 1996), which the International Reading Association revises every 3 years or so, make finding good books extremely easy. Increasingly, so do Internet resources—including such nonglitzy resources as on-line card catalogues. Most teachers are familiar with these and many other sources of books for children, but these resources do not seem to get used as much as they might.

A third step is to make sustained silent reading a frequent activity (McCracken, 1971). If many children do not read at home—and unfortunately many do not—then it is imperative that they read in school. Linda Fielding and colleagues (Fielding, Wilson, & Anderson, 1986) have shown that about 10 minutes of independent reading a day—a little more than an hour a week—can produce significant gains; and a little more than an hour a week seems a very reasonable and manageable amount of time to devote to sustained silent reading.

There are a number of different recommendations for encouraging sustained silent reading—different ways of getting books into students' hands, different places to read, and different ways to monitor students' reading—but it seems unlikely that any one way is superior in all situations. There is, however, one frequent injunction that seems likely to be particularly important—for the classroom teacher to read along with students. It is doubtful that it makes a lot of difference whether the janitor reads, or whether the principal's secretary reads, or even whether the principal reads. But it is probably very important that students not see that the classroom teacher has more important things to do than read.

Of course, sustained silent reading is by no means the only approach to encouraging, facilitating, and promoting wide reading. Teachers can and should frequently read to students, model their enthusiasm for reading, get parents and other caregivers involved in reading to and with their children, encourage reading outside of school, be sure that students do a variety of reading in all content areas, and do everything possible to lead all children to become committed and engaged readers. Together, these and a myriad of other activities suggested in such texts as *The Read Aloud Handbook* (Trelease, 1995), *Promoting Reading in Developing Countries*

(Greaney, 1996), and *Reading Engagement* (Gruthrie & Wigfield, 1997) can greatly increase the amount of reading students do.

Teaching Individual Words

Teaching individual words is the second part of the vocabulary program outlined here. Teaching individual words is the part of a vocabulary program that typically gets the lion's share of attention in the classroom, and it is the part of a vocabulary program on which we have the most concrete and practical advice (see, e.g., Graves, Juel, & Graves, 1998; Nagy, 1988). For these reasons, I will deal with only two aspects of the matter here. First, I discuss selecting vocabulary to teach. Second, I illustrate the fact that the task of learning individual words is actually a variety of different learning tasks that require quite different teaching procedures.

Selecting Vocabulary to Teach. Unfortunately, once students get beyond the first or second grade, there is no such thing as a convenient list of words to teach. Instead, the vast majority of words to be taught are ones teachers identify in the texts students are reading. In general, of course, teachers need to teach the words students do not know.

The best source of information about what words students do and do not know is the students themselves. Teachers can identify words in upcoming selections that they think will be difficult and build multiple-choice or matching tests to find out whether or not the words are difficult. Of course, constructing such tests is time-consuming and certainly not something to be done for every selection. However, after several experiences of identifying words that they think will be difficult and then checking students' performance against their expectations, teachers' general perceptions of which words are and are not likely to cause their students problems will become increasingly accurate.

In addition to testing students on potentially difficult words using these traditional types of tests, teachers can take the opportunity to ask students which words they know. One easy way of doing this is simply to list potentially difficult words on the board and have students raise their hands if they do not know a word. This approach is quick, easy, and risk-free for students; it also gives students some responsibility for their word learning. Moreover, research indicates that students can be quite accurate in identifying words that they do and do not know (White, Slater, & Graves, 1989).

Once potentially difficult vocabulary is identified, criteria for identifying the most important words to teach need to be established. The answers to the following four questions can be helpful in winnowing down a list to the words most worth teaching:

- "Is understanding the word important to understanding the selection in which it appears?" If the answer is "No," then other words are probably more important to teach.
- "Are students able to use context or structural analysis skills to discover the word's meaning?" If they can use these skills, then they should be allowed to practice them. Doing so will both help students consolidate these skills and reduce the number of words teachers need to teach.
- "Can working with this word be useful in furthering students' context, structural analysis, or dictionary skills?" If the answer here is "Yes," then your working with the word can serve two purposes. It can aid students in learning the word, and it can help them acquire a strategy they can use in learning other words. One might, for example, decide to teach the word *regenerate* because students needed to master the prefix *re-*.
- "How useful is this word outside of the reading selection being currently taught?" The more frequently a word appears in material students read, the more important it is for them to know the word. Additionally, the more frequently a word appears, the greater the chances that students will retain the word once the teacher has taught it. (Graves, Juel, & Graves, 1998, pp. 10–11)

Differences in Word-Learning Tasks. As I noted at the beginning of this section, the second point I want to make about teaching individual words is that the task of learning individual words is actually a variety of different learning tasks that require quite different teaching procedures (Graves & Prenn, 1986; Graves & Slater, 1996). If teaching individual words is to be as effective as possible, we need to match the teaching procedures we use to the learning tasks different words present to students. In the remainder of this section, I illustrate such matching by discussing two word-learning tasks that represent very different learning.

Teaching words that represent available concepts. Many of the words we teach do not represent new and difficult ideas. They are simply new labels for concepts students already have. In such cases, particularly robust and time-consuming teaching procedures are not needed; fairly thin procedures will do the job well. The thinnest approach likely to be effective might be called the Context Plus Use of the Dictionary Approach (Graves et al., 1998). It consists of simply giving students a word in a rich context, having them look up the word in a dictionary, and briefly discussing the definition they come up with. *Excel,* for example, might be a new label for some middle-grade students. Presenting *excel* in a sentence such as "To get to the Olympics, a person must really *excel* at an Olympic sport," hav-

ing students look up *excel* in the dictionary ("to be superior in some respect"), and then briefly discussing its meaning would constitute appropriate instruction. Note that even this thinnest vocabulary instruction
involves students' working with both context and a definition. We have
good evidence that giving students both a context and a definition is superior to either context alone or a definition alone (Stahl & Fairbanks,
1986).

Teaching words that represent new and challenging concepts. Teaching new
and challenging concepts is a very different matter from teaching new
labels and requires robust and often time-consuming procedures. One of
the most robust procedures for teaching concepts was developed by Doro-
thy Frayer and is sometimes called the Frayer method (Frayer, Frederick, & Klausmeier, 1969). Here are the steps of the Frayer method and an
example of using the method with the word *globe*.

- Define the new concept, giving its necessary attributes and, if practical,
  showing a model or picture illustrating it.
    A *globe* is a spherical (ball-like) representation of a planet.
- Distinguish between the new concept and similar but different concepts
  with which it might be mistaken. In doing so, it may be appropriate to
  identify some accidental attributes that might falsely be considered to be
  necessary attributes of the new concept.
    A *globe* is different from a *map* because a map is flat.
    A *globe* is different from a *contour map*, a map in which mountains and
    other high points are raised above the general level of the map, be-
    cause a contour map is not spherical.
- Give examples of the concept, and explain why they are examples.
    The most common *globe* is a globe of the earth. Globes of the earth are
    spherical [display a sphere or spheres such as a ball or an orange] and
    come in various sizes and colors.
    A much less common *globe* is a globe of another planet. A museum
    might have a spherical representation of Saturn.
- Give nonexamples of the concept and explain why they are nonexamples.
    A map of California.
    A map of how to get to a friend's house.
- Present students with examples and nonexamples, and ask students to distinguish between the two.
    An aerial photograph of New York. (nonexample)
    A red sphere representing Mars. (example)
    A walking map of St. Louis. (nonexample)
    A ball-shaped model of the moon. (example)
- Have students present examples and nonexamples of the concept, have
  them explain why they are examples or nonexamples, and give them feedback on their examples and explanations. (Graves, Juel, & Graves, 1998,
  pp. 12–14)

The Frayer method is admittedly an involved and time-consuming procedure, and there are certainly simpler procedures for teaching new concepts. But there are also considerably more involved ones. Teaching new and challenging concepts requires time and effort, and using a quick and easy teaching procedure is unlikely to accomplish much.

There are, of course, other word-learning tasks and many other ways to teach individual words. But I believe that by describing these two quite different word-learning tasks and a teaching method appropriate for each of them, I have made my main point. When we teach individual words, we need to use methods appropriate to the word-learning tasks we are trying to accomplish.

Teaching Word-Learning Strategies

Unlike teaching individual words, which is a very frequent activity in schools, teaching students strategies for learning words themselves is a very infrequent activity. In fact, I know of no detailed archival description of a well-planned, serious, powerful, and long-term attempt to teach students word-learning strategies. This is very bad news. If, as I argued, students have the task of learning tens of thousands of words and we can only teach them a few hundred words a year, then they have to do a lot of word learning on their own. Moreover, if students are to really profit from the wide reading that is so important to vocabulary growth, they need to be adept at learning words as they are reading.

Three word-learning strategies are particularly worth spending time on—using context to infer word meanings, using word parts to arrive at word meanings, and using the dictionary to learn or verify word meanings. Of these three, using context is almost certainly the most important (Sternberg, 1987), and using context is the strategy I discuss here—both because it is the most important strategy and because teaching students to use the other strategies is much simpler and can be modeled on the procedures used in teaching them to use context.

Although a recent meta-analysis indicates that efforts to teach students to use context to infer word meanings have generally had a positive effect (Fukkink & de Glopper, 1998), research has not indicated the most effective approach for doing so. However, there is a huge and very solid body of data on how to teach *comprehension* strategies. In the remainder of this section of the chapter, I suggest how that approach looks when applied to the matter of teaching students to use context.

Here are what I consider to be the key characteristics of the approach, taken from my own experiences and reading of the literature, as well as from papers by Donald Deshler (1997), Jan Dole, Kathleen Brown, and Woodrow Trathen (1996), Barak Rosenshine (1997), and Michael

Pressley (1997). Following the description of each characteristic, I comment on what it means when applied to teaching context clues and give an example of its application.

- *From the beginning, the teacher recognizes the difficulty of teaching and learning complex strategic behavior and is prepared to help students with the challenging task they face.*

  This means that the instruction is going to require a considerable amount of planning and preparation. Among other things, teachers need to locate or create (1) descriptions of context clues and how to use them, (2) ways of motivating students to learn about context clues, (3) sample contexts which include a variety of sorts of context clues and contexts that span a range from very directly revealing word meanings to only hinting at word meanings, and (4) practice materials and activities that give students opportunities to work with these contexts.

  It also means that the instruction is going to take a considerable amount of time. Two to four days of instruction a week over 3 weeks is a reasonable estimate of the time needed for initial instruction in using context clues. More specifically, it seems likely that four 30-minute sessions the first week, three 30-minute sessions the second week, and two 30-minute sessions the third week would provide students with solid grounding in using context clues.

- *From the beginning, the teacher recognizes that getting students to generalize their use of the strategies taught so that they use them independently with various materials and in various settings is a major challenge.*

  If we want the sort of transfer that leads to independent use of context clues in real reading situations, we need to give students opportunities to use context in reading different sorts of materials, in different settings, and over substantial time periods. This means that the 3 weeks of initial instruction described above is only the beginning. Students need opportunities, prompts, and feedback in using the strategy with narratives as well with expository texts, with geography as well as with science, and at home as well as in school.

- *The approach employs direct explanation.* Students are told what the strategy is, why it is worth learning, how to use it, when and where to use it, and how to evaluate its effectiveness.

  The teacher's initial explanation to students about what using context clues is and why learning to use them makes sense is likely to sound something like this:

  "Today, we're going to begin working with using context clues to figure out the meanings of words we don't know or aren't sure of. Context clues are clues and hints that the words and sentences surrounding an unknown word give us about the meaning of the unknown word.

"Learning to use context clues is important because much of the time when we read we will come upon at least some words we don't know. And learning words we don't know is important because knowing the words in something we're reading helps us understand it. Also, learning more words and using them helps us speak and write clearly."

- *The approach makes extensive use of scaffolding.* Initially the teacher provides support that enables students to do things they couldn't do without that support. Tools or procedures available as scaffolds include modeling the strategy, thinking aloud while using it, beginning with simplified material, using concrete prompts, coaching with verbal prompts, and completing parts of the task for students.

Modeling and Thinking Aloud. The teacher's modeling of the strategy for the sentences:

> "Rusty *scowled* angrily at Mary and then stamped out of the room. 'I'm never coming back!' he shouted as he left."

might go something like this:

> "Hmm. *Scowled* is something Rusty did at Mary. He was angry, and he did this *scowling* just before he stamped out of the room, and then he shouted at Mary. I'm not sure what *scowled* means, but it must have something to do with showing anger. Maybe it means the same thing as *shouted*, or maybe it means *sticking out your tongue*, or maybe it means *giving a mean look*. I'm still not sure what *scowled* means, but I think it's related to anger, that it's a way of showing anger."

Beginning with Simplified Material. As Jere Brophy points out in Chapter 9 of this volume, it is a mistake to expect novices to function immediately like experts. And as John Anderson and colleagues (J. Anderson, Reder, & Simon, 1995) note, both decomposition and decontextualization can be appropriate features of cognitively motivated instruction. Having students begin to work with context clues in simplified texts that are briefer and include more revealing context than many of the actual texts they will encounter is consistent with both of these observations. Working with simplified material allows the teacher to focus students' attention on the relevant parts of the text and to maximize their chances for initial success. Thus, for example, the following two sentences might be used during instruction to provide strong context clues to the meaning of *summoned:* "As soon as dinner was over, Mr. Haskins *summoned* a taxi. And once it arrived, Tim said goodbye quickly and was soon on his way back to his apartment."

Using Concrete Prompts. In most instances, the primary concrete prompt used with context clue strategy instruction will be a chart with a succinct list of the steps in the strategy put up in a prominent place on the classroom wall. A chart for using context clues might show these steps: (1) Recognize that you don't know a word. (2) Look for clues to the word's meaning in the same sentence. (3) If you don't find clues in the same sentence, look for clues in the rest of the paragraph. (4) Guess the meaning of the word. (5) Try the meaning you guessed to see if it fits.

Coaching with Verbal Prompts. As students attempt to use context to glean word meanings, the teacher can frequently support their efforts verbally. If, for example, a student is stumped as he attempts to guess the meaning of *wept* in the context "When Jenny heard her dog had been hit by a car, she *wept* for a long time," the teacher might use a prompt like "As the author explains, Jenny had just heard some really bad news. What's something people often do when they hear really bad news?"

Completing Part of the Task for Students. In initially modeling the strategy, the teacher will complete all of its steps herself. As instruction and practice continue, she will at various times complete some steps and leave others to students. For example, at one time she might (1) identify the unknown word and (2 and 3) think aloud as she looks for clues to the word's meaning, leaving students the tasks of (4) guessing the word's meaning and (5) trying out the meaning they guess in the sentence. At another time she might do nothing but (1) identify the unknown word and leave all the other steps to the students.

- *The procedure follows the gradual release of responsibility model.* Over time, the teacher dismantles the scaffolding she initially used. This means she increasingly allows and requires students to use the strategy on their own. It also means that she increasingly gives students more difficult tasks.

  Initially the teacher does all the work, modeling how she would use context to arrive at word meanings. Later she does some of the work and lets the students do some of it. Later still, the students might work in pairs. Finally, the students work independently.

  Over this same period of time, the teacher gives students increasingly challenging contexts to work with. This means moving from one- or two-sentence passages in which context quite obviously reveals the meanings of the unknown words to much longer passages in which context provides much less obvious and much less rich clues.

- *After initial instruction, the teacher makes extended and special efforts to help students make the strategy their own and use it as part of their normal reading.* This last characteristic is redundant to the first two listed. However, I believe that the difficulty of transfer and the infrequency with which strategy instruction is followed up in ways that promote transfer and give students real proficiency in the strategies taught warrants the redundancy. Students need to be prompted to use the strategy and perhaps have its use modeled—in math, in history, in science, in the morning, in the afternoon, in study hall, and so forth. If we want to maximize or, in fact, make very likely their wide and independent use of the strategy, we have to take some definite steps to do so, and we have to take these steps in many different contexts and over a substantial period of time.

This list of key characteristics of a well-planned, serious, powerful, and long-term attempt to teach students to use context clues to unlock word meanings suggests why such instruction is seldom seen: It is difficult, it is time-consuming, and it requires both fairly extensive materials and a rich repertoire of teaching techniques. If many teachers are going to employ such instruction, they need more readily available materials and more instructional support than are typically available.

Fostering Word Consciousness

Fostering word consciousness is the fourth and final part of the vocabulary program outlined here. As defined by its most prominent advocates—Richard Anderson and Isabel Beck (Anderson & Nagy, 1992; Beck, McKeown, & Omanson, 1987)—word consciousness is a disposition toward words that is both cognitive and affective. Students who are word-conscious know a lot of words and know them well. Equally importantly, they are interested in words, and they gain enjoyment and satisfaction from using them well and from seeing or hearing them used well by others. They find words intriguing, recognize adroit word usage when they encounter it, use words skillfully themselves, are on the lookout for new and precise words, and are responsive to the nuances of word meanings. They are also well aware of the power of words and realize that they can be used to foster clarity and understanding or to obscure and obfuscate matters. Admittedly, such students are quite something—certainly stalwart models of word consciousness. But I describe them as an ideal. Perhaps we do not even want students who are this crazy about words, but we certainly want students who are more interested in words than they are likely to be without our encouragement.

Compared to a difficult task like teaching word-learning strategies, fostering word consciousness is something that can be done quite easily. In fact, a huge step toward fostering word consciousness comes from simply recognizing that we want to make students consciously aware of words and their importance. There are a myriad of ways of doing this. Let me suggest just a few of them, taken from some of the work that my colleague Susan Watts and I have recently done (Graves & Watts, in press; Watts & Graves, 1996).

Modeling Adept Diction in Our Own Speech and Writing. One good starting point in encouraging and nurturing word consciousness lies in teachers' attitudes toward words and the attitude they project to students. We want children to feel that adept diction—the skillful use of words in speech and writing—is something worth striving for. We want them to see that we care about words and how we use them. Thus it makes sense for teachers to deliberately use and perhaps explain words that at least some of their students might not yet know.

In describing how he was startled by a low-flying jet on the way to school, for example, a teacher might tell his fourth-graders that the jet made a *thunderous* noise and point out that *thunderous* is sometimes an excellent word for describing a really loud noise because it reminds us of the great booming sound of thunder. Or, in talking about a movie she had just watched with her sixth-grade class, a teacher might comment that the *cinematography* was outstanding and then pause to discuss with students what *cinematography* is. At other times, a teacher might simply use a word that he thinks students might find useful but that some of them probably don't know. For example, in writing the directions for an essay assignment on the board for eighth-graders, a teacher might write that students' essays should *delineate* as fully as possible the factors leading up to the Boston Tea Party, knowing that some students are almost sure to ask about the meaning of *delineate*.

Recognizing Adept Diction in Texts Students Are Reading. Good authors, of course, employ appropriate and often colorful words in their writing, and it makes good sense occasionally to point out particularly felicitous or interesting word choices. For example, if a class of fifth-graders were reading the chapter on D-Day in Joy Hakim's award-winning history text *War, Peace, and All That Jazz* (1995), a teacher might point out that Hakim chose to use the word *armada* in the sentence "The largest armada ever assembled appeared off the French coast," ask why *armada* might be a more powerful word than *fleet,* and then explain that *armada* refers specifically to a fleet of warships rather than to any sort of fleet if none of the students supplied an answer.

Or, if a group of seventh-grade students were reading and discussing Russell Freedman's *Eleanor Roosevelt: A Life of Discovery* (1993), a teacher might give special attention to these lines: "Franklin remembered Eleanor as a skinny girl in a *hopeless* party dress. Now she was wearing a stylish outfit from Paris." How, the teacher might ask, could a party dress be *hopeless?* Why has Freedman chosen this particular word to describe Eleanor's dress? Of course, with only this fragment of context, one is forced to do a lot of inferring, but it seems likely that Eleanor herself, and not just the dress, seemed rather hopeless to Franklin at the time.

Recognizing and Encouraging Adept Diction in Children's Speech and Writing. Another opportunity for recognizing and promoting adroit word usage comes from children's own speech and writing. Thus a teacher might compliment a fourth-grader for describing banana slugs as *gigantic,* give a little recognition to a sixth-grader who noted that the odds of winning the lottery are *astronomically small,* and recognize the verbal skill, if not the tact, of the tenth-grader who writes that the new principal seems to be a real *curmudgeon.* During writing conferences, a teacher might encourage students to rethink word choices in an effort to make their writing more colorful, precise, and on-target for a particular audience. I find in my own writing that word choice is a very important consideration when I get to the point where I am really trying to polish something. In one of my revisions of this chapter, for example, I found that I had used the word *concrete* in three consecutive sentences, and I searched a thesaurus and came up with the alternative of *tangible,* which actually turned out to be a somewhat better word for my purposes and which I used in two out of the three sentences. Unfortunately, I seldom see word choice given much attention in school writing programs.

Promoting Word Play Such as the Use of Clichés and Puns. Clichés, are, as the dictionary points out, dull, trite, and outworn. In many instances they are also—as Peggy Rosenthal and George Dardess note in *Every Cliché in the Book* (1987)—"dead on their feet," "good for nothing but the garbage bin," and "not worth the paper they're printed on." Yet the very fact that they are familiar and have "stood the test of time" means that originally they constituted a unique and interesting way of saying something. Moreover, as I may repeat "until the cows come home," they can be a lot of fun and they give students many opportunities to play with and appreciate words.

One activity that children are likely to enjoy might be called "Cliché Characterizations." A lot of clichés refer to character traits, making it possible to describe characters or character types solely with clichés. Thus, for example, we might ask students to contrast two characters, one of whom is friendly and outgoing and the other of whom is quiet and careful, entirely with clichés, starting them off with a few such as a "real dynamo" and a "ball of fire" for the outgoing character and "down to earth" and "a straight arrow" for the careful one.

Like clichés, puns constitute a particular sort of word play that often meets with derision. As Richard Lederer (1988) points out, although many adults make a point of grimacing and letting out a big sigh when they hear a pun, puns are often used by talented writers and speakers. Shakespeare, for example, used them extensively. In *Romeo and Juliet*, for example, Mercutio can't resist a pun, even though he is dying. "Look for me tomorrow," he says, "and you will find me a grave man." And during the signing of the Declaration of Independence, it was no less a wit than Benjamin Franklin who quipped, "We must all hang together or, most assuredly, we shall hang separately." Also—as Robert Greenman notes in *Words in Action* (1983)—first-rate newspapers use puns with some regularity, as exemplified in one *New York Times* article noting that "Bird watchers from as far away as Denver have flocked to the Merrit Island Wildlife Refuge" and another *Times* article reporting that "Balloons have become a high-flying business and sell at inflated prices."

Children love puns, begin playing with puns as early as the first or second grade—"What's black and white and re(a)d all over?"—and continue to be interested in them throughout their school years and beyond. Here is one of many pun games middle-grade students are likely to enjoy. It is taken from Lederer's *Get Thee to a Punnery* (1988), which contains a plethora of thought-provoking activities for punsters and would be punsters.

Lederer calls the game "The Sign of the Times." A teacher might begin by talking with students about the fact that signs abound in today's world—in business windows, on cars and trucks, and on front lawns—and that many of these make use of puns. Then he could give a few examples, such as these:

- On a diaper service truck: *Rock a dry baby.*
- On a peanut stand: *If our peanuts were any fresher, they'd be insulting.*
- In a butcher shop window: *Never a bum steer.*

Next, students could try their hand at creating similar signs; or, if creating them from scratch proved too challenging, they could complete partial signs such as these:

- At a planetarium: *Cast of thousands. Every one a* _____ .
- In a billiard parlor window: *Try our indoor* _____ .
- In a garden shop: *Lighten up your garden, plant* _____ .

Again, the goal of activities like this one is simply to get students interested in words and involved with words.

Promoting Word-Play Books. Word-play books abound—a typical branch library or a large bookstore might have a dozen of them—and they deserve a place in classroom and school libraries. Richard Lederer's *Pun and Games* (1996) is one of the newer and I think better ones, and it is a good one to mention in closing this discussion on word consciousness, both because it is specifically written for middle-grade students and because it lets me end on a light note that I think is quite appropriate when considering word consciousness. As noted on the jacket, *Pun and Games* contains a wealth of "jokes, riddles, one-liners, and games to enhance language skills and tickle the funny bones of kids ten and up." Here is one of my favorites, taken from the wonderful Victor Borge routine on inflationary language. Borge created this routine based on the argument that everything else goes up in price, so language should go up too. In English there are words that contain the sounds of numbers, such as wonder (one), before (four), and decorate (eight). If we "inflate" each number by one, we come up with *twoder, befive,* and *decornine*—as well as with the following rendition of "Jack and the Wonderful Beans."

"Jack and the Twoderful Beans"

Twice upon a time there lived a boy named Jack in the twoderful land of Califivenia. Two day Jack, a double-minded lad, decided three go fifth three seek his fivetune.

After making sure that Jack nine a sandwich and drank some 8-Up, his mother elevenderly said, "Threedeloo, threedeloo. Try three be back by next Threesday.

Jack went fifth and soon met a man wearing a four-piece suit and a threepee. Fifthrightly Jack asked the man, "I'm a Califivinian. Are you two three?"

"Cerelevenly," replied the man," offiving the high six. Anytwo five elevennis? (Lederer, 1996, p.40)

The playful attitude toward words in particular and language in general that Richard Lederer and Victor Borge demonstrate is not the only attitude we want to cultivate in guiding students toward word consciousness. But it is certainly one reasonable attitude we would like to cultivate. If we can get students interested in playing with words and language, then we are at least half way to the goal of creating the sort of word-conscious student who will make words a lifetime interest.

CONCLUDING REMARKS

In the beginning of this chapter, I noted that a vocabulary program ought not to constitute a huge part of the curriculum. In concluding, I want to make it clear that the vocabulary program I have described does not consume an inordinate amount of time. Here are estimates of how much time the four components of the vocabulary program might consume.

An hour of sustained silent reading a week, of course, takes an hour. But because the benefits of silent reading are not limited to vocabulary growth, not all of the time spent reading silently should be counted as time devoted to vocabulary. It seems reasonable, in fact, to consider only a fourth of the total time devoted to silent reading—15 minutes—as time spent on vocabulary.

Teaching individual words is something that is done only as the need arises. That typically means when the entire class or a group of students are reading materials with particularly challenging, important, or intriguing vocabulary. Approximately 20 minutes a week should be enough time to spend teaching individual words.

Teaching word-learning strategies will take a lot of time during initial instruction—perhaps 2 to 4 hours a week. But this is only during initial instruction, which is likely to be about 3 weeks out of a year. Averaged over the whole of a year, that amounts to only about 20 minutes a week.

Finally, fostering word consciousness is almost free, with much of your effort there coming in little asides, as when you compliment a student for a particularly adept word used in an essay. An average of 10 minutes a week should be sufficient to nurture students toward really caring about words.

Together, the time spent on these four activities adds up to an hour and 5 minutes a week. My very best judgment is that this hour and 5 minutes will be time well spent, time that will both help students develop substantial vocabularies and complement the comprehension work and other literacy experiences they engage in.

REFERENCES

Allington, R., Guice, S., Michelson, N., Baker, K., & Li, S. (1996). Literature-based curricula in high-poverty schools. In M. F. Graves, P. van den Broek, & B. M. Taylor (Eds.), *The first R: A right of all children* (pp. 73–96). New York: Teachers College Press.

Anderson, J. R., Reder, L. M., & Simon, H. (1995). *Applications and misapplications of cognitive psychology to mathematics education.* Unpublished manuscript. Department of Psychology, Carnegie Mellon University, Pittsburgh.

Anderson, R. C. (1996). Research foundations to support wide reading. In V. Greaney (Ed.), *Promoting reading in developing countries* (pp. 55–77). New York: International Reading Association.

Anderson, R. C., & Nagy, W. E. (1992, winter). The vocabulary conundrum. *American Educator,* pp. 14–18, 44–47.

Anderson, R. C., Wilson, P. T, & Fielding, L. G. (1988). Growth in reading and how children spend their time outside of school. *Reading Research Quarterly, 23,* 285–303.

Anglin, J. M. (1993). Vocabulary development: A morphological analysis. *Monographs of the Society for Research in Child Development, 58* (10, Serial No. 238).

Beck, I. L., & McKeown, M. G. (1990). Conditions of vocabulary acquisition. In R. Barr, M. L. Kamil, P. Mosenthal, & P. D. Pearson (Eds.), *The handbook of reading research* (Vol. 2; pp. 789–814). New York: Longman.

Beck, I. L, McKeown, M. G., & Omanson, R. C. (1987). The effects and uses of diverse vocabulary instructional techniques. In M. G. McKeown & M. E. Curtis (Eds.), *The nature of vocabulary acquisition* (pp. 147–163). Hillsdale, NJ: Erlbaum.

Blachowicz, C., & Fisher, P. (in press). Vocabulary instruction. In R. Barr, M. L. Kamil, P. Mosenthal, & P. D. Pearson (Eds.), *The handbook of reading research (Vol. 3).* New York: Longman.

Cassidy, J., & Wenrich, J. K. (1997, February/March). What's hot, what's not for 1997. *Reading Today,* p. 34.

Cassidy, J., & Wenrich, J. K. (1998, February/March). What's hot, what's not for 1998. *Reading Today,* pp. 1, 28.

Deshler, D. D. (1997, April). Teaching students with learning disabilities to be strategic learners. Paper presented at the annual meeting of the American Educational Research Association, Chicago.

Dole, J. A., Brown, K. J., & Trathen, W. (1996). The effects of strategy instruction on the comprehension performance of at-risk students. *Reading Research Quarterly, 31,* 62–88.

Fielding, L. G., Wilson, P. D., & Anderson, R. C. (1986). A new focus on free reading: The role of trade books in reading instruction. In T. E. Raphael (Ed.), *The contexts of school-based literacy* (pp. 149–160). New York: Random House.

Frayer, D. A., Frederick, W. D., & Klausmeier, H. J. (1969). *A schema for testing the level of concept mastery* (Working Paper No. 16). Madison: Wisconsin Research and Development Center for Cognitive Learning.

Freedman, R. (1993). *Eleanor Roosevelt: A life of discovery.* New York: Scholastic.

Fukkink, R. G., & de Glopper, K. (1998). Effects of instruction in deriving word meaning from context: A meta-analysis. *Review of Educational Research, 68,* 450–469.

Graves, M. F. (1986). Vocabulary learning and instruction. In E. Z. Rothkopf (Ed.), *Review of Research in Education* (Vol. 13, pp. 49–90). Washington, DC: American Educational Research Association.

Graves, M. F., Juel, C., & Graves, B. B. (1998). *Teaching reading in the 21st century.* Boston: Allyn & Bacon.

Graves, M. F., & Prenn, M. C. (1986). Costs and benefits of different methods of vocabulary instruction. *Journal of Reading, 29,* 596–602.

Graves, M. F., & Slater, W. H. (1996). Vocabulary instruction in content areas. In D. Lapp, J. Flood, & N. Farnan (Eds.), *Content area reading and learning: Instructional strategies* (2nd ed.; pp. 261–275). Needham Heights, MA: Allyn & Bacon.

Graves, M. F. and Watts, S. M. (in press). The place of word consciousness in a research-based vocabulary program. In S. J. Samuels & A. E. Farstrup (Eds.), *What research has to say about reading instruction* (3rd ed.). Newark, DE: International Reading Association.

Greaney, V. (Ed.). (1996). *Promoting reading in developing countries.* New York: International Reading Association.

Greenman, R. (1983). *Words in action.* New York: New York Times Books.

Gruthrie J.T, & Wigfield, A. W. (Eds.). (1997). *Reading engagement.* Newark, DE: International Reading Association.

Hakim, J. (1995). *War, peace, and all that jazz.* New York: Oxford University Press.

International Reading Association. (1996). *More Teens' Favorite Books.* Newark, DE: Author.

International Reading Association. (1997). *More teachers' favorite books for kids.* Newark, DE: Author.

Lederer, R. (1988). *Get thee to a punnery.* Charleston, SC: Wyrick & Company.

Lederer, R. (1996). *Pun and games.* Chicago: Chicago Review Press.

McCracken, R. A. (1971). Initiating sustained silent reading. *Journal of Reading, 14,* 521–524, 582–583.

Nagy, W. E. (1988). *Teaching vocabulary to improve reading comprehension.* Newark, DE: International Reading Association.

Nagy, W. E., & Anderson, R. C. (1984). How many words are there in printed school English? *Reading Research Quarterly, 19,* 304–330.

Nagy, W. E. & Scott, J. A. (in press). Vocabulary processes. In M. Kamil, P. Mosenthal, P. D. Pearson, & R. Barr (Eds.), *Handbook of reading research* (Vol. 3). New York: Longman.

Petty, W. T., Herold, C. P., & Stoll, E. (1967). *The state of knowledge about the teaching of vocabulary.* Champaign, IL: National Council of Teachers of English.

Pressley, M. (1997, April). *Why do transactional strategies instruction? The state of comprehension instruction research and practice in the late 1990s.* Paper presented at the annual meeting of the American Educational Research Association, Chicago.

Rosenshine, B. (1997, April). *The case for explicit, teacher-led, cognitive strategy instruction.* Paper presented at the annual meeting of the American Educational Research Association, Chicago.

Rosenthal, P., & Dardess, G. (1987). *Every cliché in the book.* New York: Morrow.

Ryder, R. J., & Graves, M. F. (1994). Vocabulary instruction presented prior to reading in two basal readers. *Elementary School Journal, 95,* 139–153.

Stahl, S. A., & Fairbanks, M. M. (1986). The effects of vocabulary instruction: A model-based meta-analysis. *Review of Educational Research, 56,* 72–110.

Sternberg, R. J. (1987). Most vocabulary is learned from context. In M. G. McKeown & M. E. Curtis (Eds.), *The nature of vocabulary acquisition* (pp. 89–105). Hillsdale, NJ: Erlbaum.

Trelease, J. (1995). *The read aloud handbook* (4th ed.). New York: Penguin.

Watts, S. M. (1995). Vocabulary lessons during reading lessons in six classrooms. *Journal of Reading Behavior, 27,* 1–26.

Watts, S. M., & Graves, M. F. (1996). Expanding your vocabulary program to foster word consciousness. *WSRA Journal, 40*(2), 19–24.

White, T. G., Graves, M. F., & Slater, W. H. (1990). Growth of reading vocabulary in diverse elementary schools: Decoding and word meaning. *Journal of Educational Psychology, 82* (2), 281–290.

White, T. G., Slater, W. H., & Graves, M. F. (1989). Yes/No method of vocabulary assessment: Valid for whom and useful for what? In S. McCormick & J. Zutell (Eds.), *Cognitive and social perspectives for literacy research and instruction* (pp. 391–397). Chicago: National Reading Conference.

7

Classroom Talk About Texts: Is It Dear, Cheap, or a Bargain at Any Price?

DONNA E. ALVERMANN

A brief story that explains the origin of this chapter title is in order. The setting was a large conference room in one of New York City's major hotels, where the American Educational Research Association was holding its annual meeting. My colleagues and I, who had worked on a year-long multisite case study involving middle-school students' perceptions of how they experience text-based discussions (Alvermann et al., 1996), sat with pen and paper ready to take notes as our discussant for the session, Madeleine Grumet, walked to the podium. We had asked her to comment on our work because we believed she could help us think critically about phenomena that had taken on a "that's-just-the-way-things-are" sort of meaning in our studies of classroom discussion aimed at helping students comprehend what they read. She did not disappoint us. After the customary opening in which Madeleine summarized our project and alluded to the benefits of such research, she posed this question: "What does talk have to do with learning, or more specifically, is classroom talk dear or cheap?" (Grumet, 1996). Looking back, I am almost certain she asked other pertinent questions that day, but I do not remember them. What mattered most to me then, and now, is exploring the implications of her question for classroom instruction. Although far from exhaustive, this exploration, as the title suggests, presently considers the possibility that beyond being dear or cheap, classroom talk might just be a bargain at any price.

The chapter is divided into three parts. In the first part, I provide examples from research that point to students' positive perceptions of discussion as a means of fostering comprehension and interest in subject-matter reading in the middle grades. Second, I focus on how voices get

Reading for Meaning: Fostering Comprehension in the Middle Grades © 2000 by Teachers College, Columbia University. All rights reserved. ISBN 0-8077-3896-4 (paper), ISBN 0-8077-3897-2 (cloth). Prior to photocopying items for classroom use, please contact the Copyright Clearance Center, Customer Service, 222 Rosewood Drive, Danvers, MA 01923, USA, telephone (508)750-8400.

silenced in peer-led discussions by analyzing students' talk from a post-structural perspective. Finally, I argue that as teachers we help students comprehend better and more completely when we instruct in ways that challenge them, as readers, to view texts as offering them positions they can either take up or resist. Throughout, I attempt to address Grumet's (1996) troubling question about the dearness or cheapness of classroom discussion, always with an eye toward kindling further interest in troubling the status quo in literacy instruction.

STUDENTS' PERCEPTIONS OF DISCUSSION AS HELPFUL TO COMPREHENDING TEXT

Students in the middle grades view discussion as helping them comprehend what they read (Alvermann et al., 1996; Wells, 1996). This finding also seems to hold for English-as-second-language (ESL) and bilingual learners, as well as students typically served through inclusion and/or special pull-out programs (Floriani, 1994; Goatley, Brock, & Raphael, 1995). The connection between classroom talk and learning, an area of study typically traced to the work of Barnes and colleagues (Barnes, Britton, & Rosen, 1971; Barnes & Todd, 1977), has been the object of intense inquiry lately among literacy researchers. Writing about peer-group interactions and literature discussion groups at various grade levels, these researchers (e.g., Almasi, McKeown, & Beck, 1996; McMahon & Raphael, 1997; O'Flahavan, 1989; Santa Barbara Classroom Discourse Group, 1992) have repeatedly linked students' improved understanding of what is read to classroom talk about texts.

Scholarly interest in classroom discussion has also led a few philosophers of education (e.g., Bridges, 1979; Dillon, 1994) to devote entire books to the subject, while several psychologists (e.g., Inagaki, 1981; Perret-Clermont, 1980) have written articles about the relation of youngsters' social interaction patterns to their cognitive development. One of several significant findings from this body of research is that classroom discussion has the potential to induce cognitive conflict in students, which in turn may lead to cognitive restructuring and growth in understanding. This finding has implications for middle-grade instruction, particularly in classrooms where teachers expect students to read and discuss material found in assigned content-area texts. One might expect, therefore, to find teachers in the middle grades using a fair amount of discussion as a follow-up to assigned readings. In reality, this does not seem to be the case. According to Grant (1996) and others (Finders, 1997; Goodlad, 1984; Young, 1998), student-centered discussion is anything but common practice in most content-area classrooms at the middle-grade level. Commenting on this fact, Grant (1996) observed:

> It is curious (indeed) that educators seem more likely to encourage conversation among preschoolers and university students and more likely to suppress it in the years in between—precisely during those years in which people like nothing better than to spend their time talking to one another. (p. 475)

Liking and Needing to Talk

From the perspective of some middle-grade students themselves, how accurate is this perception that they like nothing better than to talk to one another? In a study conducted by Wells (1996), students in a graduating eighth-grade class maintained that they had learned best when they were allowed to talk about things. They also claimed that dialogues *among* students, rather than just *between* teachers and students, had kept their attention and made classes which were not that interesting seem more fun. In another study involving eighth-graders (Alvermann et al., 1996), students' fondness for talking can be inferred by what they had to say about its limited sanctioning in their workaday world. They spoke, for example, of being talk-deprived. In a focus group interview involving Brad, an affable and above-average learner, we heard this exchange:

Brad: Talking is one of the things that we are pretty deprived of at school.
John (correcting Brad): We *do* talk, but you aren't allowed to . . .
Desuna (finishing for John): Without getting into trouble. (Alvermann, et. al,
     p. 253)

For these three students and others like them, classroom talk was dear. They valued having opportunities to argue with their peers over some point in a common text they were reading in their English language arts class. Argument was an acknowledged fact of life in their eyes, and they spoke freely of how it helped them to comprehend their assigned readings. They were ardent defenders of their right to interrupt and talk over one another, believing as they did that this practice opened up new avenues of thinking for them. As one student put it,

> There are a lot of things in our minds that we aren't thinking of, and [other people's] words can trigger them, and . . . when you have the whole classroom talking and someone says something it can trigger [other ideas] and it keeps on going. (Alvermann, et al., p. 257)

Thus what might have seemed like worthless chatter, or even cheap talk, to an uninformed observer passing by Room 201 was in these students' minds an essential element for comprehending and building on one another's ideas. For sure, this kind of free-flowing, "open-forum discussion" (Alvermann, O'Brien, & Dillon, 1990, p. 301) is not for every classroom; nor is it for every lesson in even the most discussion-oriented classrooms. It can be, however, when used judiciously, a means of engaging nearly all learners—even the most reluctant ones—in talking about texts. Reading for meaning, students in the middle grades have told us, is made easier when teachers provide opportunities for talking about assigned work.

Research for Students' Perceptions of Needing to Talk

A growing body of education research on the nature of engaged reading supports students' perceptions of the dearness of classroom talk and its benefits to them as learners (Almasi et al., 1996; Baumann & Duffy, 1997; Guthrie & Alvermann, 1999). Other researchers working in fields related to literacy education—for example, in the area of cognitive engagement—have also reported findings that seem to support students' perceptions that talk is valuable when it comes to comprehending their assigned texts. For instance, the results of Pintrich and DeGroot's (1990) study of seventh-graders' motivated and self-regulated learning suggest that students who believe their schoolwork is interesting and who value opportunities to respond to (and even challenge) other students' thinking are more readily engaged in academic tasks.

Important as they are to student engagement in general, cognitive and motivational factors alone cannot fully account for students' willingness to engage in academic tasks that require reading for meaning. As Almasi and colleagues' (1996) study of elementary-age students has clearly shown, the culture of the classroom plays a significant role in engaged reading and follow-up discussion groups. Similar findings apply to students in the middle grades as well. For example, in our work (Alvermann et al., 1996) with two distinctly different eighth-grade language arts classes (one in an urban center and the other in a more rural area of the state), students demonstrated through their interviews and everyday actions that they were well aware of the conditions they believed to be conducive to discussions that had an impact of their comprehension. One such condition was *working in small groups.* Students believed that small-group discussions, unlike whole-class discussions, provided them with more opportunities to talk and be heard. Following are examples of what students told us in a focus group interview about their preferences for small-group discussions:

John: I kind of like those [small groups] because you don't have to fight over, you don't have to wait and wait and wait before you have a chance to talk. You only have like five people in the group and everybody is close enough to hear you, so you just kind of say your thing when you feel like it.

Alice: The small group is kind of nicer [sic] because it is more personal and people kind of listen to you more and get interested in it.

Christy: It seems like it takes forever for [the teacher] to call on me, and by that time we have gone on to another subject, by the time I get to say anything [in whole-class discussions].

Melanie: It [whole-group] gets me nervous to talk in front of a whole lot of people about, like, opinions and stuff. But then, small group, it's like me and my friends, so it is easier. (Alvermann, et al., p. 254)

Classroom cultures that support students' perceptions of needing to talk have a second characteristic in common. They afford students *the right to have a say in how discussion groups are formed and the rules for participating in them.* According to the eighth-graders we interviewed, student input on forming and sustaining small-group discussion is critical to the success of the group. Equally important, they say, is for students to have read their assignments in advance of the group meeting so that they will be prepared to do their fair share of the talking and to stay on-task rather than deliberately causing the group to stray from the topic at hand. Although characterizing effective small-group discussions in this way is hardly news, it is noteworthy that in the classrooms where students had a hand in setting discussion practices, peer-group pressure was an important factor in how the groups used talk to mediate their comprehension of assigned materials. Overall, students in the middle grades whom we interviewed were adamant in their belief that "they had a better understanding of what they read when they listened to their peers discuss a selection" (Alvermann, et al., p. 260). From their considerable and informed perspective, then, it seems reasonable to entertain the notion that discussion is a bargain at any price.

PEER-LED DISCUSSION AND MEANING PRODUCTION

Currently, there is much talk of a crisis of authority and meaning that some theorists associate with the postmodern condition and others with poststructuralist theory. Poststructuralist perspectives on meaning production push us to think in different ways about what we in the reading community generally refer to as comprehension or reading for meaning. In this section and the next, I intend to elaborate a bit on poststructuralist theory—first in relation to peer-led discussions, and then in relation to the assumptions we hold when teaching students that comprehending texts is about "personal" response.

In introducing poststructural theory to my content literacy classes at the University of Georgia, I remind students that it is not my intention to impose on them a new or better way of "doing reading instruction"; nor is it a thinly disguised attempt to colonize a little piece of the reading world for myself and my ideas. I tell them that I fashion myself, in Edward Said's (1994) words, "[not] like Robinson Crusoe whose goal [was] to colonize his little island, but more like Marco Polo . . . who [was] always a traveler, a provisional guest, not a freeloader, conqueror, or raider" (pp. 59–60). As venturer, not colonizer, then, my goal is to explore some of the assumptions underlying peer-led discussion—one of our most valued but perhaps least understood approaches to decentralizing the authority structures in classroom talk about texts.

Peer-Led Discussion

We know from the literature on student-led discussion groups in grades K-12 (e.g., Almasi, 1995; Alvermann et al., 1996; Goatley et al., 1995; McMahon & Raphael, 1997) that peers, acting as "more knowledgeable others" in the Vygotskian (1978) sense of the term, can facilitate meaningful interpretation of texts. However, what is less well understood is that the manner in which these more knowledgeable others do their facilitating work can sometimes silence their less confident peers.

For example, in a study reported elsewhere (Alvermann, 1995/1996), an eighth-grader known as Laura (a pseudonym) confided in several individual and group interviews over the course of a year that she was less and less interested in being part of peer-led discussions. Despite her reputation for being outspoken (or perhaps partially as a result of it), Laura increasingly silenced herself. At one point she claimed that she preferred teacher-led discussions to peer-led ones because, in her words, she could "just sit back, watch, and not be a part." As I observed Laura in weekly visits to her gifted language arts class, her self-imposed silences reminded me in many ways of the work that Rogers (1993) and others (e.g., Finders, 1997; Gilligan, Lyons, & Hanmer, 1990) have done on girls' loss of voice, resiliency, and self-esteem as they approach adolescence. In the following excerpt from an audiotape transcription of a group interview with Laura and four of her peers after they had watched an earlier videotaped discussion, Laura commented on how she was positioned in the group:

Interviewer: What about you, Laura? I think we have heard from everybody but you.
Laura: Hmmm . . .
Peers: (in undertone and in unison) She likes talking.
Laura: Um, I think I used to like talking. I don't like it as much anymore because it is like I have gotten to the point that I get tired of people telling me how I talk or when I am wrong and stuff like that. . . . So I just don't like to talk as much anymore.
Interviewer: You are worried about what other people say?
Laura: No, it's just like people don't let me talk as much anymore, you know. Because I could usually like, talk—like I can talk to my mom a lot. Because we, we pretty much agree on stuff, and—like in class and stuff, people don't always agree and they don't, I mean—
Jonathan: (interrupting) There is more criticism.
Laura: Right. There is more criticism and—
Jonathan: (interrupting) Your mom is not going to disagree.
Laura: Your mom is not going to say, "Golly! How could you say something like that," you know. I think your peers are lots more critical. I mean it's always like that.
Brad: They don't know you as well either. I mean you have known your mom for a long time. (An undertone of laughter is heard in the group.)
Laura: This is true. I mean I have known—
Brad: (interrupting) Your mom understands you better.
Sandra: And your mom wouldn't put you down, either.
Laura: Really! She wouldn't say, "you're stupid."
  (Alvermann, 1995/1996, pp. 283–284)

Meaning Production

Laura is discovering that what is ordinary and acceptable talk in conversations with her mother is open to criticism among her peers. Her sense of being positioned as outrageous ("Golly! How could you say something like that") and being put down by her peers ("Really! She wouldn't say 'you're stupid'") is part and parcel of the storyline, or discourse, that others in her peer group (and, most pointedly, Laura herself) are learning to take up. From a poststructural perspective, it could be said that Laura is going "through a process of *subjectification* . . . [in which] each person actively takes up the discourses through which they and others speak/write the world into existence *as if they were their own"* (Davies, 1993, p. 13; emphasis in original). The difference between this perspective and socialization theory is that the latter would have us focus on the process used by others (in this case, Laura's peers) to shape her behavior. In contrast, poststructuralist theory focuses attention on how Laura willingly takes up the storyline that she and others are inscribing. Another way of saying this is that Laura is reading and writing herself into existence through the discourses (or storylines) that are available to her. This point will be developed further in the next section, where I attempt to show that readers comprehend (i.e., produce meanings from texts) not so much through their personal experiences and backgrounds as through their taking up of the discourses available to them (Patterson, Mellor, & O'Neill, 1994). For now, however, a point worth remembering from the Laura excerpt is that in poststructuralist terms, students, speakers, readers, and so on can be thought of as discursively located "subjects." Recognized as such, the Lauras in the world are better positioned to imagine other possible storylines for themselves.

At a later date during an individual interview with Brad, one of the boys in the group from which the excerpt was taken, I learned that he attributed Laura's increasing dislike of peer-led discussions of their assigned readings to her argumentative nature. Commenting on this point, Brad said:

> Laura is really outgoing and she is a nice girl, but she argues a lot. Her way always has to be right. I mean, nobody else can even dare oppose her or anything. I mean she always has her idea, and if it is not her idea, then she just goes into this desperate pout—I mean she whines. . . . And so it just, I don't know. I think she likes a fight. I mean she wants to be the first woman president. I don't have any problem with that. I mean that's just the way she is. She just, I mean I guess she is pretty liberal I would say, and she argues about a lot of stuff. (Alvermann, 1995/1996, p. 287)

Interestingly, Brad went on to contrast Laura's style of arguing with that of Alice, the fifth member of the group:

> Alice, I don't know, she argues in a cheerful way. And she, I have actually seen her do this, she goes, "Okay, well, you are getting too mad so I will stop this." But she can get pretty annoying sometimes. I guess everybody can. I don't know, it's just sometimes, sometimes she does it because she is pretty liberal, too. . . . I think Laura is more liberal [because] she thinks women should play football. And Alice is more of a liberal in the nature side, like rain forests and whales and stuff like that. (Alvermann, 1995/1996, p. 287)

Although Brad's gendered comments are telling in their own right, here, I am more interested in his perception of the dearness of classroom talk. In his words:

> I love to talk and discuss things. When something comes up, and we get a chance to talk about it, I always do. I love to participate. This is because I feel you get a lot more out of learning when you get into the topic rather than mope around in the corner. (Alvermann, 1995/1996, p. 285)

Compared to Laura, for whom discussion is becoming anything but a bargain, Brad sees it as an opportunity to learn more, to engage with the various issues that arise from the readings his teacher assigns in the class anthology. Producing meaning through talk allows Brad to be active—a condition for learning that he views as superior to sitting back and moping.

POSTSTRUCTURAL READINGS AND CLASSROOM TALK

Teachers who involve students in thinking and talking about texts in ways that challenge authoritative or dominant readings provide access to understanding how different sets of meanings are produced. These different sets of meaning are what some call alternative or oppositional readings. Creating spaces for such readings is made easier if students come to see texts[1] as offering them positions that they can either take up or resist.

Reading Positions and Texts

As a point of departure into thinking about poststructural readings and classroom talk, it is helpful to consider a situation that arose in Bob Fecho's[2] class and is reported here in his words:

> It was my eighth period English class that led me to reconsider the way in which language was taught and learned in my classroom. We were reading "Beautiful Black Men," a poem by Nikki Giovanni. Although its lines contain such dated terms as "outasite Afros" and "driving their hogs," the poem is a celebration of African American identity in straight forward street language and dialect. It was, I thought, safe—meaning that it seemed to have no political edge relative to other poems by the author and her contemporaries—and would stir no controversy in my class. While I often pick provocative texts, the purpose for studying this poem was to examine the vivid and colloquial use of language by Giovanni.

Yet, as my students finished the read-aloud, I could see that they were unsettled. There was a terseness about their responses to my questions that was quite unlike the usual affability of this group. Through the year they had challenged me, kidded me, and questioned me, but had rarely shut me out. However, this poem that I thought would set them talking about life "back in the day" and the positive African American images inherent within the verses, instead had made them tight-lipped and seemingly disgruntled. Moreover, when I mentioned their disquietude, their response was that it was really nothing and I shouldn't worry.

I could have let it drop, ignored the awkwardness as I have done in the past, and gone on to the next poem. But I didn't—couldn't—and I pressed the issue. Finally, Latonya, who was always upfront about her opinions, blurted, "She making fun of the way Black people talk."

There it was. I thought the poem to be a celebration. I believe Nikki Giovanni intended it as such. But my students saw it as a put down, a parody. My "safe" poem had heated up in ways that were both political and personal. And life in my classroom would never be the same. (Fecho, 1998, p. 75)

Although Bob proceeded to describe a year-long class project that involved his students as inquirers into the political nature of language, with the goal being an increased understanding of the role language played in their lives, what is important here is this situation's illustrative account of how, unlike Laura in the earlier example, the students in Fecho's classroom resisted reading themselves into existence through the storyline that was available to them. Even after learning that Giovanni (whom they had at first assumed to be White) was of their race, they refused to take up a storyline that positioned them in ways that contradicted their own beliefs and values.

A Poststructuralist Reading

From a poststructuralist perspective, the students' response to Giovanni's poem can be explained in terms of competing discourses. As Beach (1997) has noted, "this [perspective] differs from much of reader response pedagogy in which students are taught to respond by applying their own subjective experience to the text" (p. 1) without considering how authors are positioned by the discourses they draw on. Before offering a poststructuralist reading of the incident that occurred in Fecho's classroom, it is instructive, I believe, to look at Ivanic's (1994) work on the discoursal construction of writers' identities.

Ivanic's example of how a college student's writing simultaneously identified her with contrasting discourses is helpful in understanding how writers in general are positioned by the various discourses available to them. In the following excerpt from the student's essay in which she assessed the way that Blacks have redefined themselves through literature and the mass media, there are vestiges of at least three discourses:

> Despite such imagery, Black women have resisted these externally defined images of their social realities, that portray them as worthless, insignificant and inferior. Black women challenged these external definitions of their lives, by having sought to construct their own, thereby telling their own "herstories" and asserting their social realities like it is. (Ivanic, 1994, p. 7)

Evidence that this writer identified with the academic community is visible through her choice of the third-person plural ("their") and her distancing of herself from the very group of women to which she belonged—Black women. At the same time, she announced her membership in the feminist ("herstories" in place of "histories") and Black communities ("telling [them] . . . like it is"). The identities that writers (or speakers, readers, and listeners) take up more often are determined by the discourses that are available to them than by matters of free choice (Ivanic, 1994). Although some discourses are valued over others and not all discourses are available to everyone, still, as Ivanic has noted, all writers do "have a hand in the . . . construction of their own identities by the selections they make among the discourses they are familiar with in the socio-cultural context within which they [write]" (p. 5).

By analogy, then, Nikki Giovanni contributed to the impression that the readers in Bob Fecho's class constructed of her when they listened to the read-aloud of "Beautiful Black Men." Giovanni's carefully selected words, such as "outasite Afros" and "driving their hogs," were part of an identity she deliberately chose to construct "back in the day" when Blacks were very much interested in building solidarity and pride in their race. That the students in Fecho's class some two decades later did not appreciate Giovanni's vivid and colloquial use of language is understandable, especially given their initial belief that the poet was White. However, even when they discovered Giovanni was of their race, Latonya still resented what she presumed to be, in her words, "making fun of the way Black people talk."

It is interesting to speculate what Latonya and her classmates might have learned from the highly charged incident if they had been made aware of the fact that Giovanni had several discourses available to her but that in selecting the one she did, she opened herself to being misinterpreted and, in this case, dismissed. As Ivanic (1994) has noted, having options available in writing (reading, speaking) one's identity into being does not preclude the limitations and consequences that stem from exercising those options.

A Different Reading

One might also explain what happened in Fecho's class using Fish's (1980) concept of interpretive communities. Such a reading would characterize the students' response to Giovanni's poem as illustrating what can happen when readers who bring similar personal experiences to bear on a text form their own interpretive community. However, I find this reading less compelling pedagogically for the very reasons that Patterson and colleagues (1994) have outlined below. To their way of thinking, the concept of interpretive communities, as argued by Fish, fails to make problematic the traditional reader response notion that students should be encouraged to bring personal experiences to bear when interpreting texts. Because reader response theory does not concern itself with the economic, political, and social forces of the different discourses present in our institutions and in society at large, teachers are less apt to make clear how those forces can color students' perceptions of their experiences. In Patterson and colleagues' (1994) words:

> The problem with [Fish's] argument is that it simply produces a group version, rather than an individualist version, of reader-response. Rather than claiming that individuals produce different readings because everyone is personally different, [Fish argues] that a specific group produces a particular reading because its members share something which is *intrinsic* to the group. That "something" is often conceptualized in essentialist terms as "essence": the distillation of all that makes women what they are, for instance, or Australians what they are, or [African Americans] what they are.
>
> Rather than conceptualizing readers as unique individuals who are capable of generating interpretations out of a private existence in a space outside language, we could begin to think about readers as discursively located "subjects." Both texts and readers are assumed, within this frame, to be governed and produced in particular historical circumstances of time and space.
>
> If we propose that readers may not produce personal interpretations out of their individual experiences so much as produce readings which are positioned by particular sets of values and beliefs, then we can begin to reconceptualize reading as a social practice. It is in this sense that students of different races, different social classes, and different genders may produce readings which challenge dominant or authoritative meanings because they have available to them different sets of values and beliefs. . . . Readers construct readings, not as originators of meaning, but as human subjects positioned through social, political, and economic discursive practices that re-

main the location of a constant struggle over power. (pp. 65–66; emphasis in original)

A PARTING THOUGHT

To think of reading as a social practice, as Patterson and colleagues (1994) propose, takes us back to Labov's (1972) early work on sociolinguistic patterning, Au's (1980) exploration of participation structures in reading groups, and Bloome's (1985) characterization of reading as a social process. About the same time that these authors were taking issue with some of the commonsense propositions undergirding literacy practices in the English-speaking world, an influential group of writers in Great Britain were delving into children's oracy development in the schools (Barnes et al., 1971; Delamont, 1983; Stubbs, 1983). More recently, Freebody, Luke, Gee, and Street (in press) have argued that literacy *is* critical social practice—an argument that I elaborate on elsewhere (Alvermann, 1998) in relation to the need for reconceptualizing the literacies in adolescents' lives.

A commonality shared by those just mentioned, as well as others, is the belief that "social interaction surrounds and influences interaction with a written text" (Bloome, 1985, p. 134), and it is this belief that drives much of the current research on classroom talk about text. Although much work remains to be done before we more fully understand how classroom talk mediates what students comprehend, I am prone to argue from the point of view that discussion is a bargain at any price. Perhaps more than any other literacy practice currently in vogue, classroom discussion serves as an antidote to what Aoki (1997) labels as that most dreaded of practices—"a dentistry of the text, in which reading proceeds by the extraction of meaning and ideas" (p. 22) at the expense of classroom talk that may at times be a little more cheap than we would ideally have it.

NOTES

1. Texts, as used here, refer to the conventional print materials that are available in most classrooms as well as the "texts" of videos, films, and the like. Conversations among students in peer-led discussion groups also produce "texts," as do nonverbal behaviors that can be read by others.

2. Bob Fecho, then an English language arts teacher in the school district of

Philadelphia, described himself as "a male of Eastern European descent [whose] students now and always have been African Americans" (Fecho, 1998).

REFERENCES

Almasi, J. F. (1995). The nature of fourth graders' sociocognitive conflicts in peer-led and teacher-led discussions of literature. *Reading Research Quarterly, 30,* 314–351.

Almasi, J. F., McKeown, M. G., & Beck, I. L. (1996). The nature of engaged reading in classroom discussions of literature. *Journal of Literacy Research, 28,* 107–146.

Alvermann, D. E., (1995/1996). Peer-led discussions: Whose interests are served? *Journal of Adolescent and Adult Literacy, 39,* 282–289.

Alvermann, D. E. (1998). Imagining the possibilities. In D. E. Alvermann, K. A. Hinchman, D. W. Moore, S. F. Phelps, & D. R. Waff (Eds.), *Reconceptualizing the literacies in adolescents' lives.* (pp. 353–372). Mahwah, NJ: Erlbaum.

Alvermann, D. E., O'Brien, D. G., & Dillon, D. R. (1990). What teachers do when they say they're having discussions of content area reading assignments: A qualitative analysis. *Reading Research Quarterly, 25,* 296–322.

Alvermann, D. E., Weaver, D., Hinchman, K. A., Moore, D. W., Phelps, S. F., Thrash, E. C., & Zalewski, P. (1996). Middle and high school students' perceptions of how they experience text-based discussions: A multicase study. *Reading Research Quarterly, 31,* 244–267.

Aoki, D. S. (1997, April). *Teaching and the artless letter: Lacan, plain language and the matheme.* Paper presented at the annual meeting of the American Educational Research Association, Chicago.

Au, K. (1980). Participation structures in a reading lesson with Hawaiian children. *Anthropology and Education Quarterly, 11,* 91–115.

Barnes, D., Britton, J., & Rosen, H. (1971). *Language, the learner and the school* (rev. ed.). Harmondsworth, UK: Penguin.

Barnes, D., & Todd, F. (1977). *Communication and learning in small groups.* Boston: Routledge & Kegan Paul.

Baumann, J. F., & Duffy, A. M. (1997). *Engaged reading for pleasure and learning: A report from the National Reading Research Center.* Athens: University of Georgia Press.

Beach, R. (1997). Critical discourse theory and reader response: How discourses constitute reader stances and social contexts. *Reader, 37,* 1–26.

Bloome, D. (1985). Reading as a social process. *Language Arts, 62,* 134–142.

Bridges, D. (1979). *Education, democracy and discussion.* Windsor, UK: National Foundation for Educational Research.

Davies, B. (1993). *Shards of glass.* Cresskill, NJ: Hampton Press.

Delamont, S. (1983). *Interaction in the classroom* (2nd ed.). London: Methuen.

Dillon, J. T. (1994). *Using discussion in classrooms.* Buckingham, UK: Open University Press.

Fecho, B. (1998). Race, literacy, and the critical inquiry classroom. In D. E. Alvermann, K. A. Hinchman, D. W. Moore, S. F. Phelps, & D. R. Waff (Eds.), *Reconceptualizing the literacies in adolescents' lives.* (pp. 75-101) Mahwah, NJ: Erlbaum.

Finders, M. J. (1997). *Just girls.* New York: Teachers College Press.

Fish, S. (1980). *Is there a text in this class? The authority of interpretive communities.* Cambridge, MA: Harvard University Press.

Floriani, A. (1994). Negotiating what counts: Roles and relationships, texts and contexts, content and meaning. *Linguistics and Education, 5,* 241–274.

Freebody, P., Luke, A., Gee, J., & Street, B. V. (in press). *Literacy as critical social practice.* London: Falmer.

Gilligan, C., Lyons, N. P., & Hanmer, T. J. (Eds.). (1990). *Making connections: The relational worlds of adolescent girls at Emma Willard School.* Cambridge, MA: Harvard University Press.

Goatley, V. J., Brock, C. H., & Raphael, T. E. (1995). Diverse learners participating in regular education "Book Clubs." *Reading Research Quarterly, 30,* 352–380.

Goodlad, J. I. (1984). *A place called school.* New York: McGraw-Hill.

Grant, R. W. (1996). The ethics of talk: Classroom conversation and democratic politics. *Teachers College Record, 97,* 470–482.

Grumet, M. (1996, April). Discussant's response to symposium titled *Troubling what we know in secondary students' participation in classroom talk about texts.* Presented at the annual meeting of the American Educational Research Association, New York.

Guthrie, J. T., & Alvermann, D. E. (Eds.). (1999). *Engaged reading: Processes, practices, and policy implications.* New York: Teachers College Press.

Inagaki, K. (1981). Facilitation of knowledge integration through classroom discussion. *Quarterly Newsletter of the Laboratory of Comparative Human Cognition, 3*(3), 26–28.

Ivanic, R. (1994). I is for interpersona: Discoursal construction of writer identitites and the teaching of writing. *Linguistics and Education, 6,* 3–15.

Labov, W. (1972). *Sociolinguistic patterns.* Philadelphia: University of Pennsylvania Press.

McMahon, S., I., & Raphael, T. E. (1997). *The Book Club connection: Literacy learning and classroom talk.* New York: Teachers College Press.

O'Flahavan, J. F. (1989). *An exploration of the effects of participant structure upon literacy development in reading group discussion.* Unpublished doctoral dissertation, University of Illinois, Urbana-Champaign.

Patterson, A., Mellor, B., & O'Neill, M. (1994). Beyond comprehension: Poststructural readings in the English classroom. In B. Corcoran, M. Hayhoe, & G. M. Pradl (Eds.), *Knowledge in the making* (pp. 61–72). Portsmouth, NH: Boynton/Cook.

Perret-Clermont, A. N. (1980). *Social interaction and cognitive development in children.* New York: Academic.

Pintrich, P. R., & DeGroot, E. (1990). Motivational and self-regulated learning components of classroom academic performance. *Journal of Educational Psychology, 82,* 33–40.

Rogers, A. G. (1993). Voice, play, and a practice of ordinary courage in girls' and women's lives. *Harvard Educational Review, 63,* 265–295.

Said, E. W. (1994). *Representations of the intellectual.* New York: Vintage.

Santa Barbara Classroom Discourse Group. (1992). Constructing literacy in the classroom: Literate action as social accomplishment. In H. H. Marshall (Ed.), *Redefining student learning: Roots of educational change* (pp. 119–151). Norwood, NJ: Ablex.

Stubbs, M. (1983). *Language, schools and classrooms* (2nd ed.). London: Methuen.

Vygotsky, L. S. (1978). *Mind in society: The development of higher mental psychological processes.* Cambridge, MA: Harvard University Press.

Wells, M. C. (1996). *Literacies lost: When students move from a progressive middle school to a traditional high school.* New York: Teachers College Press.

Young, J. P. (1998). Discussion as a practice of carnival. In D. E. Alvermann, K. A. Hinchman, D. W. Moore, S. F. Phelps, & D. R. Waff (Eds.), *Reconceptualizing the literacies in adolescents' lives.* (pp. 247–264) Mahwah, NJ: Erlbaum.

8

Literacy Lessons Derived from the Instruction of Six Latina/Latino Teachers

ROBERT T. JIMÉNEZ

Educators, policy makers, and the general public are paying increased attention to the literacy learning needs of Latina/Latino students (Crawford, 1997; El Nasser, 1997; Hispanic Dropout Project, 1996). These needs are multiple but are perhaps best illustrated with the following statement: Latina/Latino students are reading at significantly lower levels than other students, they comprise three out of four of the approximately 10 million students learning English as a second language in the United States, and they are losing ground in terms of academic achievement and high school graduation rates (Hispanic Dropout Project, 1996; National Center for Educational Statistics, 1997). Finding workable solutions to address the literacy learning needs of these students will almost certainly require researchers to examine the situation from a variety of perspectives. One possibility is to examine the instructional practice of teachers who are exceptional or distinctive in one way or another and who work with the population in question (Erickson & Mohatt, 1982; García, 1994; Ladson-Billings, 1994).

In this chapter, I present selected findings from three previous research studies in which my colleagues and I identified, described, and implemented productive literacy practices for Latina/Latino students (Jiménez, 1997; Jiménez, in preparation; Jiménez, Gersten, & Rivera, 1996). In these three studies, I worked directly with six Latina and Latino teachers who engaged in productive, or at least thought-provoking, strategies with their students. These literacy practices and teacher characteristics consisted of the following: These teachers adapted and modified newer conceptualizations of recommended literacy practices, developed trust and rapport with their students, communicated in intriguing ways with their students, and promoted the transfer of information acquired through native-language instruction to English-language contexts.

While European American teachers of African American students can turn to an emerging body of literature that examines the practice of creative and innovative African American teachers, teachers of Latina/Latino students have not been as fortunate (Foster, 1993; Ladson-Billings, 1994; McElroy-Johnson, 1993). Because the majority of teachers working with Latina/Latino students are both European American and novices who have not received training in working with children from diverse backgrounds (de la Rosa, Maw, & Yzaguirre, 1990; National Education Association, 1990; Zimpher, 1989; Zimpher & Yessayan, 1987), I felt that this chapter could provide these teachers with potentially useful information for improving the literacy learning and instruction of Latina/Latino students.

Teachers from the Latina/Latino community are an increasingly scarce resource. Presently only 3% of all teachers are Latina/Latino; there are about 64 Latina/Latino students for every 1 Latina/Latino teacher in the United States (de la Rosa et al., 1990). At the same time, fewer persons from minority backgrounds are enrolling in teacher education programs (Gay, 1993; McCurdy, 1987). Yet these Latina/Latino teachers may hold great potential for enhancing the knowledge base on teaching Latina/Latino students. Research on the instructional practice of Hawaiian, Native American, and African American teachers, for example, has led to the development of suggestions for culturally responsive instruction (Au & Mason, 1981; Erickson & Mohatt, 1982; Ladson-Billings, 1994).

Perhaps paradoxically, teachers from mainstream backgrounds may be the ones with the most to benefit from such research because cultural and linguistic interaction patterns can be extraordinarily difficult to determine. Such knowledge, when available, has previously been used to modify and adapt the instructional practice of mainstream teachers to more meaningfully involve culturally and linguistically diverse students in their own learning (Au & Mason, 1981; Heath, 1982).

METHODS USED IN PREVIOUS RESEARCH

The methods used for conducting the three research studies reported in this chapter were similar, with a few notable exceptions. As a result, I integrate and summarize the description of these methods whenever possible in order to avoid redundancy. More complete accounts of the methods used can be found in Gersten and Jiménez (1994), Jiménez, Gersten, and Rivera (1996), and Jiménez (1997).

Settings

Data for the Jiménez, Gersten, and Rivera (1996) report were gathered in one elementary school of a large urban school district in southern California. The school had a large student enrollment (approximately 1,000 students), and a Latina/Latino population of approximately 82%. Three Latina/Latino teachers participated in this research project. They were Rogelio Cárdenas, Elisa Montoya, and Rosa Mata (all names used are pseudonyms).

Data for the Jiménez (1997) report (see also Jiménez & Gámez, 1996) were gathered in a large semi-urban school district in northern Illinois. All the students in this study attended a school with a predominantly minority enrollment. Of 819 students, 533 were students of color, the majority of whom, 407, were Latina/Latino. Laura Estrada was the Latina teacher involved in this project.

Data for the Jiménez (in preparation) report were collected in the same school district as that for Jiménez (1997). The teachers, however, worked in a school on the other side of town. There were 517 students enrolled in this school, 290 of whom were Latina/Latino and 186 of whom received bilingual education services. Two Latina teachers, Claudia Contreras and Diana Orozco were, were involved in this project.

Description of Participating Teachers

Both Elisa Montoya and Rogelio Cárdenas were of Mexican origin. Elisa was raised in southern California, while Rogelio was raised in Mexico just south of the California border. Both teachers were certified to teach in elementary education, with a bilingual credential. Although both teachers were fluent speakers of Spanish and English, Rogelio was more comfortable speaking Spanish while Elisa was more comfortable speaking English. Rogelio had taught for 8 years, and Elisa for 16 years; both had taught only in the United States.

Rosa Mata was also of Mexican origin. She was raised in El Paso, Texas, held an elementary and bilingual credential, and had taught for 12 years at the time of the study. She was also fluent in English and Spanish. She taught students in a Grade 3 classroom.

Laura Estrada was of Puerto Rican heritage (Jiménez, 1997). She was also a fluent speaker of both English and Spanish, but perhaps a bit more comfortable with Spanish. She had been raised in both the mainland United States (New York) and in Puerto Rico. She held a transitional bilingual teaching certificate. Her undergraduate university training was in library science, and at the time of the study she was in her second year of teaching and was completing coursework required by the state for approval of bilingual teachers.

Diana Orozco was of Mexican origin (Jiménez, in preparation). She had been raised in Chicago but had ties to relatives in northern Mexico. Diana was more comfortable speaking English, even though her Spanish-language proficiency was high. A second-year teacher when I first met her, Diana was certified to teach in elementary education, with a bilingual credential. Claudia Contreras was Puerto Rican. While living in Puerto Rico, she had been recruited by the district to teach in Illinois. Claudia was therefore more comfortable speaking Spanish, but she also spoke English. She held a special education credential, with a bilingual endorsement. Claudia had 28 years of teaching experience, most of it in Puerto Rico.

Data-Collection Procedures

Classroom Observations. I observed all the teachers over a period of between 1 semester and 2 years, depending on the research project. Data collection included multiple in-depth qualitative observations of the teachers in their classroom environments. Between four and ten observations were conducted, typically ranging in duration from 1½ to 2 hours. Handwritten field notes were used to record classroom activities. Although the original purpose of the observations was to capture students' responses to the participating teachers, the result was that a large amount of data also documented teachers' literacy instruction. These literacy learning events were recorded for evidence concerning the language or languages used by the students and the teachers, the characteristics of that language use, the nature of interactions between teachers and students, and the nature of instruction.

Interviews. All of the teachers were interviewed at least once and, in some cases, twice using semistructured interview protocols. Teachers were also interviewed informally throughout each of the research projects. Interviews occurred in multiple settings: before and after school, during lunch breaks, driving to and from district presentations, and, on a few occasions, in restaurants. The teachers were specifically asked to share their approaches for designing instruction and their rationales for choice of reading materials. They were also asked to describe their beliefs concerning teaching language-minority students to read and write, their thoughts on the use of children's literature with language-minority students, their ideas on the effects that culture has on instruction and student learning, their understanding of how parents can be involved in school and classroom activities, and their ideas about what teachers need to know to work effectively with language-minority students.

LESSONS LEARNED

The findings of the previously described research studies are organized under the headings of three general topics that emerged during analysis: the ways that teachers used their two languages as media of instruction, some promising instructional practices, and teachers' understanding of and attitudes toward Latina/Latino students and their families.

Language Usage

García (1994) described how effective teachers of culturally and linguistically diverse students use Spanish and English:

> They use English and Spanish in highly communicative ways, speaking to students with varying degrees of Spanish and English proficiency in a communicative style requiring significant language switching. Direct translation from one language to another is a rarity *but utilization of language switching in contexts which require it is common.* (p. 237; emphasis added)

Of particular interest in García's statement is the information he provides on language switching, sometimes called code-switching or code-mixing (McClure, 1981). Early research in bilingual education noted the problems involved when bilingual teachers provided students with concurrent translations of instruction (Legarreta, 1977). Specifically, students paid no attention to instruction in their weaker language, thus negating any potential second-language learning.

Legarreta's (1977) research has had a profound effect on the field of bilingual education as a whole, and many bilingual teachers still work hard to maintain a strict separation between the two languages. Legarreta's influence could be discerned in the comments of Elisa Montoya. Elisa explained during an interview that she provided a clearly defined period of time each day for speaking and using English in the classroom, and another time for speaking Spanish. During English time, she encouraged students to use English as much as possible in her transition classroom, and she praised students when she heard them communicating informally in English. However, she did not discourage students who chose to speak in Spanish during English time. Interestingly, however, she did discourage students from using English during Spanish time. She stated that students needed more support to not abandon Spanish. She explained her approach as follows:

> When we're together as a class, they are expected to use English. It is okay, though, to use Spanish. . . . The kids need to feel comfortable communicating. They definitely should feel comfortable asking questions. . . . *I want them to use their Spanish if that's what they feel comfortable using.*

In contrast, Elisa said that, although the students might switch freely between languages, as a teacher she operated primarily in one language or the other depending on the activity to clarify the focus. So during math instruction, she spoke in English (unless there was a clear problem); for social studies, she used Spanish.

All the teachers considered it their responsibility to teach their students English. In other words, rather than simply insisting that students speak English, they saw their role as showing students how to go about doing so. Activities were often structured to provide opportunities to practice and use English. However, when students seemed flustered in answering complex questions in English, they would ask the student to answer in Spanish and then help them express at least some of the ideas in English.

Rosa Mata accomplished this task while working with a student in grade 3. When an 8-year old child, Ana, stood in front of the class and was asked by Rosa to deliver a one- or two-sentence description of a book she had read at home, she was silent. The teacher's prompts and knowledge of what this child knew and could report appeared to guide her scaffolding (support) of this short exchange.

Rosa: What is it you don't know how to say? Say it in Spanish first.
Ana: Los niños están asustados porque su abuelito les contó un cuento.
   (The children are frightened because their grandfather told them a story.)
Rosa: Okay, because grandfather told them a story about a dragon. Was there a real dragon? What happened?
Ana: Ellos estaban corriendo y se encontraron con sus abuelitos. *(They were running and they met their grandparents.)*
Rosa: Okay, they were running and they met their grandparents. Do you have anything else to say, Ana? Okay, your next book report is going to be in English because I've heard you talk English outside and you do a good job.

García's (1994) finding that effective bilingual teachers make use of both languages within and across utterances appears at first to be contradictory to Legarreta's (1977) conclusions. His views on language use seem to provide teachers with the possibility of making greater use of both languages while at the same time giving students an incentive to heed all instruction. Diana Orozco, for example, perhaps because she was newer to the profession of bilingual education, made frequent use of English–Spanish code-switching when interacting with her students. Diana's use of both languages was quite distinct from that observed in Elisa's and Rosa's classrooms. Notice how her use of Spanish softens her directive:

Diana: Voy a ser mas estricta, mas firme, okay? Go and get into your
groups. *(I'm going to be stricter, more firm, okay?)*

During the same lesson in which her students were reading a science text, Diana asked a question in Spanish and provided the answer in English. In both of these examples, and indeed in almost every example in which Diana made use of code-switching, her language switch had the effect of providing the students with new information. She was not simply translating, even though, at times, some information was repeated.

Diana: ¿Qué es un hipótesis? *(What is a hypothesis?)* It's an educated
guess.

Laura Estrada also occasionally engaged in the same kind of behavior. She explained the water cycle to her students and then asked them a question:

Laura: ¿Por qué? *(Why?)* Why does it rain?

Other research appears to confirm the importance of building rapport with students through the use of the Spanish language (Carter & Chatfield, 1986; Lucas, Henze, & Donato, 1990; Moll, 1988). Lucas and colleagues (1990), for example, placed language use and the importance of valuing culture as the category of first importance when determining why some high schools were effective in their teaching of Latina/Latino students. Factors that these researchers identified included the following: Teachers viewed the speaking of Spanish as an advantage rather than a disability; they refused to attach stigma to the speaking of Spanish; they made efforts to learn Spanish if they were monolingual English speakers; they made classes on Spanish-language grammar and literature available to native Spanish speakers; and they made classes in Spanish as a second language available to native English speakers.

Finding ways to meaningfully incorporate the use of the Spanish language into the curriculum is perhaps the greatest challenge facing monolingual European American teachers of Latina/Latino students. Teachers, however, need not be fluent Spanish speakers to make progress in this area. A willingness to learn some basic Spanish vocabulary can provide teachers with sufficient material to engage in substantial code-switching. In addition, many of the factors identified by Lucas and colleagues (1990) do not require any knowledge of Spanish at all but rather simply a positive appraisal of the language's utility. In other research Lucas and Katz (1994) identified multiple classroom activities that monolingual English-speaking teachers can use to validate students' Spanish-language abilities, such as providing students with Spanish-language books and other texts, inviting Spanish-speaking volunteers into the classroom, and encouraging the use of Spanish during cooperative learning.

Instructional Practices

With respect to instructional delivery systems, everything from direct instruction to whole language has been reported as successful for teaching Latina/Latino students (Hudelson, 1984; Silbert, Carnine, & Alvarez, 1994). Because researchers have covered the pros and cons of various approaches to teaching literacy so extensively, I will not repeat their efforts. Instead, I will highlight a few of the more salient characteristics related to the effective instruction of Latina/Latino students. These characteristics need not be limited to any one instructional approach. They include a high regard for instruction and instructional innovation, a demand for high student performance, and the provision of a demanding and challenging curriculum.

Several studies have shown that effective teachers of Latina/Latino students are knowledgeable about both more traditional and more current conceptualizations in literacy instruction (Gersten & Jiménez, 1994; Goldenberg, 1996; Moll, 1988). Lucas and colleagues (1990) and Carter and Chatfield (1986) indicated that teachers in these studies emphasized and made use of sheltered English instruction, cooperative learning, and reading and writing in content areas. Both of the previous studies also reported that the continual improvement of instruction was emphasized by the schools as a whole and by individual teachers.

The instructional conversation is a technique recommended as an innovative approach to literacy instruction (Cazden, 1988; Goldenberg, 1992/1993; Ramirez, 1992; Tharp & Gallimore, 1988). Classroom conversations and dialogues can serve several purposes—as a way to prepare students to read a text, as a device for discussing a text, as a means of incorporating children's cultural backgrounds into the curriculum, and, at times, as a vehicle for conveying information. One intriguing conversation that Rogelio Cárdenas conducted in his classroom focused on the problems caused by urban development. All the individuals in the classroom—Rogelio, a student teacher, and 27 students—were engaged in reading a book, Kurusa and Doppert's *La Calle Es Libre* (1981), or *The Street Is Free* (1995). Rogelio provided necessary information in a manner that combined teacher-directed instruction with student-generated production of information. The following short excerpt illustrates a fairly sophisticated level of discussion around an abstract topic:

Rogelio: ¿Qué clase de problemas causa el desarrollo? *(What kind of problems are caused by development?)*
María: Los animales no pueden tomar el agua y se mueren. *(The animals can't drink the water and they die.)*
Aleja: Hay unas personas que no más hacen casas y no las usan. *(There are some people who just make houses and they don't use them.)*

Demand for high student performance and the provision of a demanding and challenging curriculum were also evident in Elisa Montoya's classroom. She made productive use of her knowledge of students as competent Spanish readers: "I don't insult them with books in English that are too easy. They are good Spanish readers." For example, we observed students in her class reading several books, including, *A Wrinkle in Time* (L'Engle, 1962). Moll's (1988) view that Latina/Latino students learn English to the extent that they are motivated to learn the content presented in their classrooms provides a further rationale for providing these students with a challenging curriculum.

In conjunction with her emphasis on providing students with high-quality children's literature, Elisa also emphasized vocabulary instruction. She described instruction that mirrored strategies for determining the meanings of unknown vocabulary items verbalized by proficient Latina/Latino readers of English (Jiménez, García, & Pearson, 1995, 1996). She stated that she chose only key vocabulary words, that she did not waste students' time by going over all unknown words, and that she encouraged students to discuss new words extensively (see also Gersten & Jiménez, 1994).

Diana Orozco also presented her fifth-grade bilingual education students with a challenging curriculum parallel to that presented to native English-speaking students in her school. In other words, she did not omit information that the school viewed as necessary for success but instead combined this information within an overall culturally responsive framework. The following quote provides an idea of the content-rich nature of her instruction:

Diana: ¿Qué es fotosíntesis? C'mon, we know what *fotosíntesis* is. Es el proceso cuando . . . *(What is photosynthesis? C'mon, we know what photosynthesis is. It is the process when . . .)*

When her students encountered difficulty learning from the science text, she created an engaging activity in which each of her students received a number of statements describing important science concepts and vocabulary. The students then read the statements to their partners, who did their best to name the concept or vocabulary item. After each trial, the students' success was charted on the chalkboard. They repeated this process by reading and rereading the statements until they achieved a high rate of success. The students' enthusiasm was palpable. Those well-versed in literacy research will note the creative application of Samuels's (1988) multiple rereading technique for the purpose of attaining automaticity in word recognition.

These teachers also provided their students with specific instructional supports to assist them in transfering information and skills they had learned in Spanish to English-language contexts and tasks. Elisa referred to this procedure as "taking students back to their Spanish" to get them first to articulate their thoughts. For example, during writing assignments, students might be encouraged to write a draft in Spanish first, or they might write most of the draft in English and insert Spanish words when they wanted or needed to do so. Students would then be encouraged, perhaps with help from Elisa or from a more English-proficient peer, to write the assignment in English.

In an English reading lesson, Rogelio Cárdenas's students demonstrated one of the difficulties facing second-language learners when they read in their new language. The technique he employed modeled one possible solution to this problem. He was conducting an instructional conversation with his fifth-grade students in preparation for a story they were about to read about cowboys and cowgirls. Rogelio and his students collaboratively created a list of *English* vocabulary related to this topic. Rogelio's technique is simple but effective, as the comment by his student José attests.

Rogelio: If you don't understand all those words, raise your hand.
Cristina: Holster

Cheli: Chaps (Rogelio draws a picture of chaps and a holster.)
José: O, sí, sí, sí. Ya sé que son. *(Oh, yes, yes, yes. Now I know what they are.)*

Elisa Montoya described this phenomenon facing second-language learners: "For the most part, they have the language [both English and Spanish], they just need to try and connect it." Thus, she sees facilitating transfer of knowledge that students possess in Spanish into English as an explicit instructional goal.

Attitudes Toward Latina/Latino Students

Carter and Chatfield (1986) reported that the teachers at Lauderbach School—noted for the sustained, high levels of academic achievement of their Latina/Latino students over a six year period—almost universally rejected a deficit view of minority students. Instead, they believed that if children did not learn the school was at fault. Of more interest, perhaps, were the different ways that the teachers who participated in my research studies demonstrated their positive outlook on students and their families. Elisa, for example, described her relationship to students' parents as that of a partnership and she frequently made home visits. Elisa said that parents often told her after a home visit that they had never before been visited by a representative of the school.

In addition, Elisa scheduled open-ended parent conferences to maximize her contact with parents. In other words, she told them, "I'll be here Wednesday from 1 PM to 4 PM" without assigning to each a specific time. She said that parents did not mind waiting to speak to her if more than one parent arrived at a time, but they did resent being *told* to arrive at a specific time. Because respect for individual dignity and autonomy is so high in Latino culture, culturally competent members often refrain from making explicit demands on others, particularly when the other is an adult and the demand has to do with his or her daily schedule.

Rogelio also expressed enthusiasm when he described different ways to involve students' parents in their literacy learning. When interviewed, he shared that he enjoyed visiting his students' homes so that he could communicate school expectations. He believed that his students' parents were very willing to get involved in their children's education. But he added that it was a teacher's responsibility to reach out to the community, especially when parents felt alienated by the school system.

In addition, he said that occasionally parents came into his classroom and taught culturally familiar activities, such as making piñatas. Grandparents also were invited to tell traditional Mexican stories to his class.

Over and over, however, Rogelio stressed the school's obligation to reach out to the community. In contrast, some European American teachers I interviewed during this same project (see Gersten & Jiménez, 1994) often ascribed home–school problems to language differences or to the limited educational attainments of parents.

Lucas and colleagues (1990) described the high levels of commitment and personal attention provided by teachers from high schools known for their effectiveness in teaching Latina/Latino students. This commitment took the concrete form of advocating students' interests by supporting activities like MEChA (Movimiento Estudiantil Chicano de Aztlán), Latino clubs, Spanish-language newspapers, and athletic events. Moll (1988) provided examples of how this concern was translated into instructional activities, such as making frequent connections to students' backgrounds by incorporating culturally familiar information into the curriculum. The commitment also included more personal touches, such as a willingness to carefully monitor students' personal and academic progress.

Diana demonstrated a highly personal interest in students' welfare, which became evident when she disciplined them. She reprimanded Juan, for example, by saying "A poco haces así en la casa" *(You wouldn't dare do that at home)*. Although Juan reacted with a rather angry look, it was clear to me from this and subsequent interactions that he appreciated Diana's concern. She used the expression "I'm gonna be on you like white on rice" about five or six times. She made this statement specifically to Juan and loud enough for all to hear. She asked the students, "Do you know what that means? You're gonna find out."

In another incident, Diana pulled three girls into the room—and it was clear she was angry. First, she required that the three copy the slogan hanging on the bulletin board: Lo popular no es siempre lo mejor *(The popular thing is not always the best thing)*. They were also told to write a two-paragraph explanation of why that statement was true and how it applied to them. So far, a rather pedestrian example of discipline. But then, Diana called Elena. She called three or four times in a stern, firm voice. She told Elena to come and stand next to her. Elena came over. Diana stared at her intently. Elena began to sway back and forth. After what seemed like an eternity, probably a full minute or so, Elena's face reddened and a tear appeared. Diana told her to return to her classroom. It was a powerful demonstration of discipline without punishment. It was a demonstration of profound disappointment. It caused Elena to tremble. It moved me deeply.

During an interview, Laura described her concern for her students. Her statement provides hints of Laura's intimately personal involvement in her students' lives. Her statement was also backed up by my knowledge of home visits she made to students in trouble and her willingness to work with social agencies responsible for some of her students' welfare.

> They get to know me so much, they know that I can be the most loving person, but they learn to know my physical expressions and I just look at them, straight ahead. But they know that I love them. And I fool around with them, I fool around with the kids, and I get involved. . . . I had one [student] this year, but he had a conflict. His mother lo había abandonado, se crió con el padre, estaba todo el tiempo hablando de la mujer *(had abandoned him, he was raised by his father, he was talking all the time about women)*, so he had a conflict with women. He thought that I was his teacher and he could just manipulate me. And the best, the most loving that I got that year was from that student. He gave me this huggy *peluche,* teddy bear. So, he was always fighting with me, but he bought it with his own money.

CONCLUSIONS

These examples from the instructional practice of six Latina and Latino teachers were chosen to provide concrete illustrations for enhancing the instruction of teachers who work with similar students. The examples depicted how these teachers moved beyond deficit models of learning by holding high expectations for their students. More specifically, they used language to communicate more than just information, they adapted and modified newer conceptualizations of recommended literacy practices, and they developed trust and rapport with their students. My hope is to encourage more dialogue about these topics as part of a larger effort to improve the academic achievement of Latina and Latino students in the United States (Hispanic Dropout Project, 1996; National Center for Educational Statistics, 1997).

Sensitivity to the Linguistic Needs of Students

Language rights, and more specifically the status conferred upon or denied to the Spanish language, have always been an issue of central importance to Latinas and Latinos (San Miguel, 1987; Walsh, 1991). Spanish-language rights have, at various times, been guaranteed by treaty, forbidden within schools, grudgingly tolerated, and, most recently, subjected to intense hostility and legal sanction (Crawford, 1992; Valencia, 1991). Weber (1991) cogently summarized how this unpleasant history has manifested itself in U.S. schools: "In the view of American education, knowledge of a mother tongue other than English has been perceived until recently as a liability to learning, a factor in low intelligence, and an indicator of poverty and questionable academic potential" (p. 98). Perhaps not surprisingly, all the teachers included in this chapter found multiple ways to affirm their students' Spanish-language abilities.

Elisa Montoya and Rosa Mata, for example, ensured that students had access to open lines of communication. They found ways to probe students' knowledge using both Spanish and English. They made sure that students felt successful before they gently encouraged them to express their thoughts in a second language. These two teachers did *not* demand public performance in English on command, but they did provide students with multiple opportunities for using English and they did consistently communicate to their students that they wanted and expected them to make use of their fledgling English-language abilities. Diana Orozco illustrated this gentle approach when she chided one of her students for using only English with a new arrival who was Spanish-dominant. The message was that learning English takes time, and communication takes priority over use of the second language.

These teachers embodied in their practice a general principle articulated by Nieto (1992). She described teachers who made a difference in the lives of culturally diverse students as follows:

> Students remembered those teachers who had affirmed them, whether through their language, their culture, or their concerns. Teachers who called on students' linguistic skills or cultural knowledge were named most often [as teachers who had made an important difference in their lives]. (p. 242)

Provision of Instructional Opportunities

These teachers made sure that their students received a wide range of learning opportunities, including the means to comprehend instruction, a framework for interacting verbally, a challenging menu of reading materials, and an interesting and conceptually dense curriculum.

Rogelio Cárdenas, for example, made use of drawings to enhance his English-language literacy instruction. Students were able to confirm and solidify their comprehension of an overall conceptual set or schema of information prior to being presented with a text. Diana made use of code-switching between English and Spanish, which gave students a little more information than they would otherwise have had while still maintaining an incentive to pay close attention.

One of the teachers, Rogelio, made extensive use of an instructional conversation approach that provided his students with opportunities to talk. This approach was used during both his Spanish and English literacy instruction. His literacy instruction allowed students to transfer a framework they had learned in their first and stronger language to their second language, English. A major criticism of all instructional programs provided to students who are learning English is that they do not receive adequate opportunities to use either their first or second language (Arreaga-Meyer & Perdomo-Rivera, 1996; Goldenberg, 1992/1993; Ramirez, 1992).

Finally, students had opportunities to read interesting and challenging materials. Elisa, for example, used high-quality children's literature books in her classroom. Diana also adapted a repeated reading technique for use with science texts. Her students were able to work on improving their reading fluency and word-recognition abilities while at the same time learning an important part of the curriculum.

An Emphasis on Relationships

The educational community has found the task of creating a welcoming environment for students from linguistically and culturally diverse backgrounds particularly difficult (Nieto, 1992). The teachers whose practice I examined communicated respect for their students, their families, and, by extension, their communities. They never blamed their students' families for difficulties experienced at school. Elisa made sure that parents felt welcome at parent–teacher conferences. Rogelio believed it was his responsibility to know his students' parents. He also found ways to integrate parents into his classroom and to showcase their talents. Creating good relationships with parents is a significant accomplishment for any teacher. The task is complicated for teachers of linguistically diverse students, but the rewards can be measured in higher student achievement (Carter & Chatfield, 1986; Goldenberg, 1987).

These teachers also demonstrated an intensely personal interest in their students' welfare. Diana showed concern for her students by disciplining them, using community norms as her standard. Her statement to Juan that he wouldn't dare misbehave at home like he was trying to do at school had an immediate effect on his behavior. Her profound disappointment in Elena visibly moved this young teen. In essence, Diana and Laura provided indications that they viewed their jobs as teachers as including relentless monitoring of troubled students. These teachers described the discipline they used with their own children in very similar terms. Yet, in spite of its seeming severity, Laura, for example, communicated a deep concern and love for her students. The concern these teachers showed for their students, while distinctly Latina, was also reminiscent of the behaviors reported by Ladson-Billings (1994) for effective teachers of African American students.

In sum, while it is clear that research is only just beginning to identify potentially useful information for teaching Latina/Latino students, it seems to make sense to examine carefully the practice of exemplary Latina/Latino teachers for ideas, possibilities, and particular instructional practices. The examples presented in this chapter, however, are not meant to serve as prescriptions for how to teach Latina/Latino students. Rather, it was my intention that they stimulate thought and provide a range of possibilities for teaching literacy. It is my hope that more research will be devoted to this topic and that such information will be viewed as useful by teachers and others who have the responsibility of teaching Latina/Latino students to read and write.

REFERENCES

Arreaga-Mayer, C., & Perdomo-Rivera, C. (1996). Ecobehavioral analysis of instruction for at-risk language-minority students. *The Elementary School Journal, 96*(3), 245–258.

Au, K. H., & Mason, J. (1981). Social organization factors in learning to read: The balance of rights hypothesis. *Reading Research Quarterly, 17,* 115–152.

Carter, T. P., & Chatfield, M. L. (1986). Effective bilingual schools: Implications for policy and practice. *American Journal of Education, 95*(1), 200–232.

Cazden, C. (1998). *Classroom discourse: The language of teaching and learning.* Portsmouth, NH: Heinemann.

Crawford, J. (1992). *Language loyalties.* Chicago: University of Chicago Press.

Crawford, J. (1997). *Best evidence: Research foundations of the Bilingual Education Act.* Washington, DC: National Clearinghouse for Bilingual Education.

de la Rosa, D., Maw, C. E., & Yzaguirre, R. (1990). *Hispanic education: A statistical portrait 1990.* Washington, DC: Policy Analysis Center–Office of Research, Advocacy, and Legislation–National Council of La Raza.

El Nasser, H. (1997, May 14). *Hispanics quit school at a rate twice the average.* USA Today, p. A-5.

Erickson, F., & Mohatt, G. (1982). Cultural organization of participation in two classrooms of Indian students. In G. Spindler (Eds.), *Doing the ethnography of schooling* (pp. 132–174). New York: Holt, Rinehart & Winston.

Foster, M. (1993). Educating for competence in community and culture. *Urban Education, 27*(4), 370–394.

García, E. (1994). *Understanding and meeting the challenge of student cultural diversity.* Boston: Houghton Mifflin.

Gay, G. (1993). Ethnic minorities and educational quality. In J. A. Banks & C. A. Banks (Eds.), *Multicultural education* (pp. 171–194). Boston: Allyn & Bacon.

Gersten, R. M., & Jiménez, R. T. (1994). A delicate balance: Enhancing literacy instruction for students of English as a second language. *The Reading Teacher, 47*(6), 438–449.

Goldenberg, C. N. (1987). Low-income Hispanic parents' contributions to their first-grade children's word recognition skills. *Anthropology and Education Quarterly, 18*(2), 149–179.

Goldenberg, C. (1992/1993). Instructional conversations: Promoting comprehension through discussion. *The Reading Teacher, 46*(4), 316–326.

Goldenberg, C. (1996). The education of language-minority students: Where are we, and where do we need to go. *Elementary School Journal, 96*(3), 353–361.

Heath, S. B. (1982). Questioning at home and at school: A comparative study. In G. Spindler (Ed.), *Doing the ethnography of schooling* (pp. 102–131). New York: Holt, Rinehart & Winston.

Hispanic Dropout Project. (1996). *Data book.* Washington, DC: U.S. Department of Education.

Hudelson, S. (1984). Kan yu ret an rayt en Inglés? Children become literate in English as a second language. *TESOL Quarterly, 18*(2), 221–238.

Jiménez, R. T. (1997). The strategic reading abilities and potential of five low-literacy Latina/o readers in middle school. *Reading Research Quarterly, 32*(3), 224–243.

Jiménez, R. T. (in preparation). Culturally and linguistically relevant strategy instruction for language minority students with learning disabilities.

Jiménez, R. T., & Gámez, A. (1996). Literature-based cognitive strategy instruction for middle school Latina/o students. *Journal of Adolescent and Adult Literacy, 40*(2), 84–91.

Jiménez, R. T., García, G. E., & Pearson, P. D. (1995). Three children, two languages, and strategic reading: Case studies in bilingual/monolingual reading. *American Educational Research Journal, 32*(1), 31–61.

Jiménez, R. T., García, G. E., & Pearson, P. D. (1996). The reading strategies of Latina/o students who are successful English readers: Opportunities and obstacles. *Reading Research Quarterly, 31*(1), 90–112.

Jiménez, R. T., Gersten, R., & Rivera, A. (1996). Conversations with a Chicana teacher: Transition from native- to English-language instruction. *Elementary School Journal, 96*(3), 333–341.

Kurusa, & Doppert, M. (1981). *La calle es libre.* Caracas, Venezuela: Ekaré.

Kurusa, & Doppert, M. (1995). *The street is free.* New York: Annick.

Ladson-Billings, G. (1994). *The dreamkeepers.* San Francisco: Jossey-Bass.

L'Engle, M. (1962). *A wrinkle in time.* New York: Ariel.

Legarreta, D. (1977). Language choice in bilingual classrooms. *TESOL Quarterly, 11*(1), 9–16.

Lucas, T., & Katz, A. (1994). Reframing the debate: The roles of native languages in English-only programs for minority students. *TESOL Quarterly, 28*(3), 537–561.

Lucas, T., Henze, R., & Donato, R. (1990). Promoting the success of Latino language-minority students: An exploratory study of six high schools. *Harvard Educational Review, 60*(3), 315–340.

McClure, E. (1981). Formal and functional aspects of codeswitched discourse of bilingual children. In R. P. Durán (Ed.), *Latino language and communicative behavior* (pp. 69–94). Norwood, NJ: Ablex.

McCurdy, J. (1987, May 27). Teacher-education reforms move ahead, but movement faces skeptics and problems. *The Chronicle of Higher Education,* p. 23.

McElroy-Johnson, B. (1993). Giving voice to the voiceless. *Harvard Educational Review, 63*(1), 85–104.

Moll, L. C. (1988). Some key issues in teaching Latino students. *Language Arts, 65*(5), 465–472.

National Center for Educational Statistics. (1997). *Dropout rates in the United States: 1995.* U. S. Department of Education.

National Education Association. (1990). *Federal education funding: The cost of excellence.* Washington, DC: Author.

Nieto, S. (1992). *Affirming diversity.* New York: Longman.

Ramirez, J. D. (1992). Executive summary. *Bilingual Research Quarterly, 16*(1 & 2), 1–62.

Samuels, S. J. (1988). Decoding and automaticity: Helping poor readers become automatic at word recognition. *Reading Teacher, 41*(8), 756–760.

San Miguel, G. (1987). *"Let all of them take heed": Mexican Americans and the campaign for educational equality in Texas, 1910–1981.* Austin: University of Texas Press.

Silbert, J., Carnine, D., & Alvarez, R. (1994). Beginning reading for bilingual students. *Educational Leadership, 51*(5), 90–91.

Tharp, R. G., & Gallimore, R. (1988). *Rousing minds to life.* Cambridge, UK: Cambridge University Press.

Valencia, R. R. (1991). *Chicano school failure and success: Research and policy agendas for the 1990s.* New York: Falmer.

Vygotsky, L. S. (1962). *Thought and language.* Cambridge, MA: MIT Press.

Waggoner, D. (1991). *Undereducation in America: The demography of high school dropouts.* New York: Auburn House.

Walsh, C. E. (1991). *Pedagogy and the struggle for voice: Issues of language, power, and schooling for Puerto Ricans.* New York: Bergin & Garvey.

Weber, R.-M. (1991). Linguistic diversity and reading in American society. In R. Barr, M. L. Kamil, P. Mosenthal, & P. D. Pearson (Eds.), *Handbook of reading research,* (Vol. 2; pp. 97–119). New York: Longman.

Zimpher, N. L. (1989). The RATE Project: A profile of teacher education students. *Journal of Teacher Education, 40*(6), 27–30.

Zimpher, N. L., & Yessayan, S. (1987). Recruitment and selection of minority populations into teaching. *Metropolitan Education, 5,* 57–71.

9

Beyond Balance: Goal Awareness, Developmental Progressions, Tailoring to the Context, and Supports for Teachers in Ideal Reading and Literacy Programs

JERE BROPHY

I was very pleased to be asked to comment on the 1997 Bond Conference contributions, gathered together in this volume, because the chapters are of unusually high quality and complement one another quite well. I refer here not only to solid research and scholarship, but to carefully phrased and tempered conclusions that are mindful of the multiple goals that need to be addressed in a complete literacy program and thus the complexities of curriculum and instruction that these goals imply.

This kind of scholarship represents what should, but seldom does, provide the basis for informed decision making about educational policy and practice. I speak as someone who came into education largely by accident and only after completing a Ph.D. in human development. Once I began to learn about education as a discipline and as a profession, I found much that was familiar and reassuring, but also much that was strange and disturbing. Knowing little about the field, I had assumed that it would function largely as an applied science, in which a well-organized and gradually increasing knowledge base was used to inform decisions about curricula, teaching methods, and other aspects of policy and practice. Instead, I found that educational policy debates typically are highly polarized and policitized, tending to produce pendulum swings between extreme and limited positions. Arguments frequently are reduced to false dichotomies, such as phonics versus whole-word methods, as if these were the only two choices available and as if one must choose between them instead of blending them within a balanced program. Worse, such arguments often imply that there is one best way to teach, when we know that different goals and situations call for different methods.

Unfortunately, such oversimplifications and polarizations seem to be especially frequent in reading and language arts. Yet this volume is refreshingly free of these defects. All of its chapters are solid, research-based contributions. In discussing them I will focus on the connections among them and on potential implications for practice. Along the way I will suggest a few cautions and alternative interpretations, but no strong objections.

Since I am a person without formal training in reading and literacy education, you may be wondering where my remarks are coming from. In part, they come from my general experiences with the field, particularly my service as a member of the Reading Commission that developed the report *Becoming a Nation of Readers*, as well as my service as co-director of the Institute for Research on Teaching at Michigan State University. In the latter role I became very familiar with the work of Taffy Raphael, one of the authors represented here, as well as the work of Gerald Duffy, Laura Roehler, Patricia Cianciola, Carol Sue Englert, Susan Florio, and other reading and literacy scholars.

My disciplinary background is in developmental and educational psychology rather than in curriculum and instruction in literacy or any other school subject. These disciplines have contributed some fundamental ideas that provide contexts within which I have interpreted the issues addressed in the chapters. Developmental psychology teaches us that learners' instructional readiness and needs change as they acquire new cognitive capacities and domain knowledge. Therefore we should expect to see evolution in both curriculum and instruction as students gain expertise in subjects taught at school. Across a school year, a curriculum unit, or even a single lesson, we should see a gradual transfer of responsibility for managing learning from the teacher to the students, gradual increases in the levels of challenge offered by the learning activities, and so on.

Educational psychology teaches us that there are qualitatively different kinds of learning, each requiring a unique set of instructional moves and learning activities to support optimal progress. For example, Gagne and Briggs (1979) distinguished among five types of learning: attitudes, motor skills, information, intellectual skills, and cognitive strategies. Also, people who write about curriculum goals typically distinguish among knowledge, skills, attitudes or values, and behavioral dispositions. Such distinctions should caution us against simplistic suggestions that there is only one kind of learning or one way to teach.

Recently, I have been learning about the field of curriculum through my involvement in social studies. Here again I have found fundamental principles that are important to keep in mind, yet easy to forget once we begin to focus on more specific issues. One such principle is that curriculum construction and implementation should be guided by clear purposes and goals, expressed as statements about desired student outcomes (the knowledge, skills, attitudes or values, and behavioral dispositions that the curriculum is designed to develop). In this view, everything involved in teaching a school subject is construed as a means to be used to accomplish the subject's goals, not as an end in itself. Thus even curricular content, as well as instructional methods, learning activities, and assessment devices, should be selected because they are viewed as effective means for enabling students to achieve the desired outcomes.

Another fundamental point is the distinction between curricular issues (what is most worth teaching and why) and issues of instructional methods (how this worthwhile content might be taught most effectively). These two sets of issues quickly become linked in practice, but it is helpful to separate them for purposes of analysis. Curricular issues are logically prior to method issues: It makes no sense to argue the relative value of different instructional methods unless such arguments are carried out in the context of agreement about the purposes, goals, and intended outcomes of the instruction. Once such clarity is achieved, research can inform our thinking about both the curricular and the instructional issues.

Some curricular issues cannot be resolved through empirical research because they involve value questions that must be argued as such. However, the curricular recommendations that emerge from these arguments contain implied assumptions that can be tested empirically. These include readiness assumptions (that students at each grade level are ready to learn prescribed content) and outcome assumptions (that accomplishing the learning goals will enable students to apply what they are learning in relevant life situations). It is important for us as educators to highlight and research the assumptions that are built into our curricular recommendations, because these assumptions may not hold up. For example, everyone might agree that certain content ought to be in the curriculum, but research might establish that students need to acquire a certain critical mass of cognitive capacities or prior knowledge before they can address this content productively. Such findings would indicate that the content should be taught, but not until students had attained the necessary cognitive developmental levels or acquired the necessary prior knowledge.

Alternatively, a given curriculum component might have strong face validity as a way to bring about some desired student outcome, but research might establish that the component does not have its intended effect. If so, follow-up would be needed to see if the problem could be corrected by adjusting the content, the instructional materials, the teaching methods, or the learning activities. If not, we might be forced to conclude that our fundamental assumptions about the value of the curriculum component were incorrect, despite their face validity. These possibilities illustrate how research can inform curricular arguments, not just the arguments about instructional methods that seem to command most of our attention.

Drawing together these fundamental ideas yields the following as my stance in commenting on the chapters collected here. First, clear purposes and goals ought to drive the development and evaluation of learning systems. Curriculum content, instructional methods, and learning and assessment activities ought to be judged with reference to their relative effectiveness in accomplishing their intended outcomes. Theories are important as bases for generating principles for educational practice and explanations for why these principles should be effective. Ultimately, however, learning systems and instructional methods need to be assessed with reference to the demonstrated trade-offs they offer as means for accomplishing worthwhile instructional goals, not with reference to the appeal of the theories that are associated with them.

A complete subject-matter program focuses on the most worthwhile goals and learning outcomes. Its mix of components evolves as students gain expertise, and it varies in its specifics according to the goals of a given lesson or activity. Different program components relate in varying degrees to different goals (such as learning versus motivation goals). An optimal program will reveal not just (1) balance among various components but also (2) tailoring of relevant components to particular situations and (3) evolution in which components are emphasized as students move through the program.

SOME COMMENTS ON THE CHAPTERS

Working within this context, I now turn attention to the individual chapters. I begin with Dole's chapter because she offers a broad status report of the field, touching on almost all the issues that other chapters address more specifically. Next, I address chapters that focus on reading comprehension, progressing from van den Broek and Kremer's broad synthesis to Pressley's review of research on strategy teaching to Fuchs and Fuchs's presentation of a specific program (Peer-Assisted Learning Strategies) that incorporates some of these strategies. Next, I consider three chapters that broaden our focus from reading comprehension to related components of a complete reading and literacy program: Graves on vocabulary teaching, Alvermann on classroom discourse and related voice issues, and Jiménez on adapting instruction to students' cultural differences. I finish with Raphael's chapter, because it reintroduces several key issues addressed in earlier presentations.

The Current Status of Comprehension Instruction: Dole

Janice Dole has written a nice history and status report on comprehension instruction within reading and language arts curricula. She includes a comparison of whole language, literary response, cognitive strategy, and direct instruction methods along a continuum from implicit to explicit instruction. Her recommendations call for balance among these different approaches and, more specifically, for a synthesis that would incorporate the best features of each. I agree with that idea, but I would qualify it to include the implication that the selection of instructional strategies for any particular curricular strand or lesson should be made with reference to the goals and intended outcomes. An ideal program will be balanced not only in the sense that it incorporates the best features of implicit and explicit instruction, but also in the sense that it uses particular instructional techniques for the purposes to which they are best suited, so that it shifts from one optimal set to another as goals and activities change.

Dole's remaining conclusions are interesting in that some of them are pessimistic (strategy instruction has not been implemented in many American classrooms, many teachers seem to have abandoned not only basal reading programs but comprehension instruction as well, and teachers seem to want easy answers to increasingly complex teaching and learning questions), but others are optimistic (many teachers want to learn more effective ways to teach, and cognitive strategy instruction has been incorporated in most recent basal reading programs). I see cause for optimism in two recent trends. One is the trend mentioned by Dole—that cognitive strategy instruction is being incorporated into basal programs. The other trend is that people are beginning to develop miniprograms or curriculum strands that incorporate judicious mixtures of related instructional strategies and are designed to be easy for teachers to understand and implement. The latter trend is represented in this volume in the chapters by Fuchs and Fuchs and by Raphael.

One minor point that Dole made in passing is that the use of implicit or indirect instruction is "supported by" literary response theory as well as theoretical perspectives on social construction models of learning. I submit that while it is desirable that our recommendations for practice be consistent with our theories, such consistency does not in itself constitute support for the validity of our recommendations. Only research in classrooms can do that. Especially in applied fields like education, there is a tendency to overvalue theories relative to empirical data. However, many theories are simply incorrect, and even when the theories are valid, many attempted translations from theories to practice are flawed. For example, consider the arguments originally advanced to justify whole-language advocates' recommendations for early reading instruction. One basic assumption was that readers pay attention only to those aspects of the text that they need to process in order to get its meaning. Early studies of expert readers seemed to support this idea. However, more recent studies done with sophisticated scientific equipment that monitors minute eye movements have demonstrated beyond doubt that even the most expert readers process every letter in every word. They do so mostly automatically and with great rapidity, but they do not skip letters or words and they divine meaning from processing just a few key subparts of texts (Adams, 1990).

Thus whole-language theorists' analysis of the process of reading as conducted by expert readers was incorrect. Speaking as a developmentalist, however, I submit that this whole controversy was never relevant in the first place to arguments about curriculum and instruction in early reading. It is simply a flawed assumption to suggest that novices in reading or any other domain of competence ought to be expected to function immediately like experts do. This ignores the strong likelihood that expertise will have to develop gradually over an extended time period, that the nature of reading and the repertoire of reading processes used by the reader will evolve in important qualitative respects as expertise develops, and that learners will need different forms of instruction and different learning activities at different stages in their progress. This is the common pattern seen for all kinds of complex learning; so, pending evidence to the contrary, advocating that we teach children to read by merely immersing them in literature is akin to advocating that we teach them to swim by throwing them into the deep end of the pool. Furthermore, this would be true even if the recently discredited ideas about the reading processes of expert readers had turned out to be accurate. Again, it is only demonstrated effectiveness in the classroom, not congruence with some favored theoretical notion, that can speak to the validity of recommended curricular or instructional practices. Failure to understand or accept this by certain prominent policy advocates, most notably by several high-profile leaders in the whole-language movement, has contributed to the crisis in reading education that has developed in recent years.

Dole also notes that literary response theorists believe that, with practice, response skills will become part of learners' internal processing of text and eventually be activated automatically. This is an empirical assumption that ought to be investigated, not simply accepted on the basis of theoretical arguments. It may turn out to be true, but bear in mind that most assessments of the relative effectiveness of explicit versus implicit methods of teaching anything, regardless of subject matter, have favored the explicit methods.

As someone whose work is sometimes cited as supportive of explicit instructional methods, I want to underscore a point made by Dole in talking about direct instruction. She notes that there are many definitions of and criteria for direct instruction, but she quotes Rosenshine and Stevens (1984) as targeting three components that cut across various definitions: demonstration, guided practice with feedback, and independent practice. It is important to recognize this and to distinguish the essentials of direct instruction from what Gage (1994) called the accidentals—features of a given direct instruction program that are not essential to the notion of direct instruction. I mention this because the DISTAR program has become synonymous with direct instruction in the minds of many reading educators, yet the features of DISTAR that many find objectionable (e.g., postural and hand-motion requirements, sing-song oral repetition patterns, and a highly structured and linearly sequenced curriculum) are "accidental" to DISTAR, not essential features of the concept of direct instruction that grew out of process–outcome research. Demonstration, guided practice with feedback, and independent practice are the essential features of direct instruction. Note that these components are not significantly different from modeling, coaching, scaffolding, and transfer of responsibility from teacher to student, the components that are commonly identified as essential features of socially mediated situated learning.

Dole's chapter is among several in this volume that led me to raise a quibble about terminology: It is probably too late to stop this now, but I find it disconcerting when reading educators speak of readers "interacting" with texts to produce meaning. The text is fixed; only the reader is acting. To me, it makes sense to speak of readers processing, interpreting, or constructing meaning from text, but not interacting with text.

Dole's comments on the literary response approach suggested another quibble. This approach is appealing to me insofar as it calls for stimulating students to reflect on what they read, generate personal responses, and engage in dialogue. However, I think it unwise for proponents of this approach to flatly rule out convergent questions to which teachers already know the answers. Sometimes such questions are needed to draw students' attention to a key element in the story or to clarify an element about which the students are confused or mistaken. This suggests that literary response approaches are likely to meet students' needs more successfully if they avoid rigidly banning these questions.

Late in her chapter, Dole notes that constant changes in recommended methodologies eventually cause many teachers to reject research and researchers. I agree that teachers are rightly confused and irritated by the seemingly continuous shifts and contradictions in the advice directed at them by supposed experts. However, I submit that the vast majority of the problem is not being caused by researchers, if we define *researchers* as the kinds of people who have contributed chapters to this volume. Researchers stay close to their data and make careful, qualified statements about implications. The kinds of overblown, polarized, and evangelical statements that cause most of the problem to which Dole refers are coming not from researchers but from people whose policy advocacy is based on strong theoretical biases and who typically have something to sell but little or no scientific support for their claims and recommendations.

An Analysis of Reading Comprehension Processes: van den Broek and Kremer

Paul van den Broek and Kathleen Kremer present a nice analysis of the processes involved in comprehending texts successfully, how these processes can fail, and how understanding these things can help us both to understand why effective reading comprehension methods are effective and to design new ones that are as effective as they can be. They begin with the important assumption that different reading situations and comprehension goals call for different mixes of comprehension processes and outcomes, and thus imply correspondingly different instructional methods.

van den Broek and Kremer review research indicating that comprehension can be affected by reader characteristics, such as readers' background knowledge, metacognitive monitoring of their comprehension as they read, and standards for coherence; by text structures that promote reader-friendliness; and by aspects of the instructional context, including the support that a teacher might provide by setting a purpose for the reading and by scaffolding students' efforts to understand what they read. In the process of analyzing the reader-friendliness of texts, van den Broek and Kremer include an important implication for the design of instructional materials: We want maximally user-friendly texts when our purpose is to convey information, but when our purpose is to help students acquire reading skills, we want texts to be user-unfriendly in controlled ways that will require students to develop the strategies we are trying to teach.

van den Broek's own research illustrates the need to match instructional methods to the skill levels of the readers. One of his studies showed that inserting questions into a text aided comprehension by ninth-graders who had mastered basic reading mechanics but interfered with comprehension by third-graders who were still novice readers. Another study showed that revising texts to make them more coherent and explicit aided the comprehension of college readers when the text was difficult and the readers' skills were weak but did not improve comprehension when the text was easy or the readers' skills were strong.

Generalizing from van den Broek and Kremer's chapter and from aspects of several of the other chapters, I would emphasize the need to tailor comprehension-improvement strategies to the purposes of the reading, the skills of the readers, and other context factors. Some strategies are used primarily to make a text clear and coherent to whoever reads it, whereas other strategies are used for developing students' comprehension skills. Some strategies are used primarily to develop the basic mechanics of reading in primarily novice readers, others are used to develop basic comprehension skills, and still others are used to develop readers' reflection on texts or response to literature. Some strategies are used to prepare readers prior to the reading, others to scaffold their reading as they proceed through the text, and still others to help them reflect on or analyze the text after their initial reading of it.

Readers at almost any level are likely to benefit from teacher structuring and scaffolding of their reading, but the nature and degree of such scaffolding needs to evolve as the readers gain expertise. Helping a primary-grade student understand a single sentence and helping a high school student appreciate and respond to a Shakespearian drama both involve assisting students in comprehending what they read, but the students and the curricular purposes and goals are very different, and the instructional strategies need to differ accordingly.

Rather than view these complexities as frustrations, researchers and teachers ought to appreciate them as indications of what we are learning about adapting instruction to students and situations. Researchers are making progress in understanding these complexities and their potential implications for instruction, and they will continue to build on this knowledge base. Still, research-based information can only inform teachers about the trade-offs involved in decision alternatives; it cannot make those decisions for them. Teachers must decide what goals to pursue with their students and what combinations of content representations, instructional methods, and learning activities will be most helpful in assisting their students to accomplish these goals.

One final aspect of van den Broek and Kremer's chapter that I would like to comment on is the way in which they apply their analysis of reading comprehension processes to help us understand why certain successful reading comprehension methods work. They single out Reading Recovery methods used in the early grades and Reciprocal Teaching methods used in the middle grades. They also refer more generally to what Pressley and others have called transactional methods for teaching comprehension strategies, in which students are prompted to ask and answer questions as they read. I submit that van den Broek and Kremer's analysis also can be applied to the Peer-Assisted Learning Strategies program presented by Fuchs and Fuchs and the Book Club program presented by Raphael. Both of these programs incorporate many of the same features that van den Broek and Kremer have identified as reasons for success in other comprehension-teaching programs. To his analysis, I would add the concept of "authentic task": These small-group and partner-reading approaches not only develop particular skills and strategies, engage readers in sustained reading of text under good motivational conditions, and use this interactive environment to offset limitations in background knowledge; they also engage students in reading and interacting about text for primarily authentic reasons, not merely to demonstrate competence to the teacher.

Research on Strategy Teaching: Pressley

I enjoyed Mike Pressley's chapter for personal as well as professional reasons. It was heartwarming to read his nice tribute to the University of Minnesota's contribution of key ideas that led to the development of cognitive strategy instruction methods. Speaking as a person who was on the scene, Pressley provides a lot of historical detail that people in the field will find interesting and enlightening.

I do not have much to say about the content of Pressley's chapter because I find everything in it to be right on. The chapter offers cogent arguments and related data citations, followed by tempered conclusions, concerning the value of decoding, word-recognition, vocabulary, and strategy instruction. Pressley also notes recent trends among researchers toward packaging sets of strategy-instruction methods within more comprehensive approaches, as well as trends among teachers toward assimilating within their reading and literature curriculum those strategy-teaching methods that seem most suited to their students and their instructional goals. As Dole noted in her chapter, Pressley has been known to express pessimism about the likelihood of widespread adoption of strategy-teaching methods that have been validated through careful research. These recent trends provide more cause for optimism.

The PALS Program: Fuchs and Fuchs

Lynn and Doug Fuchs describe Peer-Assisted Learning Strategies (PALS), a class-wide peer-tutoring method developed to help teachers cope with increasing diversity in their classrooms. PALS incorporates many of the principles and strategies identified as effective by van den Broek and Kremer and by Pressley, but it subsumes them within a method designed to be simple for teachers and students to learn.

I consider their work to be a model of programmatic research and development. Early studies assessed the effectiveness and relative importance of components being considered for inclusion in the program. Once the basic components of the original PALS program were identified, experimental evaluations of the program as a whole were conducted. Most recently, the research team has focused on fine-tuning efforts that have resulted in differentiation of a modified PALS for use in the intermediate grades to supplement the original PALS used in the primary grades. Thus their work has led not only to enhancement of the PALS program through additional components but to differentiation of separate combinations of components that are tailored to the contrasting skill sets and needs of different learners. This illustrates the need for the kinds of adaptations that van den Broek and Kremer emphasized in their chapter.

The PALS program is one example of the recent trend, which I noted earlier and which was noted by Pressley, toward packaging combinations of effective strategies into programs targeted for particular students and instructional goals. It also exemplifies many of the principles identified by van den Broek and Kremer as reasons why successful comprehension instruction programs are effective. Finally, the PALS program is noteworthy for several other characteristics: In packaging it for classroom use and presenting it to teachers, the Fuchses designed it as a supplement to whatever instructional approach the teacher uses now, offered clear and limited time guidelines (three times a week, 40 minutes per session), kept it simple for teachers and students to learn, and ensured that it remained feasible for implementation as they fine-tuned it and added enrichments.

A Comprehensive Approach to Vocabulary Teaching: Graves

Like Pressley's chapter, Mike Graves's chapter is personal and heartfelt, yet it is carefully grounded in scientific data and culminates with a wise and tempered set of recommendations. Graves argues well for the importance of attention to vocabulary, and two of the four strategies he emphasizes are ones that most of us would associate with vocabulary teaching: teaching the meanings of individual words and teaching strategies that will enable students to learn words independently. Yet his other two strategies are providing wide reading opportunities and fostering word consciousness and motivation. Most of us would associate these strategies with whole-language or reader response approaches, but, as Graves explains, they have important vocabulary-development functions as well as authentic reading functions.

Graves argues for appropriate attention to all elements of a complete reading program and for phasing instructional strategies in and out according to developmental sequences. He also makes some important distinctions between teaching a label for an already-familiar concept and teaching words that represent new and challenging concepts, as well as between focusing on the meaning of a single word and teaching vocabulary in the context of increasing comprehension of connected text. All of these distinctions and qualifications are well-taken.

Some would argue that teaching words that represent new and challenging concepts ought to be considered concept teaching rather than vocabulary teaching. In that regard, there is a useful literature in educational psychology on concept teaching, featuring such strategies as presenting prototypical examples first and then juxtaposing carefully selected examples in order to help students grasp the connotations and denotations associated with the word (Good & Brophy, 1995). In any case, whether we call it vocabulary teaching or concept teaching, this kind of teaching connects directly with comprehension instruction. Students will not be able to comprehend a passage, even if they can read the words correctly, unless they know the meanings of the words. I believe that this aspect of teaching deserves more attention than it typically gets, both from researchers interested in content-area reading and from teachers who specialize in the content areas.

As I was reading through Graves's chapter for the first time, it occurred to me that although the strategies he suggests are good ones, it would be overkill to activate them routinely. I thought about how I would save the high-powered teaching strategies for the most important vocabulary words (the ones that refer to key concepts needed to understand text). I also thought that I would not spend much, if any, language arts instructional time on promoting word play through clichés and puns or playing word games, but I would want to make these games available, along with the kinds of word-play books described by Graves, in a learning center somewhere in the classroom.

Given these thoughts, I was very pleased and reassured when I reached the section in which Graves provides situational and time guidelines for using the strategies he recommends. It would be enormously helpful to teachers if everyone who provided or reviewed evidence favoring the efficacy of particular components of a literacy program would provide such guidelines. I think that a major reason why many teachers have not adopted more of the instructional strategies developed in recent years is lack of clarity, not only about when and why these strategies might be used, but about with whom and for how long. When presented with the kinds of guidelines that the Fuchses suggest for the PALS program or that Graves suggests for use of his vocabulary-building strategies, teachers are likely to become both more motivated to incorporate new strategies into their existing programs and more confident in doing so.

Classroom Discourse About Text: Alvermann

Donna Alvermann's chapter synthesizes research on the value of classroom discourse in general and of small-group discussion of recently read text sections in particular. The peer-led discussion groups that Alvermann describes in her chapter have much in common with the Book Clubs that Raphael describes in hers. In each case, small groups of students discuss the commonly read text, operating largely independently of the teacher. Alvermann's research indicates that most students enjoy opportunities to engage in such discussions and find them helpful as vehicles for learning.

Alvermann also argues for the value of adopting a poststructural perspective for understanding how people's thinking is stimulated or restricted through access to multiple discourses and for becoming more aware of and responsive to issues of voice and silencing in group interaction. I do not find this perspective as helpful as Alvermann does, because I tend to value thought (conceptual understanding) over language (communication about those understandings), proof over interpretation, and the evidential warrants that support arguments over the theoretical elegance or creativity of the arguments themselves. Consequently, I have a difficult time seeing classroom applications of poststructural ideas, especially when the focus moves away from the highly interpretive subject of literature into subjects such as science or social studies.

Such differences in philosophical orientation fade into the background, however, when attention shifts to the case study material and implications for classroom practice that Alvermann presents in her chapter. Here I found much that I view as valuable and little to disagree with, although I have a few qualifications and suggestions to offer.

First, Alvermann is clearly correct about the value of classroom talk.

In recent years, there has been a great deal of enthusiasm for, and research on, learning that occurs outside of the classroom. This work features concepts such as situated learning, expert mentoring of novices, and social construction of knowledge in the zone of proximal development. Despite this interest in learning in nonschool settings, however, comparisons of schooled and unschooled children (Rogoff, 1990; Scribner & Cole, 1981) indicate that the learning that occurs in classrooms stimulates much more growth in general knowledge and cognitive abilities than does the nonacademic learning that occurs elsewhere (Note: Many of these comparisons were done by researchers whose sociocultural theories led them to expect a different conclusion, and they tend to downplay the magnitude and generality of the effects of schooling when they review the data. However, their own findings, as well as those of other investigators, support the conclusion I have stated here.) Thus I agree with Alvermann that classroom discourse has unique value. I would qualify this statement, however, by suggesting that such discourse needs to be academically focused and conducted reflectively. In other words, valuable classroom talk is not just any talk that happens to occur in a classroom; it is talk that is structured around the key concepts emphasized in the school's curriculum. Especially when the teacher is not present in the group, steps need to be taken to make sure that group interaction is focused on curricular issues and conducted reflectively, so that it is not just more of the kinds of talk that go on in the street and do not carry comparable cognitive benefits.

Also, steps need to be taken to address the silencing issues that Alvermann raises. Leading advocates of small-group cooperative learning methods (Bennett & Dunne, 1992; Cohen, 1994; Johnson, Johnson, & Holubec, 1994) and of social constructivist approaches to teaching school subjects (Anderson & Roth, 1989; Lampert, 1989; Palincsar & Brown, 1989) routinely emphasize the need to socialize classrooms of students into learning communities. Students are taught to view discussion as a way to help one another learn and then shown how to act accordingly. They are taught relevant skills and dispositions, such as asking and answering questions in ways that promote further understanding of the topic, staying on topic, listening carefully to one another's ideas, and responding reflectively. When challenging others' ideas, they are to do so by citing relevant evidence and arguments while avoiding derision or personal attacks.

Therefore, to help bring about the benefits and at the same time avoid the problems that Alvermann documents in her chapter, I would urge teachers interested in using small-group discussion of previously read texts to think through the kinds of discourse that they would like to see occurring in the small groups, and then communicate this to their students. For example, the students might be socialized to expect that everyone will participate actively in the group discussion, that other group members will listen carefully and respond to what a speaker is saying, and that differences of opinion will lead to appropriate but not inappropriate forms of challenge and argument.

Once such norms are in place, it will be easier to sort out the issues raised in Alvermann's chapter. For example, at one level, it is obvious that people are constrained by the discourses available to them. But schooling is about changing that, not only by exposing students to new discourses (as Nikki Giovanni was trying to do in her poem "Beautiful Black Men") but by socializing students' values and dispositions regarding the purposes and uses of literature, of group discussion, of analysis and interrogation of conflicting arguments, and so on.

The examples that Alvermann drew from her case material raised some questions for me. Was Laura simply a wrongly silenced victim deserving of sympathy and help, or were her classmates at least partly justified in viewing her as a spoiled egotist who ought not to be indulged further? Is Giovanni's poem simply a literary masterpiece and moral inspiration that the students failed to appreciate, or are there some respects in which it is unintentionally revealing of identity conflict or elitism in the author? Did Latonya simply distort the intended meaning of Giovanni's poem by projecting her own attitudes and fears onto it, or did some aspects of her reaction to it display perceptiveness and wisdom?

I realize that such questions cannot always be answered in any definitive way, but I believe that they ought to be raised, and I also believe that differing interpretations ought to be viewed not merely as unique and personal but as subject to interrogation with reference to relevant evidence and arguments. It strikes me as desirable to socialize students to expect this of discussions about literature, even though (and to some extent precisely because) literature is more interpretive than other school subjects.

Finally, Alvermann wonders what Latonya and her classmates might have learned if they had been made aware of the fact that Giovanni had several discourses available to her but selected one that opened herself to being misinterpreted. I agree that this would be interesting to find out. Even more interesting to me, however, would be to see how Black students respond to the poem when they are informed prior to reading it that it was written by a Black author. As a psychologist interested in the dynamics involved in people's attitudes and expectations, I would predict a very different response from that taken by Latonya and her classmates.

Adapting Instruction to Cultural Differences: Jiménez

In his chapter, Robert Jiménez draws on portraits of six Hispanic teachers who appear to be especially effective as teachers of Hispanic students. Jiménez illustrates three general characteristics that these teachers shared in common: (1) They used both English and Spanish as media for instruction; (2) they used effective instructional practices but adapted them to the students and the situation; and (3) they connected with the students and their families in ways that produced positive attitudes toward schooling.

These teachers were determined to teach their students English, but they also affirmed the value of Spanish. They made use of both languages, not only to translate individual words or sentences but also to elaborate or clarify at times when language switching would be helpful. They provided multiple opportunities for students to speak English and encouraged them to do so, but they did not demand public performance or forbid the use of Spanish.

These teachers also communicated high expectations and offered a challenging curriculum. Their students received a wide range of learning opportunities that included the means to comprehend instruction, a framework for interacting verbally, a challenging menu of reading materials, and an interesting and conceptually dense curriculum. The two languages were used to teach important concepts, not just to teach words or language per se. This illustrates a principle of vocabulary teaching that was emphasized by Graves in his chapter and extends it to the bilingual context.

The teachers rejected a deficit view of minority students and believed that it was the school's responsibility to see that they learned. They cultivated positive relationships with the students and their families, through open-ended parent conferences and through invitations to family members to come to class and participate in ways that helped connect the school's curriculum to the students' home cultures.

All of these observations mesh nicely with findings by other investigators on meeting the needs of minority students. This includes not only the work of Moll (1992) on teaching Hispanic students, but also the work of Ladson-Billings (1994) on teaching Black students and the work of Kleinfeld (1975) on teaching Native Alaskan students. My hope is that as such research findings accumulate, principles such as those emphasized by Jiménez will become increasingly well known and accepted—maybe even eventually attain the ultimate accolade of being dismissed as little more than common sense. We still have a ways to go in this direction, however. Unfortunately, many educational policy makers and teachers are still operating from misguided beliefs, such as that students ought to be allowed to speak only English at school or that certain classes must be conducted only in English and others only in Spanish.

Finally, debates about the educational needs of Hispanic and other language-minority students often focus too narrowly on the teaching of English and on rules for when and how the two languages are to be used at school. Jiménez reminds us that these students have the same need as other students for a conceptually rich and challenging curriculum, taught using effective instructional methods and learning activities.

The Book Club Program: Raphael

I have saved Taffy Raphael's chapter for last because it provides opportunities to revisit many of the issues raised in the other chapters. Like Dole, Raphael argues the need for balance. Dole speaks of a balance between explicit and implicit methods of instruction. Raphael calls for balance in three aspects of classroom discourse: (1) the curricular focus of the discourse (on language conventions, comprehension, literary elements, and response to literature), (2) teacher versus student control of topics and turn-taking patterns; and (3) the context for interaction (whole-class versus small-groups versus paired partners).

To illustrate variations on these dimensions, Raphael draws on case material from implementations of Book Club, a literacy program for the intermediate grades. The full program includes instruction and related activities in reading and writing as well as whole-class community share activities, but it features book club meetings in which small groups of students interact to discuss recently read texts.

Student-led discussion in small groups has been an increasingly popular component of reading and literacy curricula developed in recent years. Sometimes, as in Reciprocal Teaching or the PALS program, the discussion component is designed primarily to develop reading comprehension skills and related metacognitive monitoring and control mechanisms. Other student-led discussion components, such as those described by Alvermann and the book club groups described by Raphael, are designed primarily to develop students' knowledge of literary elements and provide them with opportunities to share their personal responses to literature. Discussion components also differ according to the grade levels for which they were developed, the degree to which the students' discourse is supposed to be structured around a standard formula or series of steps, and the scope and expected length of the conversations.

Many of these methods have been demonstrated as effective, at least for accomplishing certain purposes with certain students in certain situations. However, teachers need to accomplish at least three things in order to use these components effectively. First, they need to be clear about the components' curricular purposes and intended contexts for use, so that they can choose components that are well matched to their instructional goals and to the needs and abilities of their students. Second, they need to prepare their students to engage in desired forms of discourse by making sure that they understand the purposes of the small-group or partner interactions and the kinds of discourse that should and should not occur. Third, they may need to acquire new skills and possibly even new attitudes to prepare them to initiate and scaffold student-led discussion methods effectively.

As Raphael illustrates through her case material from the Book Club program, teachers need to function at different times as explicit instructors, scaffolders of productive discussion patterns, facilitators of discussion, or co-equal participants in discussion. Teachers who are used to holding the floor most of the time and to maintaining tight control over discourse topics and turn-taking patterns will have to become willing to relinquish some of this power and become comfortable with the notion of students acting more autonomously much of the time. Teachers who are currently experiencing serious classroom management problems might need to solve those problems before seeking to implement small-group or partner discussion methods.

Most teachers, however, ought to be able to implement the methods effectively without delay, if they are willing to do so. Teachers with misgivings about the methods should be encouraged by the growing body of research indicating that, with appropriate introduction and follow-up, students learn to function effectively in small-group and partner interactions. Once they do, they begin to derive the motivational and cognitive benefits described in Alvermann's chapter. Special follow-up may be needed with students like Laura, however, to make sure that the benefits of these methods accrue to all students and not just a subgroup who tend to dominate the interactions.

CONCLUDING DISCUSSION

Everyone concerned about reading and literacy instruction in the schools ought to be encouraged by the contents of the chapters assembled here. They indicate that a considerable knowledge base has developed about reading comprehension and related skills and dispositions, both in terms of understanding the processes involved and in terms of developing and demonstrating the effectiveness of instructional materials and programs. We still need plenty of additional research and development, as well as better organization of the knowledge base we have, but even so, the stage is set for movement away from destructive pendulum swings and toward a more orderly and scientifically grounded discipline of literacy education. Several things need to occur, however, if the potential benefits of these developments are to be enjoyed by the majority of teachers and students.

First, although researchers have made remarkable strides in generating knowledge about particular literacy processes and in developing and validating systematic instructional methods for teaching particular skills, more scholarly attention needs to be directed to the big picture. What literacy-related knowledge, skills, attitudes, values, and dispositions are most important and deserving of inclusion in literacy curricula? What curricular strands are known or at least believed likely to help students attain these desired outcomes? Given what we know about developments in students' cognitive capacities and literacy knowledge and interests, how might these strands be phased in and out of the program, and how will the program as a whole evolve as students proceed from kindergarten through grade 8 or grade 12? At the moment, such basic curricular questions are being addressed only haphazardly, mostly by instructional-materials publishers working with a few consultants. I would like to see a carefully selected consortium of scholars, teachers, and publishers attack these questions in a systematic way to produce not merely a set of standards but templates for complete and well-balanced literacy curricula, with options identified for students who have special needs and for teachers who are willing to trade off one set of desired outcomes for another.

To be effective, such a group would have to be composed of people who understand that curriculum planning needs to begin with clarification of goals expressed as intended outcomes and who recognize that curricular components are not ends in themselves but means for accomplishing those outcomes. The participants also would have to have a sophisticated understanding of literacy that includes recognition of the need for completeness and balance in identifying desired outcomes to address, the need for an evolving mixture of components as students gain expertise, and the need to tailor instructional materials, methods, and activities to goals of the teaching situation and the capacities and needs of the students. Finally, the group would need to look for evidence of effectiveness demonstrated under appropriate scientific conditions, and not just theoretical rationales or unsupported claims, in making recommendations about instructional methods and materials.

The establishment and successful execution of such a project seems unlikely to happen soon, so what might we be doing in the meantime to improve literacy education in our country? I will conclude with a few suggestions for researchers, and some for teachers.

Suggestions for Researchers

- I would urge responsible literacy researchers and scholars to become more assertive in supporting sophisticated views of literacy education, calling for complete and well-rounded programs, and demanding credible evidence to support claims of effectiveness. The literacy field has been entirely too tolerant of misguided zealots and outright charlatans.
- I think we need acceleration of the trend that was noted by several chapter authors and represented by the work of several others: the packaging of sets of instructional methods within more comprehensive approaches. Especially valuable are packages designed to be user-friendly by minimizing jargon and providing guidelines to teachers about the kinds of students for whom the program is intended, the instructional goals that it addresses, and the situations and time periods for which it is meant to be used.
- I would urge literacy researchers and scholars to work with relevant policy makers, standard-setting groups, and developers of instructional materials and assessment devices to help make sure that their activities are supportive of a sophisticated view of literacy education.

Suggestions for Teachers

What can teachers do to sort through all of the conflicting advice directed at them in order to make good decisions about what is best for their students? My advice boils down to urging teachers to take control over their search for useful materials and guidelines, so that they do not end up getting confused or turned off by the atmosphere of conflict that continues to characterize the literacy field.

- Teachers need to clarify their own goals. Given their students and where their grade-level curriculum fits within the big picture of literacy education at their school, they can begin by conducting a needs assessment. What curriculum and instruction ought to be included in the program for the school year? Which elements should receive special emphasis? Will the same curriculum and instruction be appropriate for all students, or will some students need something different or something extra?

- Once teachers have clarified their goals and developed a template of the literacy program that they would like to implement, they can compare this template with what they are doing now. They may want to retain many of their current materials and methods. However, they may want to substitute for materials or methods that are not working very well or supplement what they are doing in order to address important goals are not being addressed currently.

- At this point, teachers can begin to check instructional materials catalogues, professional book lists, and research journals to find out what is available that speaks to their targeted needs. This is a time for critical thinking and decision making. I would advise teachers to look for clear statements of purpose, guidelines for usage, and evidence of effectiveness, and to watch out for oversimplified or rigid views of literacy curricula or instructional methods as well as for gaudy claims and testimonials unsupported by any scientific evidence.

- As teachers begin to identify useful materials and methods, they might be prepared to mix and match, if doing so would best address their targeted goals. However, it will be important to pay attention to what the program developers say about the essentials of the program and the specifics of implementation that must be present to provide reasonable assurance of getting good results.

- When implementing new programs or methods, teachers should take time to prepare students for them by explaining their purposes, communicating expectations for what will occur during activities, modeling desired skills and dispositions, and scaffolding students' learning. If the programs are complicated or involve several components, they may need to be phased in gradually as students gain expertise.

- Teachers will need to assess the effectiveness of the programs as vehicles for moving students toward the targeted outcomes. Were teachers and students able to implement the programs as envisioned by their developers? If so, have these experiences brought about the desired outcomes? If not, are there adjustments that might be worth trying?

In conclusion, I believe that researchers are justified in taking satisfaction, and teachers are justified in taking heart, as they contemplate the advances that have occurred in recent years in our understandings about effective reading comprehension instruction. It is easy to lose sight of these accomplishments amid the strife that characterizes "the reading wars," but when they are brought together and synthesized in a volume such as this one, we can see them more clearly and begin to view them with the appreciation they deserve.

REFERENCES

Adams, M. J. (1990). *Beginning to read: Thinking and learning about print.* Cambridge, MA: MIT Press.

Anderson, C., & Roth, K. (1989). Teaching for meaningful and self-regulated learning of science. In J. Brophy (Ed.), *Advances in research on teaching* (Vol. 1; pp. 265–309). Greenwich, CT: JAI.

Bennett, N., & Dunne, E. (1992). *Managing small groups.* New York: Simon & Schuster.

Cohen, E. (1994). *Designing group work: Strategies for heterogeneous classrooms* (2nd ed.). New York: Teachers College Press.

Gage, N. (1994). The scientific status of research on teaching. *Educational Theory, 44,* 371–383.

Gagne, R., & Briggs, L. (1979). *Principles of instructional design* (2nd ed.). New York: Holt, Rinehart & Winston.

Good, T., & Brophy, J. (1995). *Contemporary educational psychology* (5th ed.). New York: Longman.

Johnson, D., Johnson, R., & Holubec, E. (1994). *The new circles of learning: Cooperation in the classroom and school.* Alexandria, VA: Association for Supervision and Curriculum Development.

Kleinfeld, J. (1975). Effective teachers of Indian and Eskimo students. *School Review, 83,* 301–344.

Ladson-Billings, G. (1994). *The dreamkeepers: Successful teachers of African-American children.* San Francisco: Jossey-Bass.

Lampert, M. (1989). Choosing and using mathematical tools in classroom discourse. In J. Brophy (Ed.), *Advances in research on teaching* (Vol. 1; pp. 223–264). Greenwich, CT: JAI.

Moll, L. (1992). Bilingual classroom studies and community analysis. *Educational Researcher, 21,* 20–24.

Palincsar, A. S., & Brown, A. L. (1989). Classroom dialogues to promote self-regulated comprehension. In J. Brophy (Ed.), *Advances in research on teaching* (Vol. 1; pp. 105–151). Greenwich, CT: JAI.

Rogoff, B. (1990). *Apprenticeship in thinking: Cognitive development in social context.* New York: Oxford University Press.

Rosenshine, B., & Stevens, R. (1984). Classroom instruction in reading. In P. D. Pearson, R. Barr, M. L. Kamil, & P. Mosenthal (Eds.), *Handbook of reading research* (Vol. 1; pp. 745–798). New York: Longman.

Scribner, S., & Cole, M. (1981). *The psychology of literacy.* Cambridge, MA: Harvard University Press.

About the Editors and Contributors

Donna E. Alvermann is Research Professor of Reading Education at the University of Georgia, where she teachers courses in content literacy. Her research focuses on the role of classroom discussion in content literacy instruction. Recently she has begun to explore the potential of feminist pedagogy and poststructural theory for interpreting literacy practices in middle and high school classrooms. She is currently co-chairing the International Reading Association's Adolescent Literacy Commission. She is also a member of the College Reading Association's Board of Directors, and she serves on the editorial advisory boards of *Reading Research and Instruction* and *Reading Research Quarterly*. She is an associate editor for the *Journal of Literacy Research*. Her recent books include the co-edited volume *Reconceptualizing the Literacies in Adolescents' Lives* and the co-authored second edition of *Content Reading and Literacy: Succeeding in Today's Diverse Classrooms*. In 1997 Dr. Alvermann was awarded the Oscar S. Causey Award for Outstanding Contributions to Reading Research and the Albert J. Kingston Award for Distinguished Service to the National Reading Conference.

Jere Brophy is University Distinguished Professor of Teacher Education at Michigan State University, where he was also formerly the co-director of the Institute of Research on Teaching. He has written or co-authored more than 250 articles, chapters, and technical reports on teacher expectations, teacher effects, and other aspects of teaching and teacher–student interaction. Most recently his work has focused on teaching elementary social studies for understanding, appreciation, and life application. His recent books include *Powerful Social Studies for Elementary Students* (with Janet Alleman, 1996), *Looking in Classrooms* (with Thomas L. God, 7th edition, 1997), *Teaching and Learning History in Elementary Schools* (with Bruce VanSledright, 1997), and *Motivating Students to Learn* (1998).

Janice A. Dole is Associate Professor in the Department of Educational Studies at the University of Utah. After teaching elementary school, she received a doctoral degree from the University of Colorado. Before coming to the University of Utah, she held faculty positions at the University of Denver and Michigan State University. In addition, she was visiting assistant professor at the Center for the

Study of Reading at the University of Illinois at Urbana–Champaign. Her current research interests focus on comprehension instruction, learning from texts, and beliefs and conceptual change. She has written articles for research journals such as the *Reading Research Quarterly, Review of Educational Research* and *Educational Psychologist* and practitioner journals such as the *Journal of Reading.* Currently, she is on leave of absence from the university and working on a literacy initiative project for the state of Utah. She is also working on a new text, *Understanding Nonfiction.*

Douglas Fuchs received his Ph.D. in educational psychology from the University of Minnesota in 1978. He is currently Professor in the Department of Special Education at Peabody College of Vanderbilt University, co-director of the John F. Kennedy Center's Institute on Learning Accommodations, and co-director of Peabody College's Reading Clinic. His work examines the effectiveness of strategies for helping classroom teachers incorporate academic diversity. Dr. Fuchs has more than 150 publications. He is co-editor of *The Journal of Special Education,* and he serves on the editorial boards of a variety of journals.

Lynn S. Fuchs received her Ph.D. in educational psychology from the University of Minnesota in 1981. She is currently Professor in the Department of Special Education at Peabody College of Vanderbilt University, co-director of the John F. Kennedy Center's Institute on Learning Accommodations, and co-director of Peabody College's Reading Clinic. Her work centers on how classroom-based assessment might enhance teachers' instructional planning and how peers' academic groupwork can be structured to improve student learning. Dr. Fuchs has more than 150 publications. She is co-editor of the *Journal of Special Education,* and she serves on the editorial boards of a variety of journals.

Michael F. Graves is Professor in the Department of Curriculum and Instruction at the University of Minnesota and head of the Literacy Education Program. He received his Ph.D. in Education from Stanford University and his M.A. and B.A. in English from California State College at Long Beach. His research, development, and writing focus on vocabulary development, comprehension development, and effective instruction. His recent books include *Teaching Reading in the Twenty-First Century* (with Connie Juel and Bonnie Graves, 1998), *Essentials of Teaching Elementary Reading* (with Susan Watts and Bonnie Graves, 1998), *Reading and Learning in Content Areas* (with Randall Ryder, 1998), and *The First R: Every Child's Right to Read* (co-edited with Barbara Taylor and Paul van den Broek, 1996). Dr. Graves is the former editor of the *Journal of Reading Behavior* and the former associate editor of *Research in the Teaching of English,* and he currently chairs the Studies and Research Program Development Committee for the International Reading Association.

Robert T. Jiménez is currently Assistant Professor at the University of Illinois at Urbana–Champaign. He teaches courses in research methods, second-language literacy, and issues related to the education of Latina/Latino students. Dr. Jiménez has conducted research on the strategic processing of competent and less competent bilingual readers, and on the delivery of services and instruction to language-minority students at risk for referral to special education and those with learning disabilities. In 1997 he received the Initial Career Award granted by the Office of Special Education Programs, U. S. Department of Education. He has published his work in a variety of journals including the *American Education Research Journal, Reading Research Quarterly,* and the *Elementary School Journal.*

Kathleen E. Kremer is a doctoral candidate in child psychology at the University of Minnesota. Her research interests are in cognitive development during the preschool and elementary school years and its application to educational media. Her dissertation research focuses on children's understanding of flashbacks in television and film. She has served as a consultant on the design and evaluation of numerous educational television programs, radio shows, films, and multimedia products for both children and adults.

Michael Pressley is the Notre Dame Professor of Catholic Education and Professor of Psychology at the University of Notre Dame. He has published extensively in the areas of reading comprehension and reading instruction and is currently the editor of the *Journal of Educational Psychology.*

Taffy E. Raphael is Professor in the Department of Reading and Language Arts at Oakland University, Rochester, Michigan. She received the Outstanding Teacher Educator in Reading Award from the International Reading Association in 1997. Dr. Raphael's research has focused on innovations in literacy instruction and in teachers' professional development, which has been published in journals such as *Reading Research Quarterly, Research in the Teaching of English, The Reading Teacher,* and *Language Arts.* She has co-authored and edited several books on research and practice in literacy instruction. She will serve as president of the National Reading Conference in 1999.

Barbara M. Taylor is Guy Bond Chair in Reading and Professor in the Department of Curriculum and Instruction at the University of Minnesota. She is also a principal investigator for the Center for the Improvement of Early Reading Achievement funded by the U.S. Department of Education. Dr. Taylor's current research focuses on early reading intervention and schoolwide change in reading. She has published in journals such as *Reading Research Quarterly, American Educational Research Journal, Journal of Reading Behavior,* and *The Reading Teacher.* She has coauthored and edited a number of books on reading instruction.

Paul van den Broek is currently Guy Bond Professor in Reading and the former director of the Center for Cognitive Sciences at the University of Minnesota. The focus of his research is on the cognitive and neurological processes that contribute to successful reading comprehension in adults and children, and on the implications for reading instruction of children with and without learning disabilities. He has edited several books and published numerous articles in journals such as *Child Development, Journal of Educational Psychology, Journal of Memory and Language, Contemporary Educational Psychology, Journal of Reading Behavior, Journal of Experimental Psychology, Discourse Processes,* and *Memory and Cognition,* and he serves on the editorial board of the last three.

Index